Building Organizational Capacity

Building Organizational Capacity

Strategic Management in Higher Education

J. Douglas Toma

The Johns Hopkins University Press
Baltimore

© 2010 The Johns Hopkins University Press
All rights reserved. Published 2010
Printed in the United States of America on acid-free paper
9 8 7 6 5 4 3 2 1

The Johns Hopkins University Press
2715 North Charles Street
Baltimore, Maryland 21218-4363
www.press.jhu.edu

Library of Congress Cataloging-in-Publication Data
Toma, J. Douglas.
    Building organizational capacity : strategic management in higher
education leaders / J. Douglas Toma.
        p. cm.
    Includes bibliographical references and index.
    ISBN-13: 978-0-8018-9763-4 (hardcover : alk. paper)
    ISBN-10: 0-8018-9763-7 (hardcover : alk. paper)
    1. Education, Higher—Administration.   2. Organizational behavior.
3. School management and organization.   I. Title.
    LB2341.T66 2010
        378.1'07—dc22   2010001250

A catalog record for this book is available from the British Library.

*Special discounts are available for bulk purchases of this book. For more
information, please contact Special Sales at 410-516-6936 or specialsales@press
.jhu.edu.*

The Johns Hopkins University Press uses environmentally friendly book
materials, including recycled text paper that is composed of at least 30
percent post-consumer waste, whenever possible. All of our book papers are
acid-free, and our jackets and covers are printed on paper with recycled
content.

Contents

Foreword

Two thoughts set the stage for why *Building Organizational Capacity* is an important book for those leading our colleges and universities, both academically and administratively. First is a desire that someday a new college or university president will pronounce in her or his inaugural address something along the lines of the following:

> My vision is to build organizational capacity to successfully meet today's goals and tomorrow's challenges at this institution. As president, I accept, as a primary responsibility, enhancing our administrative capacity, whether in delivering academic programs, research and outreach, or administrative services. We will accomplish this by building our individual and collective abilities in planning and, especially, implementing various initiatives, particularly those with the most strategic value and highest stakes for the institution.

This president will need, as a guide, an approach to strategic management integrating the logic of systems thinking.

Second, he or she will be well served to focus on implementation. Richard Alfred, in his recent book on higher education management, rightly focuses not just on "the big picture"—strategy at university and colleges—but also on implementation. He calls implementation, as a concept, "as important, *if not more important*, than any in the book because it is the difference between success and failure" (Alfred 2006, p. 224). In stressing that senior leaders and managers often overlook implementation, he raises another critical point: "Implementation is not a popular topic with administrators. Many, if not most, fumble in their efforts to carry it out, yet it is the glove that fits the hand of strategy" (p. 227).

I have long argued that those in senior positions in academic affairs must move away from the old notion that "administrative stuff" is either unimportant or easy—or both. (I have, meanwhile, contended that business officers must broaden their perspectives beyond mere administration.) Steven Sample, president of the University of Southern California, has it right when he says, in effect, that many want to *be* president, but few want to *do* president (Sample 2003). In the final result, leadership within any organization is measured by building the capacity to enable the successful implementation of both strategies and operations. In this book, J. Douglas Toma explains the elements that comprise the organization-as-system in higher education, providing a framework for building the administrative capacity institutions need, but so often lack. It is precisely such depth within an organization that enables its leaders and senior managers to translate vision and plans into reality and successful conclusions. Accordingly, Doug explores a strategic-management framework grounded in the notion that because the various aspects of any organization influence one another, those running universities and colleges need to consider, as a daily matter, both the whole and its parts.

Building Organizational Capacity (BOC) began as an initiative of the National Association of College and University Business Officers (NACUBO). It responds to the growing awareness that the place of the chief administrative officer within universities and colleges has evolved, shedding the singular role of "head bean counter" to become a partner with the chief academic officer and an essential counselor to the president. In doing so, those involved in administration, including in business and finance, have become more central in solving complex problems and in leading major initiatives within institutions. They are crucial to strategic planning. They also have assumed an even greater role in planning and implementing various initiatives in areas that have an increasing importance in higher education, including facilities, information technology, management information systems, and human resources. NACUBO became more interested in providing its primary constituency with a means to better understand organizational complexity and to frame their thinking and actions as leaders and senior managers. Thus began the conceptual and empirical inquiries into strategic management and systems thinking that have resulted in Doug's book—and that promise to continue to provide tools to aid in the implementation of the ideas introduced and illustrated here.

Initially, NACUBO queried the leadership of the national higher educational associations and its own volunteer leaders about what presidents and chief academic and business officers would find most helpful to better the condition of their institutions. With funding from the TIAA-CREF Institute, NACUBO held a day-long program in 2003 focused on what factors seemed to matter most as institutions purposefully moved toward improvement. The result was the kernel of the framework that Doug explains in this book. As much as anything, we began to consider that what institutions neglected was as important as what they actually did. We started to ask what factors might be included on a simple checklist to ensure that leaders and senior managers covered the entirety of their institutions in framing and making decisions. We saw equal relevance in how the various elements of any institution influenced one another, with a breakdown in one area causing a ripple effect across the organization. Accordingly, our project became that of developing a framework for strategic management—one dedicated to the unique environment in higher education.

Upon coming aboard, Doug encouraged us to approach the project more empirically. We secured a grant from the Fund for the Improvement of Higher Education (FIPSE) that enabled him to assemble a team of researchers from leading U.S. graduate programs in higher education and involve his doctoral students at the Institute of Higher Education at the University of Georgia. The project began with a review of writings about strategic management and systems thinking related to both corporations and not-for-profit organizations, which Doug synthesizes in chapter 1. We certainly encountered some sound insights and useful advice in the business literature, but something was missing, especially as we considered how writings directed toward corporations applied to universities and colleges. We concluded that to contribute to preserving what has made higher education in the United States the standard and leader in the world, we needed to focus on building capacity within universities and colleges. Strategic management, as adapted to the particular environment in higher education and as informed by systems thinking, provided the device required to do so. We saw that corporate and nonprofit approaches were an insufficient fit in higher education, as its purposes are distinct from a profit motive, it relies on shared governance and decentralized decision making, and it has a culture that fundamentally values collegiality, as well as having various operational differences from the other two settings.

With NACUBO matching the FIPSE funding we attracted, we were able to send teams of three or four members, including multiple researchers and at least one representative connected with NACUBO, to conduct research across a spectrum of eight types of universities or colleges, focusing on an initiative of high value to the individual institutions. The case studies resulting from these research visits are the core of Doug's book, exploring and illustrating BOC. As we refined and began to share the BOC framework, including with various NACUBO constituents, we questioned—based in part on the insights of our audiences—whether our way of capturing the complexity of an organization-as-system in higher education was, in itself, too complicated. We decided that, to the degree possible, we had streamlined the remarkably complex world in which leaders and senior managers at universities and colleges operate. We were reassured that strategic-management frameworks from business were about as detailed as ours.

An appointment as president, chief academic or administrative officer, vice president, or dean comes only after years of experience, but assuming these positions involves a steep learning curve and some on-the-job training. We wanted to help. BOC is intended to categorize the daunting complexity and relentless pace of the contemporary university or college, clarifying the elements of the institution that require the daily attention of its leaders and senior managers. I also hope that the framework is useful in graduate programs in higher education, introducing students to the overarching challenges in managing universities and colleges (and synthesizing what they can draw from writings in business about strategic management and systems thinking).

The elements are, ultimately, more intuitive than complex, both in their titles and even in how they relate to one another. Purposes clarify aspirations; structure arranges people productively, and governance enables them to make decisions; policies are rules, and processes are means to implement them; information provides data to support decisions and facilitates communication; infrastructure entails the needed foundation of facilities and personnel at an institution; and culture is its fundamental character. It is also important to remember that strategic-management frameworks do not work without systems thinking. While each element is distinct, with the purposes category in the middle of a web formed of the others, how each relates to the others is critical. For instance, clarifying governance—who makes what decisions—is unlikely to be sufficient in itself if areas such policies and processes (and structure, information, and the other elements) are not sound (not to mention in accord with the culture of the institution). Doug underscores these connections in the case studies he presents in chapters 3-10. The idea is to provide leaders and senior managers with a map of their institution, defining and illustrating a manageable set of elements that form the organization-as-system.

Doug provides the initial effort in what I hope will be a deeper explanation. Considering the BOC framework in the context of failed initiatives would be an interesting next step—the eight cases explored in the chapters are all, to some degree, about successful efforts. Also, studying the actual application of BOC will perhaps enable us to refine our understanding of its utility. I am also interested in the nexus between leadership and the approach presented here. The framework provides a checklist that is not dependent on one leadership style or another, just as there is no one structure or culture that is correct across organizations. BOC is not prescriptive of what leaders and senior managers should do— or avoid—but it invites them to consider the various parts of any institution and how they influence one another.

James E. Morley, Jr.
Former President and Chief Executive Officer
National Association of College and University Business Officers

Acknowledgments

The strategic-management approach for higher education here is very much the product of a team effort. James E. Morley, Jr., former president of the National Association of College and University Business Officers (NACUBO), provided vision for the project from the outset and introduced the framework that we explored. The research team included Greg Dubrow, University of California at Berkeley; Matthew Hartley, University of Pennsylvania; Adrianna Kezar, University of Southern California; Kevin Kinser, State University of New York at Albany; Christopher Morphew, University of Iowa; Kathleen Shaw, Temple University; Kelly Ward, Washington State University; and Lisa Wolf-Wendel, University of Kansas. A member of the research team contributed a sidebar to each of the eight case study chapters discussing research related to a given BOC element. Having Jay write the foreword to the book and featuring each member of the research team individually is my way, albeit too modestly, of formally recognizing their significant contributions to this work.

Anthony Knerr of Anthony Knerr and Associates was the consultant on the project; Marvin Lazerson, now of Central European University, and Kenneth "Buzz" Shaw, the former chancellor of Syracuse University, were its advisors; Karen Paulsen of the National Center for Education Management Systems evaluated it; and Theresa Wright and Michael Massey worked on the project as Institute of Higher Education graduate fellows. Several NACUBO staff also worked on the project, with Jessica Shedd and Robert Rhea participating in fieldwork, and Bob contributing to managing project logistics from the NACUBO office in Washington, DC. I offer my sincere thanks to each of you. I also thank NACUBO, several national higher educational associations, and the Fund for the Improvement of Postsecondary Education of the U.S. Department of Education for funding our research.

Additionally, I wish to thank Elisabeth Hughes, Micki Waldrop, and Adam Wyatt from the Institute of Higher Education, whose thoughtful edits have improved the manuscript; Thomas Dyer, former director of the Institute, and Libby

Morris, the current director, for their support of the project; and my faculty colleagues and graduate students at the Institute of Higher Education. Ashleigh McKown from the Johns Hopkins University Press has contributed greatly, offering insights that have made the discussion here more relevant and readable. Kathleen Capels lent her considerable editorial skills to the project. I also appreciate the efforts of two reviewers, whose critiques prompted significant improvements in the manuscript. They exemplify how important the review process is in completing a book worthy of publication.

Finally, I thank my wife, Linda Bachman, and our son, Jack, for their patience and encouragement as I spent days in the field researching—and then weekends at the office and evenings on the laptop, writing. It is to them, along with Jay, that I dedicate this book.

Building Organizational Capacity

Introduction

R are is the university or college president who has not advanced a vision for the future of his or her institution. Specific organizational-change initiatives, intended to support such aspirations, typically follow. Organizational restructuring or infrastructure improvements at a liberal arts college, for example, might support a broader strategy toward becoming more selective. A community college concerned with improving student academic achievement may focus on altering its academic culture and making various structural changes in areas such as student advising. Comprehensive institutions commonly launch or extend graduate programs with visions of raising their profiles and producing more revenue. Research universities are likely to pursue faculty who can generate resources. Selective institutions, as a whole, compete aggressively for the most accomplished students. Almost all institutions are interested in establishing new markets and launching programs in popular professional fields, often at satellite sites convenient to working students.

The administrative foundation required to support these expansive institutional aspirations, however, is less emphasized by leaders. This book offers a framework for building needed organizational capacity within higher education institutions. Building Organization Capacity (BOC) categorizes the functioning of a university or college into a manageable set of specific elements, suggesting the need for them to be in sync. This approach is consistent with the strategic-management models long applied to corporations, indicating the areas in which an organization may need to adapt as it attempts to realize an initiative and, ultimately, its mission and its aspirations. Like other strategic-management models, the BOC framework necessarily incorporates the logic of systems thinking—the notion that the components within a complex organization are interrelated and must be considered simultaneously. However, BOC does not ask leaders and senior managers in higher education to apply an actual systems framework, as most of these approaches are quite rigid, especially those grounded in quantitative modeling. Instead, systems thinking merely suggests that the alignment of components within an organization is essential to its strategic management.

BOC is thus a tool that leaders and senior managers can apply in organizing their thinking about their work. The framework offers them a checklist of sorts to use in making sure that they are covering all of the bases. In planning, it emphasizes the cluster of administrative factors, operating in concert, that are necessary for the success of an initiative. Strategic management also is instructive in implementation, helping to anticipate deficiencies and breakdowns, as well as indicating the need for the elements within an organization to operate in harmony. Managing any university or college requires considering several factors at once—and keeping them straight. For leaders and senior managers in higher education, BOC provides a means to do so.

The approach also directly addresses the meaningful differences between universities and colleges and other organizational settings, including corporations, nonprofits, and government. There is an increasingly rich literature relevant to strategy at universities and colleges, as well as on higher education management.[1] There is also a tradition of scholarship on strategic management within corporate and, more recently, nonprofit settings. Yet approaches to strategic management (and systems thinking) have been considered only sporadically, and rarely comprehensively, in writings about higher education.

BOC offers university and college leaders and senior managers a straightforward strategic-management framework particular to higher education, one that they can employ to diagnose problems and develop solutions. I illustrate the elements in this approach—and how they relate to one another—through case studies of eight institutions of different types that implemented various kinds of initiatives. In doing so, I reference contemporary trends and issues in higher education, as well as the challenges that they pose. At the end of each discussion on aligning the elements, I note specifics on how those who are leading and managing institutions might implement the framework as they develop projects and work through challenges on their own campuses.

Organizational Capacity

What is the capacity that leaders and senior managers need to build within universities or colleges? Capacity is the administrative foundation of an institution, which is essential for establishing and sustaining initiatives intended to realize its vision. Those who have sought to define the concept of organizational capacity suggest that what enables it is the application of an appropriate strategic-management framework. Doing so requires that a given set of elements be aligned, employing the logic of systems thinking and always keeping in mind the mission and aspirations of an organization.[2] For instance, in considering nonprofit organizations in the United States, Connolly and Lukas (2002) suggest that organizational capacity is the continually evolving range of capacities, knowledge, and resources needed for an organization to be effective. They note that for nonprofits, these inputs include a vital mission and a clear identity, as well as effective governance and leadership, demonstrably effective programs, productive strategic relationships, sufficient and stable resources, and efficient internal operations and management. Other strategic-management frameworks identify different elements, but the basic idea of organizational capacity is the same.[3]

There can also be an institutional-effectiveness component to building organizational capacity. Such efforts usually concentrate on planning and assessment. Nonetheless, the definition of institutional effectiveness should be broader, incorporating how an institution can employ all of its available resources to maximum effect. More specifically, these efforts must address whether an institution has built—or can build—the administrative capacity it requires to fulfill its mission and realize its aspirations (Cistone 2002). Can it perform—or is it performing—at the level required to achieve the outcomes it desires through creating and sustaining various initiatives? In seeking philanthropic support, nongovernment organizations have come to know that they must specifically address such questions regarding organizational capacity. In grant applications they now routinely make the case that they have the management depth needed to support the project they are interested in launching or continuing. Questions about organizational capacity are becoming more important in higher education as well, particularly as universities and colleges increasingly diversify the sources of their funding, using institutional effectiveness measures as a justification.

In addition, what an institution is building capacity for depends on its priorities. Suppose that a research university decides to pursue a greater number of accomplished students and more faculty members capable of securing research grants, thus improving its place in the reputational rankings. It requires a certain kind of administrative capacity to be successful in doing so. BOC suggests the questions leaders and senior managers can ask in determining whether their institution has the foundation needed to support its ambitions. In other words, are the necessary elements present and in sync?

- Is there an understanding across the institution of the aspirations that the university has articulated, as well as an acceptance that they are consistent with its mission? For instance, can people envision a more selective institution, one that now may exclude various types of students who once would have attended it?
- Is the institution configured correctly to accommodate the people it is now recruiting? Has the university invested in its honors program? Is there a sufficient research-administration infrastructure?
- Is the locus of the university's decision making reflective of the type of institution envisioned? For instance, faculty governance is generally more dynamic, and academic decision making more localized, at more prestigious institutions. Has this particular institution moved in those directions—or is it prepared to do so—with both the senior administration being willing to cede power and influence and the faculty being ready to accept some of this responsibility?
- Do policies and processes exist that support a more selective, prestigious institution? Are both the formal and informal rules related to matters such as teaching load and tenure and promotion consistent with the norms at leading research institutions? Is academic advising—another process—adequately developed, and are policies related to the curriculum sufficiently flexible to accommodate more demanding students?
- Is enough information being generated and disseminated within the institution to clarify the decision making needed to advance it toward its aspirations? For instance, have there been adequate investments in institutional research and in the management information system

infrastructure, both of which are needed to support more localized decision making?

- Has the institution addressed its infrastructure needs, enhancing its human, physical, technological, and financial assets? Has the university recently hired faculty who are oriented toward conducting funded research and built an administrative structure to support them? Are professional development opportunities available to reorient more established faculty, if they wish? Are the buildings needed to support the aspirations of the institution in place, such as facilities devoted to student life—student residences, dining commons, fitness centers, and commercial districts—that parallel those at the institutions with which the university is now competing? Has it committed the necessary resources to aggressively raise funds, matching efforts at the top universities nationally?

- Is the culture of the institution—its norms, values, and beliefs—consistent with that of a leading research university? Has the university built the self-confidence needed to act in ways that its aspirational peers do? Are people ready to answer the "who are we" question in the ways that those at a leading research university would?

Finally, when answering the "capacity for what?" question, the response is bound to be different at various times. Institutional priorities, and the organizational capacity required to support them, also tend to change. For instance, during moments requiring resilience, a university or college needs to ask questions related to efficiency to be certain that it has the capacity needed to sustain its objectives. At other times, a university or college may need to focus on demonstrating effectiveness, perhaps in response to external pressures connected with accountability. Enhancing the legitimacy of an institution may become a priority, including by improving student learning, faculty governance, or external perception. Such initiatives may be concurrent, with various ones coming to the forefront at different times. Also, given the loosely coupled nature of universities and colleges as organizations, different units may concentrate on different priorities. No matter what the initiative, strategic management suggests a means by which leaders and senior managers can identify vulnerabilities in their organization. Addressing weaknesses within an element, or disconnects between or among multiple ones, provides the administrative foundation needed to support ambitions and sustain accomplishments at an institution.

A Framework for Building Capacity

How do leaders and senior managers within a higher educational institution actually build organizational capacity? This is where strategic management can contribute, integrating the notion of systems thinking into the process. BOC articulates—and considers how to align—eight elements intended to cover the waterfront of leading and managing an institution. These elements are similar to those in other strategic-management frameworks but are specific to higher education, as opposed to corporations or nonprofits:

1. Purposes—why are we here and where are we headed?
2. Structure—how are we configured to do our work?
3. Governance—who makes what decisions?
4. Policies—what rules do we proceed under?
5. Processes—how do we get things done?
6. Information—what do we need to inform our decision making?
7. Infrastructure—what are our human, physical, technological, and financial assets?
8. Culture—what is our essential character?

One way to consider these elements is as an index to what constitutes the foundation needed to support the ambitions and functions of an institution. Another way is to look at them as an inventory of what aspects, if they are missing, can lead to a breakdown within an organization, whereby an initiative struggles or basic operations are less effective.

The BOC framework is thus a diagnostic tool. It provides leaders and senior managers with a type of control panel. A pilot continuously scans instruments indicating the status of various essential functions, each of which operates in conjunction to keep an aircraft aloft—speed, direction, attitude, altitude, fuel, and so on. If the aircraft is going to reach its destination as planned, the pilot cannot consider only some of the instruments on the panel. In a similar fashion, those responsible for organizations can check a set of critical components regularly and, if indicated, improve an element. Moreover, it is not sufficient to just check elements one by one. A leader or senior manager must also consider how they relate to one another, adding the notion of systems thinking to strategic management. Part of his or her overview should be to better align the various elements with one another, just as a pilot considers the influence of speed on altitude or distance on fuel, making any needed adjustments. A breakdown in one area can influence

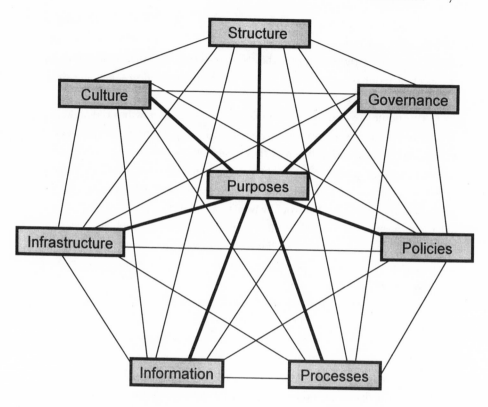

everything else, sometimes considerably. Any strategic-management framework is thus not linear, but instead is a web formed by the connections of each element with the others (see figure). Purposes is at the center of the web, as clarity with regard to this element is essential before an organization can move forward in other areas.

For example, consider the strategic decision by a dean of arts and sciences to commit resources toward building fund-raising capacity within the college, recognizing institutional priorities in this regard as well as considering his or her own aspirations for the school (*purposes*). The dean hires an experienced associate dean to manage this area, positioning that person to interact with the other associate deans (*structure*) and empowering him or her to make needed decisions to advance the initiative (*governance*). The dean adopts the recommendation of the new associate dean to develop a system to identify and track prospective donors (*information*); approves changing a few rules (*policies*) and streamlining some systems (*processes*) within the college that might have slowed the work of fund raising; and invests in needed support staff in this area (*infrastructure*). The dean also secures the backing of the faculty—who are enthusiastic about the prospect of more resources becoming available to the college—keeping them informed of progress.

At this point the dean is comfortable that the college now has the organizational capacity needed to be more active in fund raising. He or she has considered the various elements, as well as how they have to align. The dean recognized, for instance, that a sophisticated management information system for fund raising only works when there is a manager with the experience to employ it, as with the new associate dean. Yet what would have happened if the dean neglected to consider whether the college had developed the norms, values, and beliefs (*culture*) needed to focus on fund raising? For example, was the college, especially the faculty, prepared to have some areas emphasized over others, based upon their respective fund-raising potential?

In addition, the dean—and the new associate dean, particularly if hired from the outside—may not have thought about the difficulties associated with how prospective donors identified by one college may also be considered as potential targets by other colleges within the institution. Moreover, what if the base of prospective donors at the college is interested in areas that do not align with the aspirations of the dean? Even the most elegant system developed within a unit can be upset by such external influences. Just as our pilot must not only keep his or her own aircraft on the right course, but also watch for other aircraft coming too close to it (and account for the weather), organizations need to consider their affairs in the context of the overall environment.

As with our hypothetical arts and sciences college, the management of universities and colleges is particularly daunting in its complexity, given their inherently diffuse nature. Even the most capable leaders and senior managers can become so overwhelmed by details that they can sometimes miss the whole. Like any strategic-management framework, BOC offers a necessarily simplified approach toward comprehending an otherwise seemingly impenetrable organization. It divides an institution into a manageable number of functional categories, while reminding those running it to consider both how these align and what influence outside factors sometimes have upon them. Thus the BOC framework is useful to leaders and senior managers in getting organized, whether it be in planning an initiative or in scanning for breakdowns. With it, they can better avoid bypassing or neglecting something that may hinder advancing aspirations and sustaining gains.

BOC aids leaders and senior managers in avoiding the common analytical challenge of oversimplifying organizations by considering only their structure (Bolman and Deal 2003). In addition to matters such as how those within an institution are configured to do their work (structure) and who is charged with making what decisions (governance), BOC addresses symbolic matters such as purposes and culture, as well as more operational functions that are less recognized as organizational assets: policies, processes, infrastructure, and information. It is a reminder that effective management is more than simply perfecting the organizational chart.

The framework is thus potentially useful to leaders and senior managers operating in a variety of institutional contexts and functional areas—and to those confronting various types of challenges. It should encourage business officers to ask not only "how" questions, but also the "why" ones that are more pronounced when academic administrators consider issues and approaches. BOC can also remind those in academic affairs, especially those newer to administration, to focus on operations as well as on educational concerns; and prompt everyone to keep the purposes of their organization firmly in mind. Strategic management, above all, invites leaders and senior managers to consider the essential question of whether their institution has an adequate administrative foundation to support various initiatives and operations—and where it may need to make adjustments. In doing so, it tends to keep leaders, in particular, more balanced in their work. Pursuing an institutional vision can be more captivating than steadily building and regularly adapting the management capacity on which those aspirations must rest. Strategic management offers a means to balance such impulses. Architects realize that the foundation under the structures they design is essential, even if it is hidden from view and perhaps not as conceptually interesting. Leaders and senior managers in higher education must be equally perceptive regarding their own institutions.

Situating, Illustrating, and Applying the Framework

I begin with a brief review of important writings about strategic management and systems approaches, both because it is helpful to situate BOC within them and as these areas have received limited attention in scholarly works about higher education. My discussion of strategic management focuses on parallel approaches addressing corporate and nonprofit settings, which can differ from the environment at universities and colleges. I include the section on systems approaches not to provide the tools to apply a given model, but instead to reinforce the logic of systems thinking that is so essential in strategic management. Strategic-management frameworks often tend to be more of an inventory, listing a series of elements but not adequately accentuating the connections between and among the aspects of an organization.

In chapter 2, I introduce contemporary trends and issues in higher education, as well as various strategies that institutions have adopted in response to them. This discussion provides the foundation for my later chapters, which consider how current environment influences the application of strategic management. I also briefly examine how leadership and organizational change relate to BOC, as these two topics have received considerable attention in the literature, including that addressing higher education. I then address the peculiarities of applying strategic management within higher education, before concluding chapter 2 with a note about how we developed BOC.

The cases that I consider in chapters 3-10 provide a vehicle for applying the logic of strategic management, as informed by systems thinking, to real-world situations, especially in the context of the broader environmental challenges that institutions are attempting to overcome. The book proceeds element by element, with each emphasized in a chapter featuring a different case study. The cases represent a variety of initiatives, some more academic in nature and some more administrative, at a range of institutional types: two each set at a research university, a comprehensive institution, a liberal arts college, and a community college. The universities and colleges are of different sizes, are located in different settings, and have differing resources at their disposal. My intention is to make the elements more tangible, and thus accessible to leaders and senior managers, offering a vocabulary and illustrating a way of thinking.

Doing so is a departure from the usual practice of presenting a strategic-management framework as more of an annotated outline. Because the cases do not consider initiatives that applied the BOC framework directly, I neither validate the framework nor develop theory. (Going into the field to explore the approach did, however, suggest refinements.) Instead, my aim is to enable leaders and senior managers to better diagnose—and then begin to address—problems within the organizations for which they are responsible. In addition, the cases are not intended to be critical of the institutions featured, such as suggesting that they might be more democratic in faculty governance or in student influence. They represent essentially generic situations that can illustrate the elements and their alignment in the proposed strategic-management framework. The cases connect

BOC with practice, underscoring the ambiguity inherent in applying any framework within any organization—and hopefully also demonstrating the possibilities associated with doing so.

I have three primary objectives in each of these case study chapters. The first is to clarify a given element, offering an extensive definition of it, including by drawing on relevant scholarship. The second is to demonstrate how that element might apply in practice. In doing so I feature how it would relate to the other seven elements in a certain situation. Each chapter thus focuses on a particular initiative at a given university or college embodying a specific set of institutional missions and aspirations, placing it in in the context of various trends and issues in American higher education. Finally, to conclude each chapter, I offer a checklist related to how the featured element needs to relate to the others and consider how leaders and senior managers might utilize the BOC approach in their own situations.

I employ eight questions to organize my discussion in each chapter of how leaders and senior managers might gain the most leverage in applying strategic management toward realizing an initiative:

1. Given the nature and scope of the initiative, who needs to be responsible for managing and monitoring progress toward realizing it?

2. Do those managing the project have a clear sense of the mission and the aspirations that the initiative is intended to advance?

3. Does the person or team managing the project have a clear understanding, relative to the initiative, of each element and how they align?

4. Both among those responsible for a project, as well as across an institution, what kinds of efforts tend to further understanding about the elements and how they relate to one another?

5. How might understanding differ in various parts of the university—and what are the possibilities for strategic management, especially purposes and culture, to connect to the institution?

6. Apart from those leading the project, who else needs to be involved in it, including external constituents, so that each of the elements is addressed and aligned with the others?

7. Given the initiative and the type of institution involved, where are breakdowns likely to occur, and which connections between and among elements are the strongest?

8. What is the time frame for planning and developing the initiative, what are the major steps along the way, and what is needed to measure progress and, ultimately, impact?

I return to these questions in the concluding chapter, following a final review of the eight elements and how the cases illustrate the connections between and among them.

The subsequent discussion explores how leaders and senior managers in higher education can build the capacity needed to support the initiatives intended to advance institutional aspirations. The book provides a diagnostic tool for planning and implementing an initiative: identifying and defining the elements in it that require attention, illustrating how these elements must align with one another, and posing a standard set of questions related to the application of BOC. The framework is akin to a control panel, enabling the user to check the elements one by one but also, most importantly, in conjunction with one another. A strategic-management approach indicates which factors, if not sufficiently addressed, can stall or even doom a project.

Because the framework is nonlinear—it is a web—readers need not read the chapters in order. In chapters 3 through 10, they may wish to focus simply on those cases illustrating the issue and the institutional type that is of most concern to them. For instance, a leader or senior manager at a liberal arts college delving into a curricular reform initiative may want to begin with The College of New Jersey and the LaGrange College cases (chapters 3 and 6). In addition, he or she might review the University of Redlands case in chapter 8, which also concentrates on a liberal arts college, and the University of Georgia case in chapter 10, which addresses intellectual culture. The table on the following page identifies the various cases.

The application of strategic management offers promise in developing the administrative foundation required to support the respective visions of the institutions discussed in these case studies.

- The liberal arts college interested in becoming more selective cannot simply reconfigure its organization or improve its infrastructure. It must also consider how an institution of the type it aspires to become makes decisions, and on what information it needs to draw to do so well; the various policies and processes that guide operations at a selective institution; and how the organizational change it envisions is associated with the evolution of institutional culture.

Table 1 Case studies

Element (and Chapter)	Institution	Case and Institution Type	Featured Areas
Purposes (chapter 3)	The College of New Jersey (New Jersey)	transforming the curriculum to a liberal arts college model at a regional public university	academic affairs, curriculum
Governance (chapter 4)	Virginia Tech (Virginia)	developing a student computing facility to teach mathematics at a research university	academic affairs, facilities
Structure (chapter 5)	Valley City State University (North Dakota)	implementing an enterprise resource planning system at a small regional public college	administration, management systems
Policies (chapter 6)	LaGrange College (Georgia)	enhancing faculty scholarship and integrating student research into the curriculum at a liberal arts college	academic affairs, faculty culture
Processes (chapter 7)	Paul D. Camp Community College (Virginia)	improving the retention of students at a small rural community college	administration, academic advising
Information (chapter 8)	University of Redlands (California)	decision support for tuition discounting at a selective liberal arts college	administration, financial aid
Infrastructure (chapter 9)	Seminole Community College (Florida)	maintaining quality with static resources at a large suburban community college	administration, resources
Culture (chapter 10)	University of Georgia (Georgia)	invigorating undergraduate education at a research university	academic affairs, intellectual culture

- The community college concerned with enhancing academic achievement among its students may focus on changing its academic culture and make structural changes in areas such as student advising. However, it is also important for it to address who makes what decisions related to the issue, the rules by which those decisions are made, and the means needed to implement them—in addition to how governance, policies, and processes in one area can influence the entire institution, even if this is not immediately apparent.

- The comprehensive institution inclined to launch or extend graduate programs in order to raise its profile and generate more revenue cannot simply state its vision. It must also operationalize this vision through the other seven elements, considering whether its faculty is ready to become involved in a different system of decision making (governance); whether its expanded programs will require new standards for tenure and promotion (policies); and whether it has invested in the infrastructure necessary for graduate education—as well as addressing structure, processes, information, and culture.
- The same needs to be done by both the research university that aspires to achieve greater prestige by pursuing noteworthy faculty and the most accomplished students, and the nonselective institution that is focusing on new markets by establishing programs in popular professional fields that are offered in settings convenient for students.

When the factors in the framework operate in concert, the resulting organizational capacity makes the success of a given initiative more likely. When they do not, strategic management can help leaders and senior managers identify breakdowns. Leaders and managers might muddle through planning, and then implementation, but still reach the outcomes they desire. However, working within an orderly framework adds confidence and enables them to better understand why an initiative was successful. It also improves the chances for success when they undertake the next important challenge.

CHAPTER ONE

Strategic Management and Systems Thinking

Before employing a series of case studies to more directly consider the elements in Building Organizational Capacity, how they align within an institution, and how leaders and senior managers might apply them to their own challenges, a review of the prominent writings about strategic management is in order. BOC is situated within this rubric, but scholarship on strategic management, as it applies directly to higher education, is quite limited, with those interested in the topic needing to draw from the broader literature. Doing so requires considering how higher education differs from corporate and nonprofit environments.

I also summarize writings on systems approaches, not to invite the direct application of specific processes by leaders and senior managers in higher education, but instead to stress that strategic management involves not only identifying elements, but also aligning them. I employ the term *systems thinking* to describe that logic, which is so essential to strategic management, and I invite others to consider how given systems approaches might apply directly within higher education.

Chapter 2 includes a brief discussion of organizational change and leadership in higher education, two other topics that are relevant to strategic management. I also suggest how these relate to trends and issues in higher education. None of these literatures alone is entirely satisfying in anticipating and responding to challenges in leading and managing organizations, including universities and colleges, but in combination they are more robust.

Strategic Management

In discussing strategic management, I begin with a few definitions of the concept and then address how BOC fits within the various schemas of strategic management. I conclude this section with review of several leading strategic-management models developed for corporate and nonprofit settings, suggesting where BOC, in considering higher education, is different.

Definitions

A generic definition of strategic management is the formulation, implementation, and evaluation of cross-functional decisions that enable an organization to achieve its objectives (David 1995). It is what is required within an organization to systematically realize the strategy it establishes for itself. Therefore, the definition of strategic management is dependent upon what one considers strategy to be. Mintzberg, Ahlstrand, and Lampel (2005) explore the "what is strategy?" question, as well as why organizations need it. In an earlier article, Mintzberg (1987a) contends that strategy is not only a plan toward attaining missions and achieving aspirations, but is also (1) a pattern, and thus consistent over time; (2) a position, locating particular products in particular markets; (3) a perspective, or the fundamental ways an organization does things; and (4) a ploy, a specific maneuver intended to outwit an opponent or competitor. Mintzberg (1987b) then notes that organizations need strategy (1) to set a direction for themselves and outsmart competitors (or at least enable themselves to maneuver through threatening environments); (2) to focus effort and promote coordination of their activities; (3) to define the organization; and (4) to reduce uncertainty and provide consistency (however arbitrary these may be) in order to aid cognition, satisfy intrinsic needs for order, and promote efficiency under conditions of stability (by concentrating resources and exploiting past learning).

Chafee (1985), in considering universities and colleges, contends that strategy includes both the organization and its environment, is complex in substance, affects the overall welfare of the organization, involves both content and process, is not purely deliberate, exists on different levels, and involves both conceptual and analytical thought processes. Like Mintzberg, she considers strategy—and thus strategic management, which is the means to the end—to be holistic, influencing an entire organization and endeavoring to align its parts. Porter (1979) focuses on how competition influences strategy, contending that a firm gains advantage through positioning, which acts to provide the best defense against others in the market, including by differentiating its products either substantively or psychologically through its marketing. Yet advantage also comes by maintaining the connections among diversified activities within a firm, relating the notion of systems thinking to strategic management (Porter 1987). He explains that positions founded on systems are the most sustainable, as it is harder for rivals to match an array of interlocked activities (Porter 1996), and that corporate wholes are more than the sum of their business-unit parts (Porter 1987).

Traditions

There are multiple conceptual and intellectual traditions in strategic management. Mintzberg, Ahlstrand, and Lampel (2005) categorize strategic management into what they call three "prescriptive" and seven "descriptive" schools.[1] Prescriptive schools are concerned with what strategy should be. They have evolved from the *design school*, which focuses on strategy formation as a process of conception, such as with a SWOT (strengths, weaknesses, opportunities, and threats) analysis. The *planning school*, associated with Russell Ackoff, formalized the process in the 1970s, viewing strategy as detached and systematic. This approach to strategy formation largely depends upon planners, who move step-by-step to develop objectives, budgets, programs, and operational plans. In the 1980s, the *positioning school*, championed by Michael Porter, came to focus more on process than on content by analyzing industries and the competition within them. The positioning school highlights a few generic strategies that can cut across firms in a sector, with concepts such as differentiation, cost leadership, and preemption important.

BOC is more consistent with the various criticisms of these prescriptive-school approaches. Achieving a perfect design is not realistic. Planners are not better positioned to formulate strategy than those who decide upon and implement it within organizations, and the idea of following just a few generic strategies may be more applicable in business than in higher education. Prescriptive approaches can be especially difficult within higher education, given the diffuse nature of universities and colleges and the unclear lines of authority and accountability within them. Also, while the step-by-step approach of the design and the planning schools is accessible, the sequence can be too rigid when applied, thus leading to the unrealistic view that implementation is linear and proactive.

BOC does encourage leaders and senior managers to clarify the mission and aspirations of an institution, using them as a starting point in developing and implementing strategy. Doing so should involve an analysis of internal strengths and weaknesses and external opportunities and threats. It also requires simultaneously relating the other seven elements not only to these purposes, but also to one another. BOC goes beyond design, planning, and positioning to prompt leaders and senior managers to ask whether an organization has the administrative foundation in place to support a strategy—and, if not, what must change? In addition, the prescriptive schools can deemphasize systems thinking, which is inherently nonlinear and more simultaneous (and complicated) than advancing step-by-step. BOC also does not assume an ideal design or a perfect plan. Instead, it anticipates breakdowns, offering leaders and senior managers (as well as planners) a regular means to identify them. Finally, while positioning in organizations is essential, especially in developing and clarifying purposes, it alone is insufficient. A position must be accompanied by enough capacity within the organization for it to be achieved. For instance, a comprehensive institution (such as the one in the introductory chapter) can aspire to be a research university, but it will not succeed in doing so unless it has not only declared its purposes but also attended to various concerns related to the other elements.

The descriptive schools come closer to the BOC approach, as these schools are concerned less with ideal strategic behavior and more with describing what strategies actually can do. The *cognitive school* stresses subjectivity and creativity in formulating strategy over mapping reality in some more-or-less objective manner—there is no perfect outcome and no ideal approach to strategy and implementation. It is best to offer a straightforward framework, leaving it up to its users to bring it to life in whatever ways fit the local context.

Given the complexity of organizations, the *learning school* contends that strategy is a process. It is incremental, emergent, and learned, and thus cannot realistically be developed all at once in the form of comprehensive visions and exact plans. Strategy is thus strategic learning, so formulating and implementing strategy intertwine. The learning school, grounded in the notion of organizational complexity, fits higher education well, especially as it promotes systems thinking (as in Senge's formulation, discussed below). It also aligns with the continual process of checking and adjusting the fit between organizational purposes and administrative capacity that BOC invites. Moreover, leaders and senior managers, as they come to understand the organization, have the advantage of both adjusting capacity to fit purposes and reshaping purposes to align with capacity. The learning school offers an important reminder that sustainable change does not happen overnight, but instead evolves through continued clarity in purposes, as well as by regular attention to structure, culture, and operations.

Other descriptive schools are informative for BOC, but they are less directly relevant to framing the approach. The *power school* considers strategy as the product of bargaining, persuasion, and confrontation within organizations, as well as between and among them. There are certainly multiple constituencies and diffused influence at universities and colleges—and some of them are even altruistic. Nonetheless, the concept of power and influence, while important in strategic management, is only one aspect of it. The *cultural school* views strategy as an emergent social process based on common interests and integration. Culture is one essential factor in strategic management, including in BOC, and alignment within an organization is important in any approach. But there are also structural and operational aspects of universities and colleges, and not just cultural ones, that must also be emphasized. An example is the tendency of academic administrators, particularly those coming directly from the faculty, to concentrate more on values and not move beyond their natural sensibilities to also address processes. Business managers are more likely to be comfortable with operations and less apt to focus on the more intangible—and thus more contested—aspects of a university or college. Lastly, the *environmental school* approaches strategy as being reactive to the external context of the organization, rather than initiated from within the organization. For instance, states play an important role in how public institutions are governed and funded. Yet universities and colleges also have sufficient autonomy to have their direction only be influenced, but not completely determined, by outside forces.

BOC is less in accord with two final types of descriptive schools. The *entrepreneurial school* is focused more on the charisma and intuition of the chief executive officer (CEO)—an approach that certainly is not uncommon across higher education, particularly at more bureaucratic institutions (Birnbaum 1988). BOC views leadership in higher education as being more environmental, and thus not an element unto itself. It is embedded across and within functions, as opposed to driving them from outside and above. (I discuss this point further in chapter 2.) Also, even with the most dynamic CEO, power and influence within universities and colleges tend to be more legislative in nature than executive.

The *configuration school* combines the others to some extent, arguing that organizations exist in "states of being," with strategy as the process of transformation from one state to another. A good illustration is a startup organization first depending on entrepreneurial leaders and visionary strategies, eventually settling into a more mature state, and finally coming to emphasize planning, structures, and managers. Higher education institutions may make such transformations, perhaps expanding their missions or pursuing entrepreneurial ventures at their peripheries, but universities and colleges are usually mature and stable organizations, often particularly so. Even in the present dynamic environment in higher education, strategy is more likely to reside in day-to-day conceptions and operations and less in the context of fundamental transformations.

Frameworks

There are various strategic-management frameworks, such as BOC, across these traditions. As mentioned previously, organizational capacity is the administrative foundation within an institution that is essential to establishing and sustaining the initiatives—and ultimately the change, and even the transformation—embodied in its vision. What enables organizational capacity is the application of an appropriate strategic-management framework by leaders and senior managers, providing them with a checklist to apply with respect to planning and implementation.

The most prominent of these frameworks have concentrated on building capacity within corporations, but more recent approaches have also considered nonprofit organizations. Both corporations and nonprofits are analogous to higher education in some respects, yet they have meaningful differences in others. Nonprofits, like universities and colleges, lack a concrete measure of success, such as a return on investment for shareholders (although prestige is a currency of sorts in higher education). Corporations resemble universities and colleges in their complexity and, like higher education institutions, are less fragile than nonprofits often are. Therefore, even applying similar models across industries requires adjustments.

McKinsey and Company (2001) designed its Capacity Assessment Grid for nonprofit organizations. It includes seven elements of organizational capacity, with several components within each one: (1) aspirations, (2) strategy, (3) organizational skills, (4) human resources, (5) systems and infrastructure, (6) organizational structure, and (7) culture. BOC is consistent with the McKinsey model in several respects. The McKinsey Grid highlights the importance of clarity and boldness of purposes in its aspirations category; addresses structure and governance in terms of boards, organizational design, interfunctional coordination, and individual job design; and includes shared values, references, and practices, particularly as they relate to performance, in the category of culture. The McKinsey model divides infrastructure first into a human resources element, including items such as staffing levels, board composition and commitment, and the dependence of the management team and staff on the CEO. It also incorporates a physical and technological aspect into infrastructure, placing it under its systems and infrastructure category.

In addressing only fund raising and financial planning, the McKinsey Grid does not hone in on a financial infrastructure as comprehensively or as deeply as BOC. Given the generally more ambitious, ambiguous, and complex nature of higher education institutions, greater attention to financial infrastructure is merited. Furthermore, the McKinsey approach confines systems to human resources and management, whereas BOC gives the category a broader reading, focusing on the informational needs of the organization—both decision support and communications. The McKinsey model concentrates specifically on (1) performance management (measurement, analysis, and adjustment); (2) planning (scanning, strategic planning, operational plans, etc.); and (3) strategy (goals and performance targets, program relevance and integration, program development and growth). BOC includes these, but as functions of governance, processes, and information. BOC also pays more attention to policies and processes than does the McKinsey framework, which lumps into organizational skills the development of organizational processes, the management of legal and liability matters, and external affairs.[2]

In another recent work directed toward nonprofit organizations, Connolly and Lucas (2002) suggest that there are six components of organizational capacity, which they define as the wide range of capacities, knowledge, and resources an organization needs to be effective: (1) governance and leadership; (2) mission, vision, and strategy; (3) program delivery and impact; (4) strategic relationships; (5) resource development; and (6) internal operations and management. As in BOC, Connolly and Lucas stress the interrelationship of the components, counseling nonprofits to examine each element in several fashions: separately, in relation to others, and within the overall context of the organization. Robert Kaplan and David Norton (1996) emphasize the same approach in their influential Balanced Scorecard framework, which focuses on measuring performance. They note that their four complementary perspectives—financial, customer, operational, and organizational—are useful alone, but they are more valuable when viewed in conjunction with each other, and when one perspective does not outweigh the others (thus the concept of balance). Kaplan and Norton encourage managers to create a balanced scorecard through a series of interviews and workshops, beginning with vision and strategy and translating these into goals and measures, and then viewing each within the four perspectives. Kaplan and Norton's (2004) more recent work is on strategy maps, adapting the balanced scorecard to even more clearly emphasize, through the use of visual representations, the connections between elements of strategy—objectives, initiatives, target markets, performance measures, and the like.

Connolly and Lucas (2002) emphasize the importance of clarifying purposes and aspirations in nonprofit organizations, like BOC when it addresses strategic management in higher education. Having done so, nonprofits can use these to determine direction. Connolly and Lucas also stress the necessity of carefully defining governance and structure. They use the delivery and impact of programs as a surrogate for profit in a for-profit setting—the reason for the organization to exist—and thus suggest that it is vital to demonstrate tangible outcomes through evaluation and assessment. BOC extends their concept to include decision support, an aspect of the information element. It also connects communications with information, as opposed to considering it as an internal operation. Given their focus on nonprofits—organizations that are typically less well resourced than universities and colleges—Connolly and Lucas accentuate the central roles of external relationships through the development of partnerships and of securing support from a diversified pool of funders. These are also crucial aspects in higher educational management, but they are subsumed within various BOC elements, given the more predicable nature of higher education funding through tuition checks arriving each semester and annual appropriations for public institutions. Both frameworks underscore the importance of efficient operations possessing strong management-support systems, particularly in financial affairs. However, BOC is more detailed in its treatment of policies, processes, and infrastructure (financial, human, technological, and facilities)—again, a product of the more complex nature of universities and colleges as organizations.

Collis and Montgomery (1997) offer a somewhat different representation of interrelated elements, putting vision, goals, and objectives in the center of a triangle comprised of (1) resources; (2) businesses; and (3) structure, systems, and processes. They contend that viewing these in combination is the key to creating external corporate advantage. BOC also includes the mission and aspirations of an institution as one of eight elements, portraying it in the center of the web formed by their connections. Doing so indicates the necessity of considering purposes as an initial matter in a strategic-management approach. The McKinsey 7S framework does the same. (As both approaches are webs formed by the connections between and among the elements, the relative location of these various elements does not matter, since each element, including purposes in the middle, connects with each other element.) Collis and Montgomery have their other three elements revolve around purposes, which places less emphasis on the notion of systems thinking. Yet even with such differences, BOC and the other approaches to strategic management generally involve similar means, each categorizing and defining elements in a sensible way for a given sector, whether it is corporations, nonprofits, or universities and colleges.[3]

While not expressly a strategic-management approach, Jim Collins's *Good to Great* (2001) is also relevant to BOC, especially in its emphasis on building the administrative core of institutions. Collins argues that "good" is the enemy of "great" in organizations—including in higher education—and that too often institutions and the individuals within them merely settle for good. While a business can merely be good, the social sector (including higher education) should aspire to more, given that the stakes are elevated. (Collins's point suggests an interesting rebuttal to those who argue that higher education should be run more like businesses.) Continuity in institutions is particularly important in Collins's model, so the cadre of long-serving faculty and managers at most universities and colleges provides an advantage. Collins's research is based on finding "fraternal twins" among organizations in a given sector, such as General Electric (great) and Westinghouse (good). Doing so enables him to measure their performances longitudinally and ask what the great organization did that the good one did not.[4]

In looking at great organizations in the social sector, Collins suggests that there are four outputs: (1) results, seen in relationship to their mission (research, for example, at a research university, or teaching at a teaching institution); (2) impact, which he defines in terms of distinctiveness (would there be a hole that would be difficult to fill if the institution closed down tomorrow?); (3) esteem, both from those within the organization (such as students) and from experts in the field; and (4) endurance (these organizations last over time). Social-sector organizations are subject to irrational forces similar to those Wall Street exerts on corporations, particularly in encouraging maximizing shareholder advantage in the shorter term. At universities and colleges, strategies that are directed toward enhancing prestige, the currency in higher education (at least at selective institutions), cause institutions to drift upward from their mission in ways that can be similarly unproductive, a matter I consider in the next chapter.

Collins concludes that those corporations (and, by extension, universities or colleges) of a similar type that ultimately emerge as great are those that are more disciplined over the long run, even in the most dysfunctional industries. Southwest Airlines, for example, was the leading corporation across industries in earnings over the past two decades. He argues that building a great company is cumulative; it does not depend on a great event, but instead relies on building momentum through disciplined people, disciplined thought, and then disciplined action. His argument supports BOC's premise of establishing the administrative core of an institution as a foundation for realizing its aspirations. In addition, great firms are "hedgehogs," not "foxes." They latch onto one great idea and stay with it, cutting those things that do not fit. There are two types of hedgehogs—content and processes. Universities fit into the processes category, which is illustrated by General Electric operating in a variety of industries but being noted for developing executive talent across them. Focusing on purposes in strategic management, as BOC demands, is thus even more essential. Finally, the key to transformation in an organization, Collins contends, is coming to an understanding of its core values and core purposes—and changing operational and cultural practices, as well as specific goals and strategies, accordingly. Organizations often confuse processes with cores. Tenure is a good example; it is a process, not a core value or purpose—it is a means to an end, not an end in itself.[5] The application of BOC's proposed strategic-management principles avoids such confusion.

Finally, Birnbaum (2001) reminds us what strategic management (hopefully) is not. In his book on management fads in higher education, Birnbaum reviews several approaches that academic managers adopted, sometimes because of federal and other mandates, only to see them later fall into disfavor. Early approaches—planning, programming, and budgeting system (PPBS), management by objectives (MBO), and zero-based budgeting (ZBB)—were based solely on rational models and accordingly failed in the irrational and ambiguous world of higher education. The next generation of management systems, Birnbaum suggests, were attempts to tweak the rational models to fix perceived challenges associated with execution, such as intransigence across institutions. Keller's *Academic Strategy* (1983) was important in introducing strategic planning to higher education.[6] Yet in the end, Birnbaum argues, strategic planning suffered from a one-size-fits-all mentality, in which plans typically ended up looking similar despite institutional differences. It thus had problems with gaining legitimacy and generating commitment within universities and colleges (Presley and Leslie 1998). Indeed, Keller can be somewhat prescriptive in an environment that requires more flexibility.[7]

Birnbaum also discusses total quality management (TQM) and CQI (continuous quality improvement), products of the late 1980s and early 1990s; business process engineering (BPR); and the work of Hammer and Champy in *Reengineering the Corporation* (1993). These promised even more fundamental changes than quality-focused approaches. Birnbaum concludes that these fads failed because of their overemphasis on quantifying what is inherently difficult to measure in meaningful ways, given the nature of higher education. They also had disconnects in other areas: offering an illusion of certainty in an uncertain world; failing to recognize that managing is often more of an art than a science; too often centralizing bureaucracy and power; and tending to create self-fulfilling prophesies by centering on accusations, such as inefficiency. They also tended to be grounded only in some values, such as accountability, and not always in concepts important to higher education, such as intellectual development and scholarly community. Birnbaum does note, however, that these fads highlight the importance of data, emphasize alternative values, upset the status quo, support managers in their self-conception, and both diversify interaction and promote activity. Similar to the strategic-management approaches in other industries, these management fads inform BOC, whether as positive or as negative models, as well as emphasize the need to build management capacity with organizations.[8]

Systems Thinking

Any strategic-management model draws on systems thinking, which focuses on the interrelated nature of the components of a complex organization. I explore various systems approaches below, not to provide the means for leaders and senior managers to apply them directly, but to reinforce the logic of systems thinking within strategic management. Strategic management does more than simply consider an inventory of elements, also examining how they align within an organization—the notion of systems thinking. My purpose in examining several systems approaches is thus to emphasize systems thinking as a broad idea. There may be possibilities for the direct application of systems approaches to higher education, perhaps in the more accessible manner that Senge (1990) offers—a notion, once again, that other writers could consider.

Concept

Systems thinking departs from the cause-and-effect explanations of traditional science. Analytic approaches are linear, isolating elements to study their nature and generating solutions by modifying one variable at a time, thus always centering on details. In contrast, systems thinking considers groups of variables simultaneously in order to study their effects, focusing on the nonlinear interactions between and among them. It views an organization as a complex whole that is also influenced by its interactions with its outside environment. This whole is not the sum of its parts, but is greater than that: a set of interconnected units in which actions in one area reverberate throughout the entire organization. A seemingly local problem may thus be a symptom of a broader issue across the organization. Accordingly, outcomes within an organization-as-system, such as those associated with a given initiative, can be unexpected, due to the complex nature of interactions within both it and with the broader environment.

The metaphor of the human body is useful in representing a complex system and its subsystems. The human body is made up of different systems—circulatory, neurological, skeletal, and the like—but to truly understand it, one must view all of the systems interacting, responding to and compensating for each other. Information about how the body relates with its external environment is also essential. Therefore, if the goal is to better understand the body's complex functioning, learning about each system independently is insufficient. Jay Forrester (1991) explains that organizations are similarly not linear, but instead are circular, with behavior occurring within various feedback loops. Within organizations, "each action is based on current conditions, such actions affect conditions, and the changed conditions become the basis for future action. There is no beginning or end to the process. People are interconnected. Many such loops are intertwined. Through long cascaded chains of action, each person is continually reacting to the echo of that person's past actions, as well as to the past actions of others" (p. 8).

Labels for systems approaches abound—most notably systems thinking, systems dynamics, cybernetics, and systems theory—and are applied with varying degrees of precision and of attention to their intellectual foundations.[9] In general, systems dynamics centers on quantitative modeling, while systems thinking, which is more descriptive of BOC and other strategic-management approaches, highlights its more prescient points in a manner that is more accessible to practitioners, often using illustrations. Those immersed in their study can discuss even the most nuanced differences between and among traditions, theories, and approaches. The common premises, however, are that organizations are complex wholes comprising many disparate parts that do not provide an adequate picture of the organization when viewed separately, in summation, or apart from the external environment.

Systems thinking in management evolved from general systems theories that were first developed in the biological and physical sciences in the 1940s and 1950s and credited to biologist Ludwig von Bertalanffy. In the sciences, systems theories countered a reductionist slant toward organisms, arguing that organisms are more than just mere amalgams of their subsystems—dividing an elephant in half does not produce two small elephants (Senge 1990). In addition, those working with biological systems began to contend that treating organisms as closed systems, distinct from their environments, omitted broader interactions, reactions, and dependencies between the two. The logic of considering wholes and open systems applies similarly to organizations, and general systems theories eventually transcended the sciences to influence management theory.[10] In encouraging managers and others to fundamentally change their thinking to view the overall picture—including both internal and external environments—and not just their part of it, systems thinking has proved constructive in addressing difficult issues in various areas (Aronson 1998). These issues consist of the most complex problems—those (as are common at universities and colleges) lacking immediately apparent solutions, having the greatest dependence on the actions of others, requiring the most number of interactions, and often stemming from ineffective coordination.[11]

The logic of systems thinking—that aspects within an organization need to be aligned—tends to resonate with people and has thus influenced most thinking about organizations since the 1970s. Peter Senge popularized the concept, framing it as the learning organization in *The Fifth Discipline* (1990), arguing that systems thinking addresses the common "learning disabilities" in organizations that other frameworks often fail to address. Senge identifies several of these disabilities, including needlessly fixating on an external enemy (unions, foreign competitors, government regulators, fickle customers); acting to take charge without first having clarity about the situation at hand; fixating on short-term benchmarks; and failing to see gradual and particularly subtle progress. Furthermore, systems thinking can work in combination with other traditions and approaches. For instance, TQM is essentially about outputs informing inputs, which in turn inform outputs (Cooper 1995). Certainly the logic of systems thinking is consistent with strategic-management approaches such as BOC, particularly in emphasizing the need for alignment among elements within organizations.

Systems approaches to management have received rather limited specific attention recently,[12] including in addressing higher education issues, where there is a dearth of sophisticated work on the topic (and really not much scholarship at all). As Senge realized in offering his more accessible version of it, systems approaches can be difficult to understand and sometimes overly rigid as applied in an environment as complex as universities and colleges. The dynamic in shifting to systems thinking may be the same as the prescriptive schools in strategic management, yielding, to some extent, to the descriptive ones—although it is important to remember that SWOT analyses, strategic planning, and positioning remain in regular use, including in higher education.

Approaches

Jackson (2003) offers a useful typology of systems approaches. His ten categories range from those grounded in functionalism and structuralism to others that embrace postmodernism and chaos theory.[13] He concludes with his own approach, one that argues for combining other approaches, wherever possible, in creative ways, particularly through the use of metaphors (see Morgan 1997).[14] Although distinct, the various frameworks do share the foundational assumption that organizations are interdependent and that actions within them, however local they may seem, tend to reverberate.[15] Jackson fits the ten systems approaches he identifies into four broad types: (1) improving goal seeking and organizational capacity, (2) exploring purposes, (3) ensuring fairness, and (4) promoting diversity. The first category is most directly relevant to strategic management and includes hard systems, system dynamics, organizational cybernetics, and complexity theory. The other three categories focus more on encouraging broad participation within organizations-as-systems. Strategic management only draws on the logic of systems thinking; it is not aligned with any given model of it. Nevertheless, there is no reason why a leader or senior manager could not apply a specific systems approach in addition to a framework such as BOC.

In discussing his first broad type—approaches to improving goal seeking and capacity—Jackson begins with hard systems, which uses mathematical modeling to identify problems, test scenarios, and eventually enhance efficiency. The approach is common in operations research, systems analysis, and systems engineering, requiring objective definitions of a given system, including its purposes and operations. Such definitions can be difficult and limiting, particularly in considering the multiple realities, viewpoints, and objectives so central to approaches that attempt to ensure fairness and promote diversity. It is equally difficult to model politics, personalities, and culture in an organization. Nevertheless, proponents underscore the advantages of an objective, systematic analysis—as opposed to more ad hoc approaches—in encouraging clarity.

Applied systems thinking is more consistent with strategic management. It addresses some of the criticisms associated with hard systems approaches by seeking to account for complexity, change, and diversity within systems. The three primary approaches to applied systems theory that focus on goal seeking and organizational capacity are systems dynamics, organizational cybernetics, and complexity theory. I address systems dynamics, especially work by Senge in the 1990s that popularized the concept, in some detail, briefly considering cybernetics and complexity in concluding the discussion.

Systems dynamics is associated with Jay Forrester and resembles hard systems thinking in its focus on rigorous modeling in the search for patterns within organizations. This approach defines systems in terms of the interrelationships among its multiple feedback loops, which structure any organization and determine behavior within it. Feedback loops are circular processes in which decisions cause changes that influence later decisions, not only locally but across the organization—thus all influences are both causes and effects (Galbraith 2001; Forrester 1998; Senge et al. 1994; Senge 1990). *Reinforcing* feedback loops amplify either growth or decline, both of which occur at an ever-quickening pace, but not indefinite, pace. They are like compound interest at a bank, where interest added to principle increases the available capital (Galbraith, 2001). *Balancing* feedback loops operate to slow, divert, halt, or even reverse reinforcing loops through some strategic action, thus moving to a state more consistent with organizational goals. Galbraith likens them to a thermostat: if the temperature falls below the set number, the furnace activates and eventually warms the room (see also Bellinger 2004; Richardson 1991).

Galbraith (2001) provides an example of reinforcing and balancing loops taken from higher education: "In a university . . . an example of a reinforcing loop is the process by which an increase in enrollments provides additional funds which supports an increase in academic staff which provides for the enrollment of more students which produces additional funds and so on. An example of a balancing loop is the process by which an increase in staff increases the salary bill which reduces the funds available to employ staff which reduces the rate at which new staff can be appointed which leads to a reduction in staff and so forth. In both of these causal loops, delays of the order of years are involved before the loops are closed" (p. 14). The idea of balancing loops emphasizes the basic notion essential to strategic management—that multiple elements influence one another in various ways and to different extents.

Balancing loops present difficulties for managers, beginning with learning to recognize them, and then in discerning which strategies to apply in order to actually provide the balancing. This latter aspect can be especially challenging when goals within an organization are implicit and cause and effect are subtle (Senge 1990). Additionally, resistance to change in an organization is often embedded within undetected or implicit balancing processes. It is also difficult to control timing in loops, so actions intended to create balance may continue longer than is necessary for them to meet a goal, or they may oscillate around a goal rather than smoothly approach it. The process is not unlike finding the optimum mix of hot and cold water in a shower (Galbraith 2001). Furthermore, delays in results from strategic decisions may cause given feedback loops to be overlooked, or such delays may be mistaken for a lack of consequences when in fact the impacts have yet to be realized.

Systems approaches thus require taking a long view (Senge 1990). Strategic management also requires patience, with leaders and senior managers referring back regularly to their checklist of elements and considering time and again how they interrelate at any given moment. In addition, there is the challenge of complexity, whether systems having many parts (detail complexity) and many connections (dynamic complexity). Complexity causes concerns, such as an action having one set of consequences locally and a very different set of consequences in another area of the system, or when obvious interventions produce nonobvious consequences. Higher education, given its decentralized nature, is rife with such complexity, a matter to consider in applying any strategic-management framework.

Systems dynamics operates logically enough, as should strategic management, by first recalling the purpose of the organization before defining the problem to solve or undesirable behavior to correct or avoid. The approach then determines the boundaries of the system (everything that does or does not impact behavior), drawing on qualitative data produced within the organization. Systems dynamics next identifies the network of feedback loops within the organization, calculating quantities within the loops (levels) based on the relationships between and among them (rates), thus developing equations for a model. The model ultimately suggests leverage points where interventions can influence behavior within the loops, and thus across the broader system (Jackson 2003; Sternman 2000; Forrester 1998, 1994b; Morecroft and Sternman 1994).[16] Applying the model involves looking back to relevant earlier steps throughout each stage of the process; using models to test alternative policies and structure; and "educating and debating" to achieve consensus about implementing changes (Forrester 1994b). Systems dynamics proponents argue that the underlying patterns of feedback loops are not necessarily apparent within organizations, only revealing themselves through quantitative modeling. Identifying these patterns can suggest unexpected interventions, and even the need for sometimes radically changed thinking by managers, while preventing managers from leaping to what appear to be obvious solutions that nonetheless could contain unintended consequences, such as treating symptoms as opposed to causes.

As with hard systems theory and other positivist modeling approaches (such as econometrics), systems dynamics is subject to the criticism that it is only as good as the models it generates—and accurate representations of something as complex as an organization-as-system are so difficult to achieve as to be unrealistic. Additionally, social systems are not static, but instead are dynamic and negotiated terrains that are constantly being interpreted, defined, and redefined through subjective means. Critics argue that attempting to reduce such an environment to a set of variables, and to measure relationships objectively, is thus of limited utility (Jackson 2003). Again, it is the logic of such approaches—in other words, systems thinking—that is relevant to strategic management, not the process involved in building an actual systems dynamics model.

In an attempt to make system dynamics more accessible, Senge (1990) replaces Forrester's computer modeling with archetypes in what he terms "learning organizations," drawing on the concept of organizational learning established by Argyris (Argyris, 1993, 1990; Argyris and Schon 1978).[17] These archetypes are frequently recurring structures—typical combinations of feedback loops—claimed to represent most system behaviors. They allow one to predict or diagnose the structures responsible for behavioral problems in organizations and address them with certain ready-made strategies (Bellinger 2004; Galbraith 2001).[18] BOC does not employ archetypes, instead offering case studies to illustrate elements and their connections, but archetypes are not inconsistent with the framework and may be useful to managers, if only as a reminder of the importance of alignment in organizations-as-systems.

Senge's (1990) learning organization has five components: (1) systems thinking, (2) personal vision (focused energies and a commitment to learning and self-improvement), (3) mental models (learning to explicitly acknowledge and evaluate inherently incomplete representations of phenomena), (4) building a shared vision, and (5) team learning (marked by dialogue and communication). As in the

BOC framework, Senge notes that it is vital to consider all five disciplines and develop them as an ensemble, with systems thinking integrating them and providing coherence and the disciplines buttressing and enriching one another. Vision without systems, Senge contends, leads to a "lovely picture," but no understanding of the forces that need to be mastered to get there (p. 12). He suggests that most managers wrongly focus on snapshots, instead of processes over time, and on details and "things" (such as tasks, positions, people, etc.), instead of complexity. They thus see only linear cause-effect chains, as opposed to taking a wide-angle view of interrelationships.

Senge emphasizes that interrelationships control behavior within any structure, with the organization itself commonly causing difficulties, rather than just external forces, as is so often presumed. Accordingly, he contends that different managers populating the same system would tend to make the same decisions. For Senge, the key to systems thinking is leverage, which involves new ways of thinking and involves changes in structures that can lead to significant and enduring improvements. The goal is for the smallest leverage to create the greatest change. Senge posits that a small change can produce big results, and that the areas of highest leverage are often the least obvious. He is ultimately interested in those within organizations creating their own reality, recognizing external influences yet acknowledging that problems are usually due to their own actions.

Consistent with systems dynamics approaches, Senge also stresses that problems are not characterized by cause and effect, but instead are in a chain of causality—a feedback loop. Like Forrester (1994a), Senge (1990) argues that cause and effect are not closely related in time and space, but instead are many interacting feedback loops and often long time delays. Thus the cause of an observed symptom may be from an entirely different part of system, perhaps even far back in time (Forrester 1994a). Also, new policies can cause reactions in other parts of a system that counteract their intent. Similarly, a response altering the behavior of a system that seems right, given human intuition, can actually make the problem worse, such as in the example from the 1960s and 1970s of public housing furthering urban decay (Forrester 1994b).[19] Once again, these notions are all relevant in applying any strategic-management framework.

Organizational cybernetics, associated with Stafford Beer, is the second applied approach that Jackson (2003) outlines. It focuses more on the effective structuring of organizations than on managing them. Beer (1966) posits that since organizations can often be black boxes, it is not always necessary to fully understand how one works in order to impose a measure of control over it by monitoring outputs and manipulating inputs, with feedback loops triggering points of intervention. Effective management involves reducing variety (or imposing consistency) at multiple levels within the system. Beer argues that all complex organizations are recursive, existing in hierarchies that repeat themselves on multiple levels throughout the organization. Once an organization has defined its identity and aspirations, it must focus on which units or subsystems, acting as autonomously as possible, must perform appropriately to achieve these goals. Only then should the organization-as-system be modeled. Organizational cybernetics is criticized for being overly functionalist: only pursuing goals, but not questioning them, and merely nodding at individualism, negotiation, and multiple viewpoints. The complexity and sophistication of its modeling is also challenged by critics coming from the opposite direction. Proponents of organizational cybernetics note the advantages associated with clarity and a shared understanding of purposes; the benefits of decentralization and of empowering local decision makers, while also maintaining a systems orientation; and the efficiency that comes with ascertaining which structures and processes are essential in an organization.

The third applied approach, *complexity theory* (originally called "chaos theory"), is inspired by the butterfly effect, Edward Lorenz's (1993) notion that a butterfly flapping its wings can change weather patterns across the planet. Even small changes in a complex system can thus alter its behavior in unpredictable and substantial ways over time. Nevertheless, there are patterns in natural and social systems that managers can discern, and organizations can adapt, evolving in reaction to their environment while also shaping that environment. In complexity theory, systems are naturally open, not closed. Therefore it is crucial for organizations to pay attention to managing their environments, inasmuch as they can. Organizations, moreover, are constantly in flux, creating only temporary stability, thus rendering long-range predictions useless. According to complexity theory, equilibrium is a state of decay and degradation in a system (Kelly and Booth 2004).

The approach thus urges managers to embrace disorder, abandoning determinism and accepting unpredictability as necessary precursors to (albeit temporary) order. Doing so, at the edge of chaos, builds capacity for creativity, innovation, and change. These ends are crucial in higher education, particularly given contemporary trends toward the greater influence of markets. Organizations can choose this "bounded instability," trying not to control everything; opt for stability (which discourages creativity and innovation), thus soon growing outdated and unresponsive; or select instability, becoming overwhelmed by disorder and eventually disintegrating or imploding.[20] More functionalist critics of complexity theory question whether an approach grounded in the sciences can be grafted onto social systems—and, once there, whether it can be adequately tested. Postmodernists challenge chaos theory's focus on success and efficiency and its premise that managers alone determine where and even what the edge of chaos is.

Exploring purposes is the second broad type of systems approach. Like complexity theory, its logic may be helpful to those applying BOC or other strategic-management frameworks. Exploring purposes employs soft systems methodology and other means to evaluate aims and objectives and promote mutual understanding within an organization. In these models, organizations act in a participative manner that integrates the views of different stakeholders, who may function as adversaries. The goal in the exploring purposes approaches is to uncover assumptions, encourage debate, and ultimately arrive at synthesis. Ackoff's interactive planning approach is inconsistent in contending that planning in any organization requires broad participation and involvement. Soft system methodology thus focuses as much on maintaining relationships as on seeking goals and answering questions (Checkland 1999).

The third type, ensuring fairness, is more emancipatory, focusing on inclusiveness. It includes critical system heuristics and "team syntegrity" approaches, the latter involving a protocol supporting nonhierarchical, participative decision making among those with some expertise about (and interest in) a topic. Jackson's fourth and final broad type, promoting diversity, incorporates postmodern ideas. It focuses not on universal solutions, but rather on local and temporary resolutions of difficulties, contending that these are all that is possible within an organization.[21]

Although not linked with or guided by a particular approach, BOC, like other strategic-management models, incorporates the logic of systems thinking.[22] Considering elements without considering their alignment is insufficient. Strategic management must employ systems thinking. In building the organizational capacity that provides the administrative foundation needed to support the initiatives that advance institutional aspirations, both strategic management *and* systems thinking are necessary.

CHAPTER TWO

Managing Increasingly Complex Institutions

E xploring the fundamentals of strategic management, as informed by systems thinking, in the previous chapter emphasizes the differences between universities and colleges and other organizational settings. Applying these ideas at any institution demands an understanding of contemporary trends and issues in higher education. In this chapter, I comment on these concerns and briefly consider literature on leading organizational change in higher education, thus providing a foundation for the discussions across the case study chapters on understanding and applying the Building Organizational Capacity framework. To conclude the chapter, I describe how we developed the BOC approach.

Strategic management might contribute to moderating some of the challenges these higher education trends and issues present. Yet there is also the risk that strategic management may accelerate the commercialization of universities and colleges, including the erosion of faculty influence across higher education and the increasingly more managed nature of institutions. Like any tool, BOC's application depends on the intentions and abilities of the user.

Trends and Issues

The strategies that underlie the initiatives discussed in the case study chapters are typically responses to the emergence of a neoliberal ethos within U.S. higher education since the 1980s, substituting a greater reliance on markets and a drive for internal efficiency for more traditional support from the state. Higher education has increasingly become a commodity, its environment marked by intense competition and its purposes becoming more connected with individual gain than with societal good (Marginson 2006; Slaughter and Rhoades 2004; Bok 2002). Within this context, even marginally selective higher education institutions employ a rather predictable set of strategies intended to simultaneously enhance the resources available to them and increase their prestige, as these two goals are thought to be mutually reinforcing (Toma 2008; Geiger 2004; Kirp 2003; Brewer, Gates, and Goldman 2002; Ehrenberg 2002).

Pursuing prestige provides universities and colleges with a surrogate for increasing shareholder value or bottom-line profits—an outcome consistent with a neoliberal frame. It can also exacerbate the mission inflation (or academic drift) that comes with institutions being naturally isomorphic (Clark 1983b).[1] Organizations, and even units within them, tend to grow more similar in structure and operation over time, preferring the legitimacy and security of attempting to replicate perceived leaders in a given field (Scott 1998; Meyer and Rowan 1985; DiMaggio and Powell 1983). Examples of this are a two-year college seeking to add four-year programs; a regional comprehensive institution aspiring to be more like a state flagship university; or a flagship competing with leading private research universities to attract star faculty. Such isomorphic behaviors provide organizations with the reduced risk that comes with staying in the herd. In increasing their prestige, colleges and universities also attempt to minimize the influence of the external entities on which they rely for support, thus enhancing their independent resource base (Pfeffer 1982; Pfeffer and Salanick 1978). Institutions tend to look increasingly like one another as they act in accord with contemporary trends, such as adding programs with market appeal or seeking internal efficiencies— and may work toward the latter through such means as considering approaches to strategic management.

In seeking prestige, selective universities and colleges now more assiduously seek to attract increasingly accomplished students, typically by employing pricing strategy, as seen in the case study of decision support for tuition discounting at the University of Redlands (chapter 8) (Geiger 2004; Ehrenberg 2002; McPherson and Schapiro 1998). Among research universities (or aspiring ones), there is also a robust market for faculty members thought to have the ability to attract significant levels of funding, especially for work that has commercial potential (Geiger 2004; Slaughter and Rhoades 2004; Kirp 2003). In both areas, universities and colleges with more limited resources tend to focus upon building a small cluster of accomplished students or enhancing particular programs in attempting to distinguish themselves strategically. They can also indicate their prestige (of a sort) and enhance resources by increasing quantity in areas such as enrollment, as do nonselective institutions that stress student convenience (Toma 2008). Across types, institutions focus on measures such as retention, including as needed to satisfy various accreditation and accountability requirements. But they are also driven by traditional values, which have hardly been abandoned (Newman, Couturier, and Scurry 2004), as can be seen in the case study of efforts to improve student success at Paul D. Camp Community College (chapter 7).

Selective (even marginally so) institutions across higher education attempt use academic initiatives to advance their "getting to the next level" visions: launching popular undergraduate majors, adding or augmenting graduate programs, encouraging faculty research, emphasizing honors programs, and enhancing study-abroad opportunities (Toma 2008; Geiger 2004; Kirp 2003). Examples include transforming the curriculum at The College of New Jersey (TCNJ) to reflect the public liberal arts college it has become (chapter 3); encouraging faculty scholarship and integrating student research into the curriculum in efforts to improve the profile of LaGrange College (chapter 6); and invigorating undergraduate education to challenge the increasingly more accomplished students at the University of Georgia (UGA) (chapter 10).

In positioning for prestige, institutions often find the available academic tools limited and uncertain. They are accordingly increasingly drawn toward more concrete strategic approaches, such as enhancing campus infrastructure (Toma 2008). Developing a student computing facility to teach mathematics at Virginia Tech (chapter 4) fits into both positioning for prestige and academic initiatives. Investments in teaching facilities, such as a science building at LaGrange (chapter 6) are increasingly common. Universities and colleges nationally, including the four-year ones among the eight featured, are also making significant investments in campus amenities, such as student residences, dining commons, fitness centers, or commercial districts. Many universities are engaged in similar efforts in intercollegiate athletics—improving facilities, upgrading to Division I, and seeking entry into better conferences—as they position themselves for the promise of greater prestige and resources (Toma 2008; Bok 2002). LaGrange, for instance, recently added Division III football as a means to enhance its external relations and its student recruitment, as well as to further situate the institution among those it aspires to resemble. Additionally, institutions are increasingly professional in framing messages for outsiders, better shaping and managing how they are perceived (Toma 2008; Kirp 2003).

Universities and colleges have supported these diverse academic and collegiate initiatives through a variety of means. One strategy is to expand—sometimes substantially—activities at their peripheries, especially when significantly increasing tuition revenue is not an option. An illustration would be a nonselective liberal arts college or a flagship state university located in a nonurban area that establishes a satellite campus near a larger city to serve part-time students studying in professional fields (Zemsky, Wegner, and Massy 2005; Newman, Couturier, and Scurry 2004; Slaughter and Rhoades 2004; Bok 2002).[2] For instance, LaGrange College has a campus in Columbus, the closest large city; Virginia Tech (located in rural southwest Virginia) offers programs in northern Virginia; and UGA does likewise in suburban Atlanta, at a facility located an hour away. Institutions are responding to perceived markets and launching programs based on student convenience, with entrepreneurial, as opposed to democratizing, ends in mind (Bok 2002)—and sometimes closing them just as fast, having come to understand the actual market when enrollments lag. Institutions are responding to student demand that continues to increase, particularly among part-time students interested in professional degrees, as individuals and employers recognize the greater need for training and credentialing in a knowledge economy (Collis 2004; Newman, Couturier, and Scurry 2004). More nontraditional students are being served in programs outside of the traditional academic core of institutions, including through e-learning (as advances in technology make this ever more appealing), at the satellite campuses that public and private institutions are aggressively developing and at the local branches of the rapidly expanding, national for-profit providers (Tierney and Hentschke 2007; Berdahl, Altbach, and Gumport 2005; Zemsky, Wegner, and Massy 2005; Collis 2004).

Managers tend to shape these peripheral academic programs, which are typically staffed by temporary faculty or core faculty on teaching overloads, and those involved are inclined to view students as clients—all meaningful cultural shifts in U.S. higher education away from traditional faculty influence (Bousquet 2008; Rhoades 2005; Zemsky, Wegner, and Massy 2005; Slaughter and Rhoades 2004).

Part of the attraction of peripheral programs is that they are assumed to be efficient—and across higher education, institutions have concentrated on finding efficiencies, attempting to cut their costs while expanding revenues. Apart from the challenge to traditional academic values these peripheral programs present, there are also strategic risks. Collis (2004) cautions against mission creep, where "each succeeding tier of the periphery pursues new directions of its own accord" (p. 63), thus risking expanding everywhere into the periphery and failing to commit a sufficient amount of scarce resources to any one venture—an inability to prioritize, in other words.

Furthermore, research universities are equally assertive in supporting faculty involvement outside of research ventures, often as individual entrepreneurs; building auxiliary enterprises such as housing and dining facilities; and pursuing corporate partnerships in research, instruction, and training (Geiger 2004; Slaughter and Rhoades 2004; Kirp 2003). Institutions of other types also envision the periphery, by generating resources, can protect the less agile, and thus perhaps the less efficient, core of the institution. Concepts such as strategic management and systems thinking may prove useful here, both in finding the right efficiencies and in bringing order to an even more diffuse institution.

Despite the promise of revenues at peripheries and efficiencies within cores, resources generally remain strained across institutions, often significantly so, especially during downturns in the national or local economy. Ever-more-intense competition has often required selective universities and colleges to discount tuition further, lowering the price paid by the most desirable students—and thus reducing the institutional bottom line (Geiger 2004; Ehrenberg 2002; McPherson and Schapiro 1998). The Redlands case addresses the university's attempt to manage costs and maximize impact with tuition discounting. Discounting has shifted the emphasis away from need-based assistance and toward merit student aid.

Nondiscretionary spending is also escalating (Dill 2003; Ehrenberg 2002). While making what, from a practical perspective, are seen as necessary investments in the various "arms races" for students, faculty, programs, and facilities (as TCNJ did in building a more selective institution), institutions are also budgeting more for basic services, including health benefits, information technology, deferred maintenance, building maintenance, and energy use (Society for College and University Planning 2005; Zusman 2005; J. Lee and Clery 2004; Ehrenberg 2002). Institutions have attempted to contain costs (aside from in various arms races), whether through outsourcing or efficiencies, as private sector management ideas have permeated the public sector (Zemsky, Wegner, and Massy 2005; Kirp 2003). The case study on implementing an enterprise resource planning system at Valley City State University (chapter 5) illustrates such trends.

Meanwhile, states are providing a diminishing proportion of budgets, and tuition and fund raising supplies an ever-greater share. State financing of public higher education has increased, but not to the degree necessary to match escalating costs (McGuinness 2005; Zusman 2005; Geiger 2004). Regular tuition hikes are replacing only some of the lost funds (Zusman 2005), especially as the cost of higher education has received greater attention from taxpayers and thus politicians (Heller 2002; Zumeta 2001). Nevertheless, states expect institutions to balance— and increasingly to demonstrate or justify—access, affordability, and quality (Schmidtlein and Berdahl 2005; Newman, Couturier, and Scurry 2004; Dill 2003). Meanwhile, expectations related to furthering local, state, and national economic development have never been higher (Altbach 2005; Altbach, Berdahl, and Gumport 2005; McGuinness 2005; Enders 2004; Geiger 2004). The case study of Seminole Community College (chapter 9) is about maintaining quality amidst dramatic growth and static resources—doing more with less. The Virginia Tech case is another example of cost savings contributing to stimulating an initiative.

Perhaps most prominently—and, ultimately, significantly—universities and colleges are cutting expenses and seeking greater agility by shifting faculty staffing away from tenure-significant positions toward temporary, part-time, and adjunct ones (Bousquet 2008; Zusman 2005; Collis 2004; J. Lee and Clery 2004; Gayle, Tewarie, and White 2003). While moving instruction to the Math Emporium at Virginia Tech was intended to improve teaching, it also controlled costs by transferring some the instructional load away from tenure-significant faculty. Non-tenure-track faculty members now constitute nearly one-half of all faculty members nationally, compared with 22 percent in 1970 (Collis 2004). What Gary Rhoades, Shelia Slaughter, and Larry Leslie term "academic capitalism" involves structural changes in academe focused on generating revenue for institutions and enhancing their competitiveness. According to Rhoades (2005), it "depends on a mode of production that fosters the growth of contingent faculty and non-faculty professionals relative to full-time, tenure-track professors. It also gives rise to a mode of management that strengthens the governance role of central academic managers relative to that of faculty" (p. 38; see also Slaughter and Rhoades 2004).

Reforms in higher education over the past two decades have primarily focused on improving management—increasing the influence of administrators while reducing that of faculty (Altbach 2005; Zemsky, Wegner, and Massy 2005).[3] The ratio of faculty to administrators is now approximately 1:1—a change from a 2:1 mix favoring faculty in 1976 (Collis 2004). Moreover, while administrative and professional staff increased nationally by 15 percent between 1993 and 2001, full-time faculty expanded by only 3.4 percent (J. Lee and Clery 2004). Whether adding administrators and reducing regular faculty has improved institutions, ultimately making them more efficient, is an open question, however.

The great change in U.S. higher education across both public and private institutions has been toward a more revenue-driven, market-responsive approach. The culture that has emerged is one of professional managers responding in more entrepreneurial ways to external opportunities. Traditional values still matter, but they are no longer the sole consideration or perhaps even the paramount one. Institutions thus need to manage greater complexity, and even ambiguity, while competing more directly and intensely, whether for people or resources (Zusman 2005; Collis 2004; J. Lee and Clery 2004). In such an environment, strategic management and systems thinking may prove useful to leaders and senior managers. Yet it can also raise concerns. Institutions have not dismantled their traditional structures of faculty governance, instead tending to supplant them with new arrangements that allow managers greater discretion in relation to academic programs. Strategic planning and administrative flexibility are increasingly esteemed, allowing a clear possibility for market criteria and revenue generation to trump educational standards (Rhoades 2005; Bok 2002). In such environments, justice can become procedural, looking not at outcomes, or even fairness, but instead at processes (Birnbaum 2004).

The approach offered here of working toward building administrative capacity through strategic management is hardly intended to further the devolution of universities and colleges away from their traditional values. A framework that encourages leaders and senior managers in better aligning the fundamental purposes and significant aspirations of institutions with how people function in them—how individuals are configured to do their work (structure), how they define who makes what decisions (governance), how they set rules to operate under (policies), and so forth—does not necessarily push universities and colleges away from their values and toward inappropriately imitating various unappealing aspects of businesses. The intention of strategic management in higher education is to strengthen the administrative foundation of an institution, but organizational capacity can be employed for any set of purposes. An institution can certainly define a set of aspirations focused on increasing its prestige and generating more revenues, employing strategic management to advance approaches such as tuition discounting for affluent students or reducing instructional costs through the use of adjunct faculty.

Alternatively, a university or college could just as easily head in the other direction, aligning the multiple elements of the organization through strategic management in order to support protecting and strengthening traditional academic values. Indeed, a president interested in positioning his or her institution in opposition to various contemporary trends, leading it away from viewing higher education in terms of individual gain, would need the same robust administrative core as one seeking advantage in the prestige race. In fact, he or she may need it even more, given the challenges associated with swimming upstream against the neoliberal current. Strategic management is a tool. It does not influence purposes, but instead supports realizing them, once defined. It is a mistake to equate strategic management with the increasingly managed university. What drives presidents toward the now standard set of aspirations and strategies focused on getting to "the next level" is a "what" question. Strategic management is a "how" one.

In addition, strategic management and systems thinking inherently concern the overall institution. Therefore, the generic situations I employ to illustrate how the framework might apply tend to feature leaders and senior managers. The case studies consider faculty members when they step into a university-wide role on a given matter. Yet faculty, especially at large institutions, are generally not directly involved in several issues, particularly those not connected with academic questions.[4] While professors are often thoughtful about how their institutions do—and should—work, their influence is primarily local (apart from the situation at consensus-driven smaller institutions).

Within academic departments, faculty traditionally determine who may teach, what may be taught, how it shall be taught, and who may be admitted to study, as Justice Frankfurter articulated in his dissent in the U.S. Supreme Court decision in *Sweezy v. New Hampshire* (1957). At the institutional level, particularly in more complex universities, formal faculty influence on management tends to be modest, with faculty senates sometimes asserting more of a moral authority than exercising formal power (Birnbaum 2004). Yet the neoliberal university or college has not abandoned the ideals associated with academe from its beginnings, even when other values have increased in prominence. The case studies on curricular reform at TCNJ (chapter 3) and on intensifying the intellectual culture of UGA (chapter 10) illustrate the importance of faculty perspectives in strategic management, as such sensibilities continue to shape the essential character of institutions across types.

Faculty influence the application of a strategic-management framework to different degrees, with that influence being characteristic of the type of institution involved and depending on the kind of question being addressed. Birnbaum (1988) categorizes institutions into four distinct types: collegial liberal arts colleges, hierarchical community colleges, political comprehensive institutions, and anarchical research universities. Faculty members at research universities exist in an anarchical environment characterized by individual autonomy. They are positioned to have influence, but they are increasingly disinterested in institutional matters. Those at traditional liberal arts colleges operate within a collegial model based on consensus, with pronounced faculty influence. In contrast, faculty members at institutions with lesser stature and fewer resources are more likely to exist in more bureaucratic environments, ones defined by hierarchy and accountability. These faculty are less likely to have enough influence to balance that of administrators on governance questions. At institutions closer to the open-access end of the spectrum, such as at community colleges, administrators frequently are the ones who define academic decisions, even those of the type Justice Frankfurter articulated. In academic programs at the peripheries of institutions, including the satellite campuses of research universities, professional managers can also have a similar influence, especially given the importance of marketability.

Accordingly, across all eight case studies, I note where the featured university or college falls on the spectrum of institutional types—and thus indicate how much influence faculty members have on strategy and management across the institution, particularly on academic matters. For instance, the TCNJ or Virginia Tech cases involve a group of interested faculty operating in an environment in which shared governance is reasonably robust—and both initiatives are concerned with academic matters. At Valley City State and Seminole Community College, faculty influence is less significant in understanding the possibilities for strategic management, given that the initiatives in these two instances involve more managerial concerns: respectively, a management information system upgrade and a combination of infrastructure improvements and their corresponding budget constraints. Even at Redlands, a selective liberal arts college, faculty are not involved in the nuts and bolts of tuition-discounting decisions; such choices are viewed as rightly delegated to the administrators charged with managing the finances of the institution.

Leading Organizational Change

The chapters that follow explore the different elements of the BOC framework and how they align with the others, as well as consider how leaders and senior managers in higher education might apply it. As context for these discussions, I briefly examine writing on leading organizational change in higher education. Unlike governance or information, leadership itself is not an element in the BOC framework. Leaders and senior managers instead set the conditions for the application of strategic management, including how it is related to the initiatives intended to advance organizational change. Strategic management tends to be most applicable to more significant initiatives—those, such as ones involving change, with the most moving parts. Writing on leading organizational change are relevant in considering strategic management and capacity building.

In applying the BOC framework, leaders and senior managers are responsible for clarifying the elements and aligning them, doing so in the context of the particular initiative they are attempting to advance. Based on the characteristics of their institution and the nature of the project involved, they should consider concerns such as who needs to be responsible for managing the initiative and monitoring its progress; whether those leading the project have a clear sense of the institutional purposes that the initiative is intended to advance; and if that person or team has a clear understanding, relative to the initiative, of the elements and how they must align. The leader or senior manager should also indicate the time frame for planning and developing the initiative and expect clarity on the major steps along the way, as well as what will measure progress and, ultimately, impact. Leaders and senior managers can also provide guidance on other matters: people who need to be involved, including externally; efforts to further clarity and cohesion in the elements; and insight into where breakdowns are likely to occur, and what connections between and among elements present the greatest challenges.

In shaping a particular initiative, leaders and senior managers can ask all of these questions in applying the BOC framework across an entire institution. For example, the president of a smaller comprehensive university may be interested in enhancing service learning. The president could manage the initiative from his or her own office, but there are several strategic priorities that also require attention—and matters arise regularly that require an immediate response. Therefore, it probably makes more sense to assign the initiative to the provost and the vice president for student affairs, as the president knows these individuals under-stand the purposes of the institution, including his or her own aspirations for it. The president might also suggest that the provost and vice president especially consider various matters: configuring people properly do their work toward advancing service learning at the institution (structure); supplying the data re-quired to make good decisions, including who might generate and communicate it; and making needed changes in the essential character of the institution in order for service learning to be successful (culture).

In doing so, the provost and the vice president will also need to examine how such questions relate to one another. For instance, should service learning be housed in a single office or managed within various units? Are existing mecha-nisms suitable for evaluating both students and the program, no matter whether the program is centralized or decentralized? Is the faculty ready to accept a new approach to the curriculum, including in matters such as evaluating students and having a service-learning office influence academic decisions? The president might also set a goal of having X many students involved in service learning in Y many years. He or she could integrate service learning into various institutional messages, including those related to fund raising, as well as consider symbolic ways to underscore the importance of the initiative.

Leadership, therefore, both enables and defines the various elements in the strategic-management framework. Management without leadership is insuffi-cient, as clarifying factors like vision and inspiration, which are captured in the BOC purposes element, matter as much as organization and accountability. Pres-idents, however, are more likely to regard effective leadership as being essential to their success—and that of their institution—rather than the improvement of management. Also, there are decidedly fewer books and articles about manage-ment in higher education (or other fields) than there are about leadership. In ad-dressing strategic management, I thus refer readers to the literature on leadership but ask them to concentrate on management—the administrative foundation within a university or college that is needed to support the initiatives that move the institution towards its ambitions.

The application of the BOC approach is consistent with contemporary think-ing on leadership. In their synthesis of research in this area, Kezar, Carducci, and Contreras-McGavin (2006)—with a nod to Bensimon, Neumann, and Birnbaum (1989)—argue that leadership in higher education over the past two decades has moved toward more process-centered, collective, context-bound, nonhierarchi-cal approaches, in which power and influence are more mutual. It is thus less leader-centered, individualistic, and hierarchical; not as concerned about universal characteristics; and less emphatic about having power over followers. Early notions of leadership focused on the personal traits of leaders, such as confidence, integrity, and intelligence. Rational-choice models of decision making assumed that leaders acted independently of their personal values (and even their ethics) in the service of the best interests of the organization.[5]

Strategic management is best portrayed as a web of relationships among elements of equal importance. It deemphasizes structure, framing it as one essential element among several. Strategic management can certainly work with a single leader resembling a conductor before an orchestra, making sure that each element has been addressed and that they are all performing in unison. Yet it works equally well—and perhaps even better—in a more process-centered, collective manner, as illustrated by the committee approach to tuition discounting policy at Redlands (chapter 8). The relevance of local context, with influence within universities and colleges diffused, only bolster such an argument. These ideas are hardly new, dating back at least to Cohen, March, and Olsen (1972) reframing leadership as a collaboration operating through networks and teams— the garbage-can approach—as opposed to the singular role of a particular individual.

Contemporary conceptions of leadership emphasize that it is neither value free nor divorced from the ethos of the organization and from society. It is acceptable for leaders, as with those in higher education, to bring their own values and convictions to the position, just as it is recognized that these leaders are the products of their institutional contexts (Birnbaum 1992). A president or dean, for instance, is likely to be criticized if he or she does not articulate a vision for his or her organization. In addition, transformational models of leadership emphasize values, as well as the importance of developing trust, consistency, and accountability (Middlehurst 1993). The concept of leadership, furthermore, has broadened to include contributing to social utility, introducing major change, giving meaning and purpose to work, empowering followers, and infusing values and ideology into organizations (House 1998). Strategic management and systems thinking are certainly consistent with attempting to realize such objectives. Building capacity within any organization involves strengthening the administrative foundation needed to support the initiatives that move an institution toward realizing its purposes. Leadership is perhaps most crucial in clarifying mission and defining aspirations—and then helping those across the organization understand their work in these contexts.

Successful leadership requires effective management—and vice versa. Kotter (1990) distinguishes between leadership and management, emphasizing, as do other contemporary commentators, that leadership is less about control than it is about empowerment. The essence of leadership is in coping with change, while management involves dealing with complexity, as in planning and budgeting or organizing and staffing. Leadership is concerned with establishing vision and generating inspiration. Management centers on systems and structures, helping "normal people who behave in normal ways to complete routine jobs successfully, day after day. It's not exciting or glamorous, but that's management" (Kotter 1999, p. 60). Leadership, according to Kotter, "always requires an occasional burst of energy. Motivation and inspiration energize people, not by pushing them in the right direction as control mechanisms but by satisfying basic human needs for achievement, a sense of belonging, recognition, self-esteem, a feeling of control over one's life, and the ability to live up to one's ideals. Such feelings touch us deeply and elicit a powerful response" (p. 60).

Leadership is not an end in itself—nor is strategic management. Both are processes toward realizing needed change within an organization. Writing almost a decade ago, Peterson (2001) defined a set of challenges necessitating change—problems that persist across higher education: (1) looming fiscal and demographic crises, (2) new institutional opportunities presented by the growth of the learning industry, (3) increased competition from other segments within postsecondary education ("the knowledge industry"), (4) persistent questions regarding the quality of educational services, (5) the need to provide educational services more efficiently, and (6) the need to adapt institutional structures to accommodate new teaching and learning roles. Cameron and Smart (1998) offer another set of impetuses for change, suggesting that less effective institutions tend to have the following characteristics: centralized decision making, a crisis mentality, less innovativeness, resistance to change, decreasing morale, politicized interest groups, across-the-board cutbacks (as opposed to prioritized ones), a loss of trust, conflict, restricted communication, a lack of teamwork, and the scapegoating of leaders. Neither more effective leadership alone nor simply employing a strategic management framework is likely to enable the change needed to solve such challenges.

There is an impressive body of research literature on transforming organizations, including work specific to higher education, synthesized ably by Adrianna Kezar (2001) and advanced, in particular, by the American Council on Education in various projects by Peter Eckel and his colleagues (e.g., Kezar and Eckel 2002;

Eckel, Green, Hill, and Mallon 1999). Nonetheless, there has been less attention, especially in higher education, to providing the organizational capacity needed to realize change. Kezar (2001) suggests six major approaches to organizational change: (1) evolutionary models highlighting the interplay between internal and external environments, including in organizations attempting to gain legitimacy; (2) teleological models emphasizing vision and defined objectives, implemented through more linear efforts toward change; (3) life cycle models centering on the importance of key individuals; (4) dialectical or political models underscoring coalitions and the informal processes related to persuasion as the crucial factors in acquiring power and influence within organizations; (5) social cognition models suggesting that there is no single organizational reality, requiring individuals to engage in sensemaking; and (6) cultural models focusing on the irrationality of organizations and the importance of organizational culture. While each model contributes to our understanding of organizational change in higher education, Kezar rightly suggests that combining the most prescient insights from several models may be the most effective way to frame and enact it.

Strategic management is not inconsistent with any of these approaches to organizational change, although it may be more useful in those that emphasize the ambiguity and complexity within universities and colleges. Bolman and Deal (2003) stress that leadership and change require a holistic approach that is open to creativity and provides options. They divide organizations into four frames: structural, human resource, political, and symbolic. As in strategic management, Bolman and Deal suggest that it is not enough to only address the structural frame, which is rational and focused on coordination in realizing goals. Leaders and senior managers must also consider the human resources frame—that organizations and people need each other and that both function better when there is a good fit between them. What causes such a fit is investments in, and the empowerment of, employees. The same is true of the political frame, with its recognition of shifting coalitions and enduring differences (and thus conflict) between and among groups—often based on the allocation of resources—that require bargaining, negotiation, and jockeying. Finally, leaders and senior managers must employ a fourth frame—the symbolic one—because of the ambiguity and uncertainty in organizational life and the recognition that symbols resolve confusion and increase predictability. In addition, the symbolic frame is important, as processes are often more important than what is produced in organizational life—what counts is not what happens, but what it means. According to Bolman and Deal, organizations are likely to be effective only by integrating these frames.

In considering strategic management, as informed by systems thinking, as a means to enable organizational change within higher education, the reframing that Bolman and Deal outline offers an important set of reminders. Organizational change demands an administrative foundation that is more complex than one simply focused on structure and governance; it should also include an examination of personnel, politics, and symbolism. Similarly, strategic management requires leaders and senior managers to consider these frames, but it also directs attention to more operational concerns—such as policies, processes, information, and infrastructure—while also emphasizing purposes and culture.

In the foreword, Jay Morley observes that presidents rarely trumpet building the management capacity of their institution as a signature accomplishment. Instead, they frame their legacy as one of increasing enrollment, building programs, constructing facilities, and so forth—and as ultimately attracting the resources that enable these to happen and fostering the greater institutional prestige that ideally results from them (Toma 2007). Jay envisioned the BOC project as a response to this tendency. Capacity within an organization can be another signature accomplishment—an important aspect of legacy. Just as building an endowment provides the financial margin needed to build reputation and offer insurance against difficult times, building capacity within an organization can serve institutional ambitions and help to smooth transitions and calm turbulence.

An Approach for Higher Education

In light of the earlier discussion, how did we arrive at the BOC framework? Jay Morley became interested in modeling the university as a system, considering this problem over several years as senior vice president and chief administrative officer at Cornell University and then as president and chief executive officer of the National Association of College and University Business Officers (NACUBO), eventually proposing a set of elements akin to those in strategic-management frameworks. I began my work on the project by holding Jay's proposed model up against various approaches in strategic management, as well as exploring writing on systems thinking and organizational change. I found much of Jay's framework to be in accord with other strategic-management models, particularly in having a web of elements as its basic architecture. The differences in the actual elements were attributable to higher education being distinct from the industries on which other approaches focus.

The next question was how to examine the proposed framework as it applied at universities and colleges. I developed a research design and Jay and I formed a team to undertake this project. The approach centered on developing case studies of various initiatives at several types of institutions and mapping the framework onto them, thus enabling the team to refine Jay's initial concept.[6] The effort clarified terms and sharpened concepts, but it did not result in the basic architecture of the framework changing. Nonetheless, developing a framework requires tradeoffs. For instance, one tradition in sociology essentially equates social processes and social structures (Scott 1970), which might suggest combining these two elements. The research team considered many such alternatives, both while the case studies were ongoing and once I analyzed the data that we gathered. However, the team ultimately retained the essence of the framework Jay had proposed, with mostly modest refinements, such as changing the labels given to a few of the elements and honing their definitions.

The case studies consisted of team members, working in groups of three, four, or five, who conducted interviews with 138 administrators, faculty, students, and trustees at seven institutions.[7] Jay and I visited each site, accompanied by one or two other members of the research team and, occasionally, by another NACUBO staff member or consultant. He and I selected the institutions purposefully, to be representative of the four major types (as NACUBO divides them): research universities (Virginia Tech), regional universities (The College of New Jersey and Valley City State University), liberal arts colleges (University of Redlands and LaGrange College), and community colleges (Seminole Community College and Paul D. Camp Community College). We did not choose the cases to represent a given element; instead, when analyzing the collected data, we came to see each of the seven studies as illustrative of one of the eight BOC elements. In order to have a case representing each element, I added the University of Georgia later in the project, working with graduate students to conduct another set of interviews.[8]

The case studies do not consider initiatives that applied the actual BOC framework directly. Instead, they represent familiar situations that can illustrate the elements in the proposed strategic-management framework. I do not intend the cases to be critical of the institutions featured. Their purpose is to connect BOC with practice, underscoring the ambiguity inherent in applying any framework within any organization—and, hopefully, the possibilities associated with doing so. In addition, the cases are more descriptive than ethnographic. The on-campus interviews on which I drew to develop the cases provided a rich source of information, as did the documents we reviewed and the observations of the research team members when visiting the campuses. In crafting the cases, I decided to focus more on explaining and illustrating the framework than on featuring the voices of the individuals we interviewed.[9] I did draw important insights from circulating the cases among our campus hosts and those on the research team involved with the interviewing, as well as at meetings of the entire research team. Also, given our purposes in the study, during the site visits we focused more on those with a better holistic sense on the institution—relatively senior administrators and faculty with formal leadership roles—and thus on those who tend to be believers in the initiatives we considered.[10] My purpose is not to develop theory, but to adapt it to a particular context—higher education—and then illustrate it. The cases consider practical issues associated with identifying an element and aligning it with others, as well as providing a context for suggestions to leaders and senior managers in applying the BOC framework.

The case studies enabled the research team to consider various necessary questions in constructing the BOC approach to strategic management in higher education. Our field work clarified the boundaries between and among the elements, suggesting that each represents a specific concept (such that it does not make sense to split a given element into multiple elements or combine two elements into one) and indicating that the elements, in conjunction, represented the whole of higher education (which is the goal of any strategic-management approach). Another crucial question is whether there are rival structures and alternative explanations—is there another way to model the organization-as-system in higher education?

Representing strategic management within an organization as consisting of eight elements is not simply science, however—there is some art involved, as well. The 7S approach, for instance, splits BOC's purposes into strategy (achieving competitive advantage) and shared values (developing a collective sense of purpose), while combining structure and governance into structure alone (grouping people, specializing tasks, distributing authority, defining reporting, and coordinating activity).[11] The 7S approach is certainly sensible—and one could use it in a university or college setting. We arrived at a different set of elements specific to higher education, yet ours are still conceptually akin to other strategic-management approaches.

Nonetheless, it is certainly possible to represent the BOC elements differently, such as in combining the elements into more general categories. For instance, one could group together the four more operational elements: policies, processes, information, and infrastructure. Similarly, structure and governance are closely related, particularly as the former is intended to shape the latter. One could also cluster elements as static nouns (structure, policies, information, and infrastructure) and active nouns (purposes, governance, processes, and culture). We kept in mind that part of the utility of a strategic-management framework is in its specificity, but it should not have too many elements to recall readily. An operations element, for instance, might include establishing rules (policies) and implementing them (processes), as well as obtaining the data needed for decision support (information) and the personnel necessary to do the work (infrastructure). Separating the static noun of policies and active noun of processes, however, seemed to us to make sense in providing leaders and senior managers with a checklist that balanced simplicity and detail. The same is true of structure and governance. Meanwhile, the four aspects of infrastructure—personnel, facilities, technology, and finances—are all static nouns and sufficiently similar to merit grouping them together.

Another question in developing a framework is whether there is a missing element—do the eight elements really cover the waterfront, or is there a ninth element (or even more)? In discussing BOC, the project team found that the most challenging question was whether leadership is, in fact, an element (a point considered in the above section on leading organizational change). A related concern was whether systems itself—the interrelationship between and among parts of an institution—is an element.

There are also questions related to the issue of the relative importance of the elements. Are they all created equal? Any strategic-management approach is based on the perils of omitting or disregarding any one element, thus indicating all are important. Furthermore, frameworks are not linear (a sequence), but instead focus on the relationships of one element with every other one (a web). Positioning purposes at the center of a web of elements underscores the premise that strategic management begins with clarity here. Not knowing what an institution values or where it is headed effectively renders consideration of the other elements worthless. How can an institution establish good rules, build the right infrastructure, or develop a productive culture without understanding in its purposes? The converse is not true—mission and vision cannot follow from policies, infrastructure, or even culture. Still, the latter two elements (and even structure and governance) might contribute to shaping the definition of purposes.[12]

Are some elements are more important than others, at least in certain circumstances or at certain times? The case studies suggest that they are. In these situations, perhaps a web portraying the elements in relation to one another might merit thicker lines or bigger circles, suggesting relative importance. However, in order for it to be useful to leaders and senior managers, a strategic management framework should be as simple as possible. In addition, as managers solve problems—and new ones arise in real time—a thick line or large circle today might be less important tomorrow. Similarly, should causality in BOC always go both ways, as it does when portrayed as a web, or does it sometimes run in just one direction? Moreover, is every element always connected with every other one? At least to some degree, each element can perhaps be seen as a dependent variable in a regression model, where all the rest of the elements are the independent variables.

Applying the conceptual framework of BOC within the context of several case studies establishes a degree of confidence in the decisions we made related to these conceptual calls. The result is a strategic-management model specific to higher education that enables leaders and senior managers to more straightforwardly capture the entire complexity of the organizations-as-systems in which they work. Aligning the elements within an organization provides the administrative foundation to support the aspirations of institutions. It is this continuity that serves as a platform for change.

CHAPTER THREE

Purposes

Redesigning the Curriculum at The College of New Jersey

In fall 2004, The College of New Jersey (TCNJ) redesigned its curriculum to better reflect the highly selective institution it had become over the previous two decades. TCNJ called the process "Academic Transformation," changing every course within every major to align its curriculum with what had become the mission and aspirations of the institution. The initiative culminated, in many respects, TCNJ's evolution from a typical comprehensive university with normal-school roots into one with the academic profile, as well as the look and feel, of a selective liberal arts college. The new curriculum shifted from a credit-based system to a course-based one, which included the creation of several more-challenging four-credit "transformed courses" to replace existing three-credit ones. TCNJ also implemented a new general education program, entitled Liberal Learning, allowing their students greater flexibility in choosing courses and facilitating minors and double majors. Furthermore, the college initiated seminars for first-year students emphasizing the serious discussion of ideas, critical reading skills, persuasive writing, and faculty mentoring; inaugurated senior capstone courses integrating every major and often involving a significant culminating project; and implemented a new scheduling format making it easier for students to meet in study or project groups outside of class.[1]

TCNJ recognized that to transform the overall academic experience at the college, everything had to change—from aspects of institutional culture to more concrete administrative functions. In realigning its curriculum to conform to its new purposes, TCNJ first and foremost needed to clarify its mission and aspirations. It also needed to address issues of structure, governance, policies, processes, information, infrastructure, and culture. Doing so was not without its challenges, especially since the evolution of the institution was somewhat incomplete and TCNJ had defined an unusual path of itself. President R. Barbara Gitenstein noted the difficulty in even classifying or labeling the institution, which is sometimes categorized as a public liberal arts college, examples of which include the State University of New York at Geneseo, St. Mary's College of Maryland, and Truman State University in Missouri. "Us[ing] the term 'liberal arts' [is] not quite accurate to the reality of TCNJ. While there may be a 'liberal arts focus' or 'core' or 'foundation,' I do not think it is appropriate to call us a 'liberal arts college' or even a 'public liberal arts college.' We have four professional schools and they are a major part of who we are and where our students study. All these students must complete a liberal learning / liberal arts curriculum, but their degrees and their majors are professional programs. Indeed, one of the most challenging aspects of Academic Transformation was creating/maintaining shared values/culture in what is essentially a comprehensive institution."[2]

Yet even when a college or university is clear about its mission and aspirations, complications tend to remain. Here and in the seven following chapters, I explore the possibilities for applying the BOC framework in the context of a given initiative, like Academic Transformation, at a particular institution, such as TCNJ, I focus on a featured element, like purposes, as well as how it relates to the others and how these connect with one another. The discussions begin by considering writings related to the element under consideration, including a sidebar in which a member of the research team offers a perspective on the research literature. After introducing the institution and exploring the initiative, element, and connections, I conclude with a discussion of how leaders and senior managers in higher education might apply the framework in diagnosing an initiative within their own organization and better aligning the eight elements toward building organizational capacity.

Purposes as an Element

Purposes indicate why an institution exists and where it is headed. BOC approaches purposes as being broader than simply the stated, formal mission of a given university or college; it also incorporates the aspirations of an institution. These ambitions include its vision and the specific practical goals toward realizing it. Mission is what an institution is; vision is broadly where it is headed; and goals are markers indicating the desired outcomes.

In recounting mission and aspirations, the purposes element is more descriptive than process oriented, especially for those individuals most directly associated with an organization. Purposes thus not only need to resonate internally with faculty, administrators, staff, and students, but also externally for alumni and other supporters. Purposes are lived within an institution, so there is a strong overlap with its culture. Beyond appealing to supporters, purposes also must fit with market realities, such as those described in chapter 2. Accordingly, they need to be at least plausible—and preferably realistic. Like any approach to strategic management, BOC begins with a college or university having clearly articulated what it is (mission) and what it wishes to be (aspirations). Such clarity ideally informs day-to-day decision making and imbues work with a necessary sense of importance and uniqueness (Hartley 2002a). In short, purposes must drive the other elements, which is why I portray it at the center of the web of elements as, so to speak, first among equals.

Seemingly everyone would agree that purposes matter greatly in organizations, especially universities and colleges. Nonetheless, Hartley asks why articulating mission, which institutions must so often do in areas such as admissions, fund raising, accreditation, and planning, is usually accompanied by a lack of enthusiasm. Citing Boyer (1987) and others, Hartley notes that universities and colleges can spend considerable time drafting mission statements, but they commonly make little direct use of them. Perhaps mission statements are so often neglected because they tend toward the rhetorical, lacking specificity and thus needed clarity (Newsom and Hayes 1991). Morphew and Taylor (2009) conclude that smaller baccalaureate institutions tend to rework their mission statement (on which so many on campus work so hard) into something more appealing to prospective students— and usually even more devoid of meaning—when disseminating it in conjunction with the *U.S. News and World Report* rankings.

Expressed institutional purposes can thus be so vague, inauthentic, or standard that they fail to inspire. Accordingly, initiatives that depend on individuals across an institution really understanding and supporting its purposes can disappoint. Universities and colleges continue to focus upon developing their mission statements, as they should, and scholars regularly emphasize how having a clear mission matters. The problem here is one of commitment. How do institutions encourage individuals to be bound to a collective effort defined by their common beliefs and values? It is essential to have leaders elucidate and senior managers appreciate why an institution exists and where it is headed, including connecting these purposes with specific initiatives intended to advance them. Purposes must also align with culture, as they only resonate when consistent with the understandings that are common across an organization (Toma, Dubrow, and Hartley 2005; Trice and Beyer 1993). In addition, the structural and functional elements in BOC (those other than purposes and culture), also contribute to the clarity that engenders dedication in organizations and enlivens them.

In addition, institutional aspirations, and the strategies employed toward realizing them, may be less inspiring because they tend to be generic across universities and colleges. Notwithstanding the relative autonomy of individual institutions and the great range in missions professed and markets served by them, the common vision across universities and colleges with even modest selectivity is to move to "the next level." In doing so, they aspire to become more like those directly above them in the prestige hierarchy broadly recognized within American higher education. Institutions not only portray their ambitions using similar rhetoric, they also attempt to operationalize them through a rather generic set of strategies (Toma 2008). These colleges and universities attempt to appeal to desirable students through launching appealing academic programs, and they also employ approaches that are more removed from academic purposes, enhancing their use of intercollegiate athletics and investing in infrastructure thought to be appealing to students.[3]

TCNJ illustrates institutional success in moving up in prestige, as its investments in academic programs and campus amenities enabled it to attract accomplished New Jersey students who formerly would not have been likely to attend a public institution. Yet the story at TCNJ is incomplete if we only consider its mission. Its aspirations, so clearly expressed and developed in concert with the culture of the institution, were just as important in guiding TCNJ. Mission and aspirations are of equal weight within BOC's purposes element. TCNJ began by carefully rearticulating its reasons for being and defining its ambitions. The college gradually reshaped its culture, aligning it with the type of institution it aspired to become, one that incorporated many of the appealing aspects of a traditional

Purposes: A Perspective on the Research Literature
Matthew Hartley
University of Pennsylvania

Organizational theory contends that mission influences organizational life in two fundamental ways. First, it is instructive. If individuals in an organization have a clear notion of some collectively desired end, they will be more able to make programmatic and policy decisions that are consonant with that purpose. They can, conversely, avoid activities inimical to that mission (Schein 1992; Ouchi 1980). Thus a clear mission provides a broad framework within which people collectively and individually organize their actions. It answers the question, what should we be doing? Of course, the specificity of the desired purpose may vary. While some institutions develop highly distinctive missions (Townsend, Newell, and Wiese 1992), others allow for looser conceptions of purpose because "being general" is less likely to alienate individuals from the organization (Davies 1986).

Second, an institutional mission can give people a sense of meaning about their work. A mission may promote a sense of uniqueness—the notion that the organization serves some special purpose or has unique qualities (Martin, Feldman, Hatch, and Sitkin 1983; Clark 1972; Selznick 1957). Mission can ennoble work, explaining to individuals how their efforts contribute to a larger cause, which, in turn, can generate greater commitment (Martin, Feldman, Hatch, and Sitkin 1983; Ouchi 1981; Pettigrew 1979). A mission may also address aspirations, expressing a bold and exciting future—a vision of what might be (Collins and Porras 1994; Nanus 1992). One quantitative study of independent colleges concluded that a clear mission correlates with high faculty morale (Rice and Austin 1988). It seems clear that organizations benefit from answering the workplace equivalent of the great existential question, why are we here?

However, developing a collective sense of purpose is no easy task. In the 1980s, countless organizations spent enormous amounts of energy drafting mission statements, only to later quietly file them away. There are myriad examples in writings about organizations, including in higher education, of mission-centered efforts at change that have come up short (Kotter 1995; Newsom and Hayes 1991; Boyer 1987; Davies 1986). A member of a prestigious liberal arts college interviewed for Boyer's (1987) landmark study on undergraduate life mockingly described the purpose-making efforts at that institution: "We've had half a dozen committees at different points in the past looking at what our goals are, were, and should be. Then, sometimes, they get as far as making a statement, which doesn't provide for any action, and of course is lost or forgotten by the time someone else decides in a year or two that we really need a committee to set goals" (p. 59). Although it is tempting to conclude that such efforts are worthless, it may, in fact, be more appropriate to term them meaningless. Although it is established that successful organizations are clear about their institutional missions, it is a mistake to conclude that developing a collective sense of purpose can be arrived at easily.

Indeed, this highlights the fact that writings on institutional purpose are limited in two ways. First, in the higher education literature, although the benefits of a clear purpose have been described (Tierney 1992; Keller 1983; Clark 1972) and recommended (Austin 1990; Smith and Reynolds 1990; Rice and Austin 1988), the process by which colleges might go about clarifying their academic missions remains largely unexplored (Delucchi 1997). This gap exists in the more general literature on organizations. March and Olsen (1981) note: "There is a need for introducing ideas about the process by which beliefs are constructed in an organizational setting" (p. 256). A second limitation is that that the term "mission" is often used simplistically, as if institutional values or goals were static. When an institution is described as "having a clear mission," the tacit assumption is that the institutional purpose is widely shared, uniformly understood, and holds constant over time. The factors that may influence a member of an organization, or groups within that organization, to either embrace or reject a "clarified" institutional mission have not been sufficiently explored. Nor do we know a great deal about how that mission is then interpreted and operationalized.

In fact, there is a clear link between institutional mission and organizational culture. In a qualitative study examining mission-centered change at three liberal arts colleges, I found that creating a clear, compelling mission requires something akin to a sociocultural movement—the organizational norms and values must be redefined and then enacted in policies and programs (Hartley 2003, 2002a). Their shared norms and values provide people with a sense of purpose (Tierney 1988). Collins and Porras (1994) have explored this link in the corporate sector. They examined a set of companies in several industries that had outperformed their peers and concluded that what set these institutions apart was their "visionary" quality. They posited two characteristics shared by all such organizations. First, they have a core ideology—a shared set of norms and values that they would not abandon, even if it became an economic disadvantage. (Hampshire College is similarly not about to start appealing to conservative students.) Second, they have an envisioned future, a bold notion of what they hope to achieve. So any robust conception of mission must view it first and foremost as an expression of organizational culture.

liberal arts college into a public, and thus affordable, comprehensive institution. TCNJ could then approach a fundamental reform of its curriculum—a significant challenge, but not an insurmountable one for a focused and committed campus. It certainly helped that the curricular change actually made the college into what it so clearly proclaimed itself to be—and actually realized it had become. Once TCNJ revised its curriculum, purposes and culture could more readily align with the other elements—structure, governance, policies, processes, information, and infrastructure—creating the administrative foundation required to advance the likelihood of a successful initiative.

The College of New Jersey and Academic Transformation

The College of New Jersey celebrated its sesquicentennial in 2005. Founded as the New Jersey State Normal School, TCNJ is primarily an undergraduate and residential college with targeted graduate programs. In 2007, the college enrolled approximately 6200 undergraduate students, almost all attending full time, and another 750 or so mostly part-time graduate students. TCNJ has a 289-acre campus in suburban Ewing, five miles from the state capital of Trenton and approximately one hour from both New York City and Philadelphia. The physical campus has been substantially renovated and expanded over the past decade, assuming the look of a classic liberal arts college. In the 1970s, the institution, then known as Trenton State College, began pursuing the standard strategy of attempting to increase its prestige—and thus its legitimacy and, accordingly, its resource base—by attracting more accomplished students and becoming more residential in nature (Toma 2008). In 2005 and 2006, TCNJ ranked as the top public institution, and fifth overall in the North, in the "top universities—master's" category in *U.S. News and World Report*; among the top 20 in the "values in public higher education" bracket in *Kiplinger's Personal Finance*; and as one of the 75 most competitive colleges nationally by *Barron's*.

Institutions commonly aspire to remake themselves toward being more selective, but TCNJ succeeded in its aspirations to a degree unusual in U.S. higher education. Over the past 25 years, it reduced the number of its undergraduate students by one-third, shifted the percentage of part-time students from nearly one-third to 6 percent, and increased students residing on campus from 31 to 59 percent. The academic profile of entering classes has risen as the college has evolved. As a result, TCNJ has become one of the most selective public institutions nationally. The college enrolls approximately 1300 full-time undergraduate students annually, accepting slightly fewer than one-half of the 8600 applicants in 2007. In 2007, the average combined Scholastic Aptitude Test (SAT) score for all entering students was 1250, the highest nationally among similar institutions. Eighty-seven percent of the freshman class ranked in the top quarter of their high school class in 2007, and 40 percent were on state-sponsored scholarships. Retention numbers are similarly impressive, as 95 percent of TCNJ freshman students return for their sophomore year, and the six-year graduation rate is 83 percent. TCNJ has one of the most successful National College Athletic Association (NCAA) Division III athletics program in the country, winning 38 championships in seven sports since 1979, the most among the over 400 institutions in the classification.

The college has achieved these outcomes while drawing 97 percent of its students from the state of New Jersey. Over 20 percent of TCNJ students are members of minority groups, reflecting the diversity of the state. The increasingly impressive credentials of the entering undergraduate students has not significantly changed either the racial and ethnic composition of the institution or the balance in enrollments across its various schools.[4] TCNJ is also a relative bargain, with 2007 tuition and fees around $5500. TCNJ has 335 full-time faculty and a 13:1 student-faculty ratio. It offers 50 undergraduate degree programs in three liberal arts and sciences schools and four professional schools.

In 1996, the institution changed its name from Trenton State College to The College of New Jersey to better reflect its transformation from a typical comprehensive institution focused primarily on teacher training to a highly selective institution with several attributes of a liberal arts college (one with selected professional schools). There is not a ready model for what TCNJ has become. The case statement on its market position (commissioned by the college) argues that TCNJ can offer "a limited number of top students throughout the nation a superior education comparable to the finest institutions, without the financial burdens associated with private education and with [comparable] outcomes." A college-wide task force on positioning TCNJ reinforced that assessment: "The College of New Jersey positions itself as a highly selective and unique public undergraduate college. It provides a transformative educational experience with the intensive faculty-student collaboration and inviting campus environment associated with the most prestigious private colleges."

Upon assuming the TCNJ presidency in 1999, arriving from her position as provost of Drake University in Iowa and with a scholarly background in English, Bobby Gitenstein was presented with a letter from the faculty identifying ten "big issues" confronting the college. Several of these related to purposes, especially developing a culture consistent with the current position of the institution and its intended future direction. Gitenstein recognized the need to change various factors, such as the college's propensity for top-down decision making, a governance system that did not encourage institution-wide decision making that involved the faculty, and a lack of shared certainty about its mission. Doing so would align the orientation of both the faculty and the administration with the more collegial approach appropriate to and typical of a highly selective, smaller college, as opposed to the more bureaucratic perspective at a usual regional comprehensive institution (Birnbaum 1988).

Given the mission and aspirations the college had assumed, Gitenstein concluded that TCNJ also had insufficient institutional support for and recognition of faculty scholarship; inadequate library resources; a "clouded" mission relating to student learning and less-than-adequate attention paid to student development; an overreliance on adjunct faculty; a need for more minority, recent immigrant, and international students; and concerns about affordability. In response, she assembled a working group to begin reviewing governance issues. The college also engaged in redefining its stated mission and developing a set of institutional commitments.

TCNJ then needed to align various academic and management functions and activities with its stated missions to become the college that it now formally professed to be. Appealing to accomplished students seeking a more intimate public college experience in a region in which private higher education significantly influences the norm, reworking the curriculum was a necessary step. The former curriculum was essentially a "legacy system," adapted as needed but never rebuilt as TCNJ evolved into a different type of institution. In anticipation, the college restructured its academic units to provide a structure more appropriate to a liberal arts college by dispersing power and influence more widely, including dividing the School of Arts and Sciences into multiple units: the School of Art, Media, and Music; the School of Culture and Society; and the School of Science. (The schools of Business, Education, Engineering, and Nursing continued with their same structures.) Faculty and administrators were also preparing the college for rethinking the curriculum and institutionalizing more collegial governance, collaborating to develop or revise policies related to new programs, promotion and tenure, student discipline, travel, and alcohol.

Meanwhile, Stephen Briggs, the provost that Gitenstein appointed the year after she arrived, reorganized the Office of Academic Affairs and worked to ready the college for the task before it, creating an associate vice president for information technology, expanding the responsibilities of the vice-provost for research and faculty development to encourage the establishment of new interdisciplinary programs, and appointing a vice-provost for academic programs and initiatives. Briggs also began an examination of the nature of faculty work through a conference committee and an advisory group of department chairs. In 2003, Briggs convened a committee to study a reduction in teaching load for administrative work that faculty performed. Planning for the new curriculum also prompted the establishment of task forces on honors programs and community building and the development, under the dean of students, of "a comprehensive first-year college experience that supports the revised curriculum." Furthermore, the college community considered facilities issues in relation to the new curriculum and, more broadly, its institutional culture. TCNJ also conducted an extensive review of nonacademic administrative structures, exploring ways to become more efficient and effective, particularly in the areas of budgeting and expenditures. Finally, the college revamped its advising systems in anticipation of the new curriculum.

Purposes at The College of New Jersey

At TCNJ, it was essential to clarify purposes before undertaking the realignment of the curriculum, recognizing that the Academic Transformation initiative would likely have floundered without doing so. Especially among the faculty, who are traditionally the guardians of the curriculum, there needed to be an unambiguous sense of what the institution had become, what this meant, and where it was headed. When Gitenstein arrived, TCNJ understood that it was moving along a path to becoming a selective, smaller public college with various liberal-arts-college characteristics and selected professional schools. Faculty and administrators no longer saw the institution as a typical regional comprehensive school, appreciating the rather distinctive route TCNJ had been moving along for several years. Because those at the institution generally understood its identity, and because the culture of the college had been evolving accordingly, the foundation needed for a set of changes as meaningful as Academic Transformation was in place.

It became Gitenstein's task, as president, to see the transformation of the institution completed. Those associated with the college understood and supported that it was not going to become another Rutgers, a research university—a path that so many other regional comprehensive universities have attempted in seeking greater prestige. TCNJ instead went in the opposite direction, toward competing directly with highly selective private colleges such as neighboring Lehigh or Lafayette, particularly for students from New Jersey. TCNJ would offer an experience approximating the privates, but at a significantly lower price for in-state students. It would intensify its undergraduate teaching mission and limit graduate programs to those necessary to serve the community. In doing so, the college would seek to attract increasingly accomplished students, thus positioning itself for greater prestige. It would earn stature not as a research university, but in the other way possible in American higher education. It had taken years to arrive at this consensus, but TCNJ was essentially there—and it appreciated that it needed to align its curriculum with what had become its purposes.

Gitenstein defined purposes for the TCNJ community accordingly, discussing both mission and aspirations: "The mission should provide a reminder about what TCNJ represents to those who already know us and send a clear message about the College to those who don't yet know us. It tells all of our stakeholders who we are, what we believe, what we want to become, and what we want to achieve. The mission will show all of us who study and work here which directions are appropriate for us and provide standards against which we will measure our progress." The college had long been considering the fundamental question of what it means to have become what it had: a smaller, public, comprehensive institution with highly accomplished students, several of the aspects of a liberal arts college, various professional schools focused on teaching, and a history as a standard regional institution. TCNJ recognized that it needed a curriculum to match "the excellent institution that we say we are" and that would match its further ambitions.

In doing so, TCNJ had to not only talk the talk, but also walk the walk. For instance, it has opted not to launch a MBA program, despite the resources and prestige that can come with such a program. Even in the context of its professional schools, TCNJ has been clear about its "teaching institution" focus, differentiating itself from a research university such as Rutgers—and the campus community understands this goal and is working toward it. Doing so enables the business school, when recruiting undergraduate students, to say that *they* are the focus at this school, unlike at larger universities. Faculty members at a teaching institution like TCNJ are not going to be distracted by MBA students or by their own consulting work, but instead will be available to undergraduates, TCNJ argues.

TCNJ both bucks national trends and is consistent with them in defining its purposes. There are countless examples of institutions in the comprehensive sector positioning for greater prestige and attempting to enhance their resource base by adding graduate programs or investing in research infrastructure (Morphew and Toma 2004; Toma and Morphew 2001). TCNJ was still interested in developing prestige and resources, but it looked in the opposite direction, toward the highly selective liberal arts colleges that are, like research universities, the most esteemed institutions in American higher education. It moved in that strategic direction through the Academic Transformation initiative, but also in how it constructed and renovated campus buildings and focused on excellence in Division III athletics (Toma, 2008, 2003). As with any upward drift strategy, faculty members and others were inclined to be supportive, prestige being an attractive ambition, especially for those acculturated as graduate students at a leading university. What mattered more than the actual path TCNJ took was that it was so clear in its mission and aspirations. Such certainly in purposes is essential in organizing the alignment of the other elements.

Connecting with the Other Elements

TCNJ is not only illustrative of the importance of clarifying purposes, but also of how it and the other seven BOC elements must align. The purposes that TCNJ adopted and the related sensibilities that it has internalized required it to reshape its structure and governance toward a more collegial model. More bureaucratic means might have been effective in pursuing Academic Transformation, but such an approach to governance and structure would hardly fit for the institution TCNJ had become. The college would need to complete the transition from being more bureaucratic in how it organized people and made decisions, as is typical of regional comprehensives, toward the more collegial orientation associated with smaller colleges and universities that enroll the most accomplished students (Birnbaum 1988).

Organizing people to do their work was important in accomplishing curricular change at TCNJ, as *structure* needed to evolve to support a more collegial approach to making decisions. The unionized environment alone at TCNJ, which is commonly associated with a more bureaucratic culture, required a particular focus on structure. The success of such an ambitious undertaking as Academic Transformation required generally productive relationships between the unions and the administration. Integrating union representatives from the faculty and staff into meaningful roles, both formal and informal, within the structure of the institution proved useful at TCNJ. Those at the college realized that if a unionized TCNJ was going to operate in a more collegial mode, the union needed to be at the table when the college made important decisions.

Restructuring also supported a more collegial approach, as with dividing the large School of Arts and Sciences into three smaller schools and thus decentralizing decision making at TCNJ. The college did pay a price in having less-experienced deans and others operating in unfamiliar surroundings during a period when stability may have been beneficial. It is reasonable to ask whether it was necessary to restructure to the extent that TCNJ did, risking confused roles when clarity may have been more useful. As the collegial model depends more on consensus than on order, perhaps the cost here was reasonable, especially given that it was curriculum reform at stake—an area over which faculty members rightly assume they will have influence.

A more decentralized structure was also better aligned with the collegial style of *governance* to which the institution had committed—and that ultimately enabled Academic Transformation to succeed. Gitenstein moved the power to make certain appointments from the president and provost to entities such as the faculty senate, staff senate, and student government, elevating these groups as decision makers in other respects. Search committees, for instance, came to include more faculty members, and even students, to encourage "a decision-making process [that] requires that everybody speak to one another," as Gitenstein put it. Such significant advisory and decision-making roles are the essence of governance. These are the kinds of reforms that few faculty members would oppose under any circumstances and that academic administrators would come to accept as necessary in TCNJ's evolution.

In order to realize its purposes, which the curriculum reform advanced, TCNJ needed to develop norms of collegiality in its governance, valuing faculty influence and building consensus wherever possible in making decisions. Even though the curriculum transformation may not have resulted in just what the faculty as a whole desired, they recognized that they owned the process, both practically and symbolically. Just as Academic Transformation was key to realizing the mission and aspirations of TCNJ, developing a more collegial approach to who made what decisions was essential in realizing a remade curriculum. It is difficult to imagine such a far-reaching curriculum reform at an institution like TCNJ had become being imposed upon a faculty.

While attention to structure and governance within the context of purposes is critical in strategic management, attention to more operational areas is also important, as with the four BOC elements of policies, processes, information, and infrastructure. In realigning the curriculum, TCNJ needed to review its *policies*, considering how its rules would need to change to align not only with the curriculum initiative, but also with its transformed institutional purposes. As a result, the institution changed or purged several outdated or duplicative policies. For instance, as a formal policy, TCNJ faculty members had a four-course-per-semester teaching load, which was hardly consistent with that of a selective liberal arts college. Without adjusting teaching load, faculty would have resisted the curriculum reform, given the additional demands on them associated with it. There is also the more formal utility of having clear rules and avoiding work-arounds, especially in a unionized environment.

In addition, Academic Transformation prompted the college to further consider and ultimately change its tenure and promotion policies to ensure that they were appropriate for an institution of its type. Unlike lowering the teaching load, changes in tenure and promotion can prompt faculty dissent, but the college had tightened its practices around faculty hiring, involving the provost to a greater extent in defining positions and hiring in ways consistent with its mission and aspirations. In student affairs, policies aligned with the curriculum reform grouped students in clusters of 15 or so for later work, according to their section in their first seminar, and encouraged greater faculty-student interaction, ideally within the residence halls.

The college also increased the transparency of its various *processes*. Gitenstein introduced more openness in the budget process, aligning it with the more participatory governance and decentralized structure that had emerged at TCNJ. People appreciated that Academic Transformation was going to add costs, but Gitenstein thought it important for the community to understand *how* it would do so, such as new faculty lines, enhanced advising, greater library needs, and the like. At a more practical level, such transparency also encouraged people to find ways to cut costs. TCNJ also coupled transparency with assessment, introducing an annual cycle of setting goals and regularly announcing results. Such assessments enabled an unusual public institution like TCNJ to withstand challenges from within the state, especially given the fact that TCNJ needs to spend more per student than other public institutions in New Jersey.

TCNJ also needed to revise more routine, but still important, management tasks, such as records management and student registration, in conjunction with the curriculum-change initiative. With the faculty increasingly embracing the teacher-scholar model, there was a new need for enhancing processes—as well as policies and infrastructure—related to supporting research and maintaining accountability in that area. For instance, TCNJ needed to expand and formalize policies regarding capturing research overhead and allocating course release. Changes in instructional processes also accompanied the new curriculum. For instance, the physics department did not change the structure of its two-semester introductory course, but it significantly reworked instruction in response to Academic Transformation by introducing a national-normed examination, the Forced Concept Inventory, that was administered to students several times during the semester. Physics also added a peer-tutoring program. In biology, the department not only restructured its introductory course, collapsing two courses into one, but it also moved to teaching it thematically, in a nonlinear manner.

There was also a process component to reshaping the curriculum itself. For instance, faculty members across units at TCNJ needed to reach consensus on how to reduce the number of courses offered, yet still accommodate their necessary content, particularly in disciplines in the sciences, where there is a more standardized and sequential body of knowledge. The TCNJ faculty arrived at a set of decisions through a formal process, culminating in a series of courses being formally approved. The process had its informal aspects as well, with some "horse trading" and some agreements to revisit changes before making them permanent. Individual faculty were also concerned about how the changes would affect their own work. The curricular reform process at TCNJ was intensive, with planning occurring while the college was still developing its overall philosophy and implementation beginning before plans were complete. For instance, faculty members were sometimes changing their courses before programs had been approved, finding that a more participatory approach to governance and a culture accentuating collegiality tend to support such ambiguity. Doing so also enabled TCNJ to move forward rapidly and in a manner that minimized using the planning process as an excuse for people not to act.

As it moved toward remaking the curriculum, TCNJ also needed to consider another BOC element, *information*. Institutional research at TCNJ needed to evolve from focusing on reporting to external agencies to providing support for the assessment of Academic Transformation and the various efforts coupled with it. The college also concentrated on areas such as student records, working toward the seamless exchange and integration of data across campus needed to fully realize the advantages of the reformed curriculum. Communication is also central to the information element, especially of the type that enables a less centralized and more participatory institution in a situation such as at TCNJ. Gitenstein approached communication, both with the trustees and across the campus, in an orderly and comprehensive yet informal manner. Doing so reached everyone associated with the college and reinforced the collegial environment she was attempting to construct. In regularly and purposefully reminding everyone in the extended TCNJ community of where they were headed and why they were going there, Gitenstein ensured that people effectively had no choice but to know the value of remaking the curriculum to align with the purposes of the institution. Communication was essential in Academic Transformation, as with the example of needing to allay student concerns about their ability to graduate in four years as the college moved from three-hour to four-hour courses, particularly while the process was unfolding and before they knew all of the details. Such a change not only involved structure, as with sequenced courses and classroom scheduling, but also the importance of disseminating and receiving information.

In accomplishing the curriculum realignment, TCNJ needed to pay attention to its *infrastructure*, another element in the BOC strategic-management framework. TCNJ had to have the right people in the right places as it moved forward with Academic Transformation. Before beginning the initiative, the college needed leaders who understood more of a liberal arts approach to higher education and could frame decisions accordingly. It also required a faculty ready to implement such an approach, which TCNJ had been building for several years. By the time it initiated the curriculum reform, TCNJ had the faculty that it needed, not only to teach the new approach, but also to envision and organize it.

The physical campus at TCNJ also emphasizes the importance of tending to infrastructure in building capacity. Over the past two decades, the college constructed the needed campus for its purposes, with the physical environment suiting the approach to teaching and learning embodied in Academic Transformation. A common criticism of the previous administration at TCNJ was that it was more interested in buildings and grounds than in academics. However, its attention to physical infrastructure, as well as to the financial infrastructure developed at the college, allowed TCNJ to shape a curriculum that required small classrooms and intimate spaces.[5]

The final element to consider in strategic management is *culture*, which is less tangible than the others, but nevertheless equally essential. TCNJ has come to have the strong sense of community that typifies a collegial institution, with the other elements having come to align with such a character. It has developed a culture consistent with its purposes, with the community, as a whole, espousing the norms, values, and beliefs commonly associated with a selective liberal arts college (but one, in this case, with selected teaching-focused professional schools). Faculty members, for instance, have come to embrace the teacher-scholar model, recognizing the utility in engaging in scholarly work that enhances undergraduate education. It has helped, of course, that one-quarter or so of the faculty have been hired since Gitenstein arrived in 1999 and thus recruited for having such an orientation. Furthermore, Gitenstein and others emphasized building culture at TCNJ around the idea of a strong intellectual community, finding ways to include not only faculty, but also administrators and even external constituents. She also underscored the importance of establishing trust in a culture based on collegiality, emphasizing communications and openness.

TCNJ made governance and culture mutually reinforcing by making both more participatory. With more diffuse leadership and influence, there is the potential for breakdowns at more levels in the organization, but the college traded that for the benefits of the collegial approach. The structure and governance now in place at TCNJ support a set of norms, values, and beliefs consistent with purposes at the college. Culture buttresses the other elements and is buttressed by them—the essence of any framework for strategic management. Clarifying purposes and aligning culture with it enables the more tangible elements—governance, structure, policies, processes, information, and infrastructure—more easily fall into place in needed ways. Without a shared set of understandings and strong relationships among constituencies built steadily over time, the success of Academic Transformation would have been unlikely.

➤PURPOSES AND ALIGNING THE OTHER ELEMENTS: A CHECKLIST
In better aligning the undergraduate curriculum with what the mission and aspirations of an institution have become, as at TCNJ, those leading and managing the institution might consider the following related to purposes:

☐ What is the mission and what are the aspirations of the institution? Clarity about the purposes element was essential at TCNJ as it transformed from a regional teachers college to a highly selective institution with a liberal-arts-college character. Developing a fitting curriculum became a more achievable undertaking once the college came to understand what it had become and what further progress that enabled. Institutions can be imprecise or unrealistic in defining missions and articulating aspirations, commonly lapsing into generic, prestige-seeking visions without providing needed context and detail. Over several years and as an entire college, TCNJ developed a sufficiently deep appreciation of what it meant to be a selective public institution, but not a research university. It was thus ready to take on the last step in its transformation, curricular reform.

☐ Does how the institution is configured to do its work align with what have come to be its purposes? Some restructuring, as with subdividing colleges, served to better align TCNJ with the collegial institution that it had become, as different structures are fitting to different types of universities and colleges. At a comprehensive institution, in contrast, consolidation may have proved to be a more productive course, toward realizing purposes.

☐ Are the right people making various decisions, given the nature of an institution? In moving toward the selective liberal arts college approach, TCNJ needed to involve its faculty more in decision making, particularly that associated with academic matters. Curricular questions at selective colleges and universities always need to involve the faculty. Peripheral academic programs offer a different model, with professional managers exerting more influence.

☐ Does an institution need to change various policies and processes in order to support an initiative such as a new curriculum and related changes at the institution? As it reshaped it curriculum, TCNJ had to rework several rules and approaches so that they aligned with what the institution had become and where it was headed. It did not want anything as readily fixable as policies and processes to hinder the implementation and ultimate success of its new curriculum.

☐ Along these lines, what data is needed to support effective decision making at the institution, and is communication a barrier to it realizing its missions and aspirations? As with policies and processes, TCNJ needed to determine information requirements associated with the new curriculum, as well as the direction culture and governance had taken at the college.

☐ What infrastructure is required to support the curriculum and, ultimately, the purposes of the institution? Over time, TCNJ changed the look and feel of its campus to reflect the institution it had become, assuming the physical character of a selective liberal arts college. It also remade its faculty, through hires aligned with advancing its purposes. As always with infrastructure, resources limit what is possible.

☐ Has the culture of the institution evolved to match its changing purposes? The essential character of the college, represented in tangible ways, slowly changed at TCNJ as its missions and aspirations developed.

Applying the Framework

In employing BOC at an institution such as TCNJ and relating to a curricular re-form initiative like Academic Transformation, leaders and senior managers might consider various questions.

Who needs to be responsible for managing the initiative and monitoring prog-ress toward it? Given the academic nature of Academic Transformation, its broad scope and essentially internal audience, and the relatively modest size of TCNJ, the provost needed to drive the process, involving the faculty to the fullest extent possible. Also, because the initiative was so linked with purposes—and the cul-ture needed to support these—it made sense for the president to assume an im-portant role. At any institution, the president and the provost are likely to have the clearest sense of the institutional purposes that an initiative is intended to advance, and thus be the most effective proponents in articulating these. A goal for Academic Transformation was certainly to improve the experience of stu-dents, but it also had strategic ends, better positioning TCNJ to attract the highly accomplished students that enhance its reputation and resources.

Additionally, given its scope, the project involved nearly the entire institution, including each school as well as most administrative units. Only the provost and president have sufficient credibility and jurisdiction—and thus leverage—to ad-vance such a broad initiative, as well as to monitor progress and make necessary adjustments. Although an initiative such as Academic Transformation is a cur-ricular matter, a faculty committee is not as well positioned to primarily move it forward. They must be involved, of course, especially at an institution with increasingly more collegial governance. The faculty, even those most engaged in governance, probably have neither the overall understanding of institutional ambitions nor the leverage to implement such a broad and deep reform by themselves.

Considering the reach of a reform such as Academic Transformation within a university or college, the provost and president are also likely to have a more ho-listic sense of what the college needs. They are best positioned to comprehend the many moving parts within the institution—the logic of systems thinking that is at the foundation of strategic management. The planning and execution related to the initiative cut across units, particularly those in academic affairs, with dif-ferent functional concerns represented by the eight elements, such as with ensur-ing that matters such as structure and governance align with the purposes that the Academic Transformation project expressly served. For instance, the restructuring of the schools that preceded the project was necessarily a college-wide decision. Such decisions made locally are more likely to advance parochial concerns, as opposed to ones consistent with overall institutional goals. In addition, momentum is important in the success of a project such as Academic Transformation. Yet its complexity, including the need to make difficult decisions, makes it a poor fit with an entirely faculty-driven process, which may be more likely to bog down or require more compromise. The president and provost are also likely to stress assessments, measuring the impact of the curricular reform so as to have needed evidence for those demanding accountability.

Despite the importance of the provost and president in advancing an initiative such as Academic Transformation, deans and faculty need to be directly involved in the project, given its academic nature. For instance, the provost and president can provide guidance on policies related to the curricular reform, but these kinds of decisions are most credible, especially with collegial governance, when they come directly from the faculty. The involvement of relevant administrative units is also important, as in process issues. These might be associated with areas such as academic advising, which could be overlooked by the faculty or even by senior administrators. The same is true of questions such as whether the institution has the data that it requires to make sound decisions and demonstrate accountability, or if its infrastructure—human, physical, technological, and financial—has kept pace with its needs, given what the institution has become. Meanwhile, when changing the curriculum, it is important to attend to another aspect of information—keeping the students informed about how the initiative will affect them. Given that the matter here is curricular in nature, it may be less important to directly involve external constituents, but with the importance of fund raising and political support, it may make sense to inform, and perhaps even consult, these outside groups.

Managing an initiative such as Academic Transformation required the provost and president communicating messages not only about the purposes Academic Transformation serves, but also about the need for alignment among the various functional areas of the college in planning and implementing the initiative. Orientations differ across an institution, as well as degrees of understanding about a curricular reform effort, so employing a variety of communications approaches is advisable. For instance, those in administrative units, such as the registrar, may be less interested in being consulted on substantive questions and more concerned with having the information they need to adapt to the new approach. Faculty will likely have the opposite orientation, with both formal channels, such as the governance process, and informal ones, such as the receptions Gitenstein scheduled at TCNJ, being equally useful. Also, culture may be the tool with the most utility in getting the entire community to understand purposes and what is required for the success of an initiative so linked with advancing them. Again, the president probably has the most leverage here, including in disseminating symbolic messages. He or she can also signal culture through references to the institutions TCNJ is most interested in resembling.

Finally, given the type of initiative and the institution involved, it is important to ask where—between and among the elements—breakdowns are likely to occur, which connections are the strongest, and which ones present the greatest challenge. Had the culture at TCNJ not evolved over time to align with its purposes, it would have offered a particularly difficult challenge, given the importance of the relationship between the two on a matter such as curricular reform. Governance is similar, as with a collegial approach being standard in a liberal arts college setting. Other matters—such as structure, policies, processes, information, and even infrastructure—are probably more readily addressed. The latter may be dependent on resources, so a breakdown may be more likely when a university or college is stretched financially. Different types of institutions and initiatives will present other opportunities and challenges in considering strategic management. Nonetheless, institutions across types will function at capacity only when elements are aligned, providing the management foundation needed to support missions and aspirations.

CHAPTER FOUR

Structure

*Rethinking the Setting for Teaching Mathematics
at Virginia Tech*

In developing the Math Emporium in 1997, a physical site for online and one-on-one instruction in mathematics, the Virginia Polytechnic Institute and State University (Virginia Tech) needed to address several factors in conjunction. The initiative had to advance its purposes: its mission as a research university and its aspirations to increase its stature and enhance efficiency. It also required an approach to structure and governance, as well as initiating various policies and processes that would enable the Emporium to function in an effective manner, both as a startup venture and in moving forward. Examining the Emporium's infrastructure and information needs was similarly important. Not only did Virginia Tech have to act upon these concerns simultaneously, but it had to do so within the institutional culture that the university had established over time. Over a decade after the launch of the initiative, Virginia Tech has generated the capacity needed to support the Emporium, but the institution still must regularly explore possible improvements and scan for potential breakdowns.

Organizing the Math Emporium involved out-of-the-box thinking at Virginia Tech, but in ways that were consistent with the character of the institution. The initiative is reflective of trends across American higher education that have only become more pronounced—developing programs, including academic ones, at the periphery of institutions in the quest for increased agility and efficiency. Launching the Emporium was a joint effort, with Virginia Tech's central administration, particularly the chief operating officer, collaborating with the mathematics faculty and various relevant academic units. The project accommodated the administration's need to reduce costs in managing an increasingly entrepreneurial university, while respecting both the tradition of faculty autonomy over academic programs and the decentralized nature of a research university.

As a peripheral program operated by a small number of faculty, the Math Emporium has become relatively disconnected from the rest of the university over its ten-plus years in existence. Those applying a strategic-management framework, especially within a research university, must often contend with a diffuse environment when employing that framework to diagnose an organization. BOC illuminates some areas that may require attention. For instance, the faculty-directed Math Emporium has a noticeable dearth of formal policies and processes to guide its internal functioning The BOC framework also suggests that aspects of the development and subsequent operation of the Math Emporium had been defined and aligned in an effective manner. Its governance and structure are consistent with general research university norms and with the particular institutional culture at Virginia Tech. In addition, the Emporium has stretched the infrastructure at the institution to accommodate various instructional and other needs, including during a period of cutbacks in state support and resulting tight budgets.[1]

Structure as an Element

Structure is how an institution is configured to do its work. As a static noun, it is a means of organization, as opposed to a form of action, like governance. Structure is relatively straightforward to grasp, especially when shown as boxes and lines on an organizational chart in a hierarchical organization. For instance, the financial and administrative unit at a university or college most likely has a vice president who reports to the president, with associate vice presidents (or directors at smaller institutions) responsible for functions such as accounting, auxiliaries, budgets, facilities, and human resources, and subunits reporting to each of these. Similarly, faculty members, who operate within the flatter organizational structure of academic departments, report to a chair, a dean, and ultimately a provost. Strategic management asks the simple question of whether such configurations serve the mission and aspirations of the institution to the fullest extent possible. In other words, are units and people arrayed in an efficient manner? Are customary or convenient ways of structuring work, even if the reporting lines are clear and seem logical, really optimal (or even just sufficient)?

Understanding structure as only linear and hierarchical—boxes and lines—is nevertheless incomplete, given the emphasis on alignment in strategic management. Leaders and senior managers must consider how structure within the context of the other elements. For instance, culture may determine structure. Even the most elegant hierarchical structure may fit poorly at a small liberal arts college, given collegial, and thus flatter, organizational norms, while a more bureaucratic means of arraying people to do their work may serve the needs and align with the culture of a large community college. Similarly, a unionized environment may emphasize formal policies that have implications for structure.

As with the other elements, BOC favors a broad definition of structure, incorporating both vertical relationships within an area and more horizontal connections with other units. For example, in launching the Math Emporium there were several decisions made up and down within the hierarchy in academic affairs, yet the project also required the direct involvement of those in administrative affairs. Structure is perhaps the most obvious and tangible of the elements in strategic management. Accordingly, restructuring is commonly an initial activity in organizational change endeavors. Gumport and Sporn (1999) note that universities and colleges tend to modify structures in response to problems of change and innovation, quality and effectiveness, and decline and equity (see also Gumport and Pusser 1999; Balderston 1995; Peterson and Mets 1987). Contemporary writing about organizations, however, contends that restructuring alone is insufficient. Bolman and Deal (2004) equate structure with three other frames (political, human resources, and symbolic), and it is one element among several in various approaches to strategic management.

Organizations across higher education tend to be structured similarly. Universities and colleges are generally isomorphic, with various organizations becoming increasingly homogeneous in an attempt to imitate those thought to be the most legitimate (Powell and DiMaggio 1991; Meyer and Rowen 1977). Accordingly, few higher educational institutions deviate from the standard organizational chart of a president, a cluster of vice presidents handling various sets of "affairs" (academic, business, external, student), a set of deans reporting to the academic affairs vice president and responsible for faculty members (who are grouped by discipline type), and hierarchies within these units managed by those with associate, assistant, chairperson, or director titles. Nevertheless, every university or college is somewhat different in structure, and there are also particular structural nuances associated with various types of institutions, such as liberal arts colleges having a dean of students or an athletic director reporting to the president of a larger university (Underwood and Hammons 1999; Levin 1998; Baker and Cullen 1993; Tolbert 1985).

Furthermore, those within different parts of organizations often work within structures that are quite unlike one another, some flatter and some more hierarchical. Although a tenured professor in a humanities department and an auditor in accounts receivable are both part of the same overall university, they are likely to experience and understand structure differently. The accountant is likely to work in a more hierarchical and bureaucratic structure focused on processes and outputs, with the professor operating in a flatter and more democratic one centered on values and status (Balderston 1995; Clark 1983a). Even with efforts to flatten hierarchies and minimize bureaucracy supported (and perhaps even inspired) by management theory, there is still a need for some degree of both in structuring a business affairs unit at a university or college. Meanwhile, even in institutions in which managers have the most influence, some amount of autonomy remains inherent in faculty work. Higher education institutions are inevitably loosely coupled, with formal, hierarchical structures embedded within an environment marked by considerable independence, particularly within academic units (Weick 1976). Large and complex institutions such as Virginia Tech offer an illustration: power and influence are likely to be diffused, no matter what the structure of the institution; there are essentially flat structures in some parts of the organization and more bureaucratic ones in others; and, given their relative autonomy, there can be resistance to coordination among units.

Nevertheless, structure matters at universities and colleges. Even with a clear understanding of its purposes and a strong sense of its character, an institution will likely falter if it is poorly structured. Strategic management underscores that in structure, as with any element, a deficiency invites a negative ripple effect across an organization. Finally, structure, like the other elements, has the potential to bridge differences within organizations. It illustrates that although universities or colleges may configure different parts of the whole in various ways, those doing the work of the institution are connected by its purposes and culture.

Structure: A Perspective on the Research Literature
Kelly Ward
Washington State University

Structure is one of those terms we assume has a common definition. Literature about this concept can be categorized into two perspectives: traditional and cultural. The traditional view considers how an organization is formally structured, as in determining "how colleges work" (Birnbaum 1988). The cultural view concentrates on how those within an organization make sense of its structure, understandings that are often not evident in organizational charts and other formal expressions of structure (Peterson and Spencer 1990). In considering structure within universities and colleges, a strategic-management framework needs to draw on both traditions. Also, there are different layers of structure in any organization, and the structure of individual units matters locally in the same way as overall structure does at the macro level.

References to structure are prevalent in the classical works in organizational theory (Birnbaum 1988, 1984; Clark 1984, 1983b; Mintzberg 1979). Mintzberg (1979) frames structure in higher education as a "professional bureaucracy"— and traditional perspectives couch organizations and their structure in terms of bureaucracy. Bureaucracies assume that there is rationality within organizations, with charts of who does what and who reports to whom being of paramount importance (Birnbaum 1988; Peterson 1985; Mintzberg 1979). Birnbaum (1988) acknowledges that bureaucracy can have a pejorative connotation—as with being perceived to prevent change, for instance—yet he recognizes the descriptive power of the term. Other terms linked with traditional perspectives include "functional," "rational," and "formal."

Duryea (1973) links a more bureaucratic orientation toward organization with the growing complexity of colleges and universities. As institutions expanded, particularly in the late nineteenth century, the college president was no longer able to assume many of the roles that have now come to be divided along administrative lines: registrar, comptroller, dean of students, dean of faculty, and so forth. It was inevitable that various roles within institutions would become more segmented and defined. The administrative side of universities and colleges became less flat and more hierarchical, but the decision to house faculty within departments offered a counterpoint and tended to divide institutions along academic-administrative lines. In the end, as demands multiplied and functions diversified, structure became more pronounced, with bureaucracy coming to shape it, as organizational charts so clearly illustrated, especially in administrative areas.

(continued)

These charts, however, only reveal one aspect of structure. Cultural perspectives offer another, concentrating on the more behavioral and thus informal aspects of organizations and the limitations of traditional perspectives (Peterson 1985). Cultural perspectives focus on how "people in higher education interpret events, how they are influenced by the setting and the content of events, and how they ascribe meaning to them" (p. 77). The cultural perspective on structure is not just about the functions of the organization, but also about the contexts in which actual people perform these functions. Structure and institutional culture are thus inherently connected. Two campuses can have very similar organizational structures, yet they might carry out their work in very different ways, based on the essential character of each institution (Clark 1984).

Weick (1976) argues that because universities and colleges are loosely coupled, an organizational chart alone does not communicate how things get done there. He notes that while there are connections within any organization, there is also individual identity and some amount of physical or logical separateness. For example, a dean might report to a provost, but he or she operates autonomously most of the time, especially as academic culture values autonomous structures. In considering academic culture and structure, Gumport (1991) identifies the importance of recognizing the interrelationship of institutions, disciplines, and specializations. Using the example of feminist scholarship, an emerging field at that time that drew from different disciplines, Gumport found that intellectual communities of faculty transcended formal structures and that departmental structures do not always function to resolve conflict or create common cause. Her work again highlights the need to consider structure simultaneously with culture (institutional and otherwise)—and even other elements. Cultural perspectives on structure create more authentic views of what actually transpires within a particular organization and thus are useful in organizational change efforts (Keup, Walker, Astin, and Lindholm 2001) and in facilitating student learning and development (Berger 2002).

In the end, the traditional focus on formal modes of organizing and rational decision making is insufficient without considering the importance of context—how people experience organizations as influenced by institutional culture, but also by the cultures associated with the overall society, academic life generally, with the various disciplines, and the like (Austin 1990).

Virginia Tech and the Math Emporium

The Virginia Polytechnic Institute and State University, founded in 1872, is the largest university in the Commonwealth of Virginia, enrolling approximately 21,000 undergraduate students and 6000 graduate students in seven undergraduate colleges, a graduate school, and a joint veterinary school. The institution, located in a small town in the mountains about an hour from Roanoke in the southwestern part of the state, offers 60 bachelor's degree programs and 140 master's and doctoral degree programs. It is the land-grant institution in Virginia, defining its mission as "instruction, research, and solving the problems of society through public service and outreach activities." It received nearly 20,000 applications for its 2007 freshman class, with an average SAT score of 1229 for those who enrolled, placing it among the leading public universities nationally. *U.S. News and World Report* ranked Virginia Tech in the top 30 among national public universities in 2007, and in the top 75 overall; several of its undergraduate engineering departments were in the top 15, and its graduate engineering program in the top 30; its architecture program has received a top-ten ranking; and its MBA program was in the 2007 *Financial Times* international top 100, 63rd overall and 43rd in the United States. The university was in the top 20 public institutions in *Kiplinger's Personal Finance* ranking of educational experiences at a bargain price.

Virginia Tech had an overall budget of just less than $1 billion, and it generated $321.7 million in research funding in 2007. Its corporate research center accommodates over 130 companies in 23 buildings adjacent to the campus, and it has five off-campus teaching facilities across Virginia and one in Switzerland. The Virginia Tech Foundation had an endowment of $941 million in 2007. The Virginia Cooperative Extension, operated jointly in the Commonwealth by Virginia Tech and Virginia State University, has 107 offices, more than 44,000 volunteers, and 160 programs focused on improving the economic, cultural, and social welfare of the people of Virginia. The institution is also noted for the Blacksburg Electronic Village project that wired the town and campus in the early 1990s. It is also one of two universities nationally (the other is Texas A&M) that offers a military-style leadership development program through its Corps of Cadets. The Virginia Tech Hokies compete in the Atlantic Coast Conference.

The Math Emporium opened in 1997 in a former department store a few blocks off campus. It is an open, 60,000-square-foot facility with 550 Apple iMac workstations (as of 2004) arranged in hexagonal pods spaced across the laboratory floor. The Emporium is open around the clock during the academic year, with shortened hours during the summer. Some 4500 students per year use the Math Emporium for what Virginia Tech terms "their principal math experience," and another 3000 use it for some portion of their academic program.

In the mid-1990s, Virginia Tech confronted resource constraints, concerns about the quality of undergraduate teaching, and the desire to increase research productivity, including in mathematics. There were also challenges associated with the capacity needed to offer a full schedule of mathematics classes. So, the timing was right for a bold initiative at Virginia Tech. The idea for something like the Math Emporium had been around for several years, but it took a confluence of pressures related to finances, quality, and research to make it happen. It also required an institution-wide commitment to a large-scale initiative and an available and appropriate empty building near campus.[2]

In the context of several rounds of budget cuts and continued increases in enrollment, the chief information officer (CIO) and the chair of the mathematics department at Virginia Tech continued a long-standing conversation about using technology to support entry-level courses. They knew they could build on the several smaller, conventional computer labs that the department already had established, as well as on pilot work at Virginia Tech using computer-based learning approaches in mathematics. Meanwhile, the provost and executive vice president (EVP), with the concurrence of the president, were considering how best to solve the overall budget problem, while moving forward with various aspirations, such as enhancing technology, strengthening undergraduate learning, and enhancing funded research. These notions converged with the realization that Virginia Tech could use a nearby vacant department store to rapidly construct what became the Math Emporium, while having the Commonwealth pay for it.

The provost then secured support, including financial commitments, from the deans whose students would use the facility. The executive vice president, Minnis Ridenour, arranged for the financing and leasing involved. With key members of the mathematics department and the CIO also behind the effort, the stars aligned in such a way that Virginia Tech could launch this initiative within an academic year. The Emporium was the right idea at the right moment. All of the relevant people at Virginia Tech, including the mathematics faculty, could agree on moving forward—and doing so quickly. The initiative aligned with the mission and aspirations of the university; various infrastructure (such as personnel, the facility, and instructional software) was readily available; and the culture at Virginia Tech embraced innovation, particularly that involving technology.

Virginia Tech teaches several courses entirely online at the Emporium, while others include significant or occasional classroom work. A course fully taught at the Math Emporium meets only once, for an orientation. After that, the course is a sequence of weekly lesson-practice-quiz cycles with periodic exams—all delivered over the Internet. Individual-lesson Web pages consist of three overlays: an explanation, examples, and a challenge problem. The default schedule for a given course requires a student to master about ten of these units per week, followed by a quiz. Additionally, there are five tests and a final examination in a typical Emporium course. Before actually taking a quiz or test for credit, Math Emporium faculty members encourage students to solve sample test problems as often as they would like, with instantaneous feedback. Students thus have a greater likelihood of doing more hands-on work with problems than they would in a lecture course. The students may proceed at their own pace, as long as they keep up with the default schedule. Michael Williams, the director of the Emporium and former associate vice president for information systems and research computing at Virginia Tech, noted that an able and energetic student could finish an entire course in a week or two. Lastly, course goals and expectations are prescribed precisely and in advance.

Math Emporium courses use online testing. The system is premised on students knowing what will be eventually tested, which requires courses to establish learning objectives. The testing system allows students an unlimited supply of practice tests constructed from the same pool of questions used for the exams, with questions made unique by randomly generating certain parts of them. An article appearing on the Apple Web page shortly before our project team visited the university quotes Williams: "Each time the application is run, it supplies you with a new problem. It can vary in wording, or any kind of variable can be written into the problem. So even if you've seen this 'type' of problem before, you still have to work the whole thing out from scratch—I do, and I write them! This allows the students to learn the whole process, in a very open way." Exams are graded immediately, so students can check their standing in the course at any time.

Doing so, Williams argues, shifts the responsibility and the authority for learning to the students, freeing faculty members to be coaches instead of assuming a more adversarial posture. At the Emporium, students have access to 80 hours per week of faculty office hours, a walk-in tutoring lab, online course materials, and a course advisor. Faculty members, graduate students, and advanced undergraduate mathematics students staff the floor of the Math Emporium, providing just-in-time, one-on-one help. The approach affords important economies of scale.

The Emporium has enabled regular faculty to reduce their teaching loads, particularly in lower-level courses, and carve out additional time for research and teaching in upper-level courses. In encouraging students to work together, as well as individually, the Emporium employs the logic of learning communities, an increasingly popular curricular approach in American higher education. Williams writes: "The structural constraint of a course / an instructor / many students has been reconfigured into many courses / many instructors / many students. In this model the faculty mindset moves from 'my student' to 'our student'; this has been difficult for some. Since floor schedules are regular, natural associations between students and faculty do form, however."

There is evidence that students are satisfied with the approach, as the Sloan Foundation reported (www.sloanconsortium.org/node/489; see also National Center for Academic Transformation 2001):

> The freedom to work at convenient times and for as long as needed probably makes the greatest contribution to student satisfaction. There is a recent indication of satisfaction with the online format. In 2001, a program of optional live lectures was replaced by online video lectures; the regular student survey indicated that use of the lectures increased from 43 percent of the students to 84 percent. The main computer presentations and the Math Emporium staff receive favorable responses in the 70 to 85 percent range.

There is some grumbling among students, of course, who can find the location inconvenient and learning mathematics challenging. In response, the Math Emporium faculty has continued to sharpen the curriculum, particularly in improving test questions.

The Math Emporium has certainly lowered costs—from $91 to $27 per credit hour for the linear algebra course, for example. The Sloan Foundation reported that shifting that two-credit course taken by 2000 first-year students in engineering, science, and mathematics produced $130,000 in annual cost reductions, including factoring in compensation for the Emporium's academic staff. The Emporium has also opened up classroom space on campus for other courses. There were, of course, capital costs associated with setting up the lab, with some of these covered by a $200,000 grant from the Center for Academic Transformation housed at Rensselaer Polytechnic Institute. The project also received funding from the Pew Charitable Trusts, the Fund for the Improvement of Postsecondary Education, and the National Science Foundation. There are also continuing operating expenses, such as the $225,000 per year the university pays to lease the building where the facility is housed. Ongoing funding is from various academic units.

The Math Emporium thus exemplifies various trends in American higher education. It offers a platform for the mathematics department to use everyone from senior faculty to undergraduate students as instructors, lowering instructional costs and affording regular faculty more time to pursue funded research. The Emporium has allowed Virginia Tech to serve more students with static or fewer resources, another contemporary challenge across institutions. It has moved an academic function somewhat to the periphery of the institution, but the mathematics faculty has retained control over the curriculum. While using increasingly temporary faculty is perhaps lamentable, albeit seemingly inevitable in a contemporary research university, the Emporium does preserve faculty governance. Finally, the Emporium exemplifies how state-level policy influences institutional-level change, given its genesis in state budget cuts coupled with the Commonwealth loosening various restrictions on all state universities, including those related to real estate.

The Math Emporium at Virginia Tech can illustrate the BOC strategic-management approach, especially in adopting a structure that aligns with purposes at Virginia Tech and connects with the other elements: governance, policies, processes, information, infrastructure, and culture.

Purposes and Structure at Virginia Tech

The Math Emporium continues to fit neatly within the mission and aspirations of Virginia Tech, advancing both research and instruction. The Math Emporium facilitates the aspiration at Virginia Tech of enhancing its standing among public research universities through enabling the mathematics faculty to teach lower-level courses more efficiently, thus creating more time for their other pursuits. In addition, Paul Torgersen, the president when Virginia Tech developed the Emporium, strongly encouraged integrating technology into teaching and learning across the university. Virginia Tech also needed to serve ever-increasing numbers of students, particularly in service courses for engineering and other professional schools, in the context of a declining amount of available resources.

The Emporium also advanced the ambition of improving its undergraduate teaching, and area in which research universities often feel vulnerable. The concept of one-on-one, just-in-time tutoring from faculty and others was compelling, signaling that the institution's seriousness about its teaching mission. It may matter less that students do not fully embrace the Emporium. The experience requires a sometimes challenging adjustment from high school patterns to working independently. What matters more is that the mathematics faculty understands the project as having the potential to improve teaching and learning, which was a significant motivation for them in launching and continuing the Emporium—and an assumption supported by later evidence. At a research university, faculty need to drive the substantive development of an academic project such as the Math Emporium. As a matter of structure (as well as governance), the senior administration needed to respect boundaries, including structural ones, with the executive vice president and the chief information officer focusing on matters such as infrastructure.

In fact, the greatest present challenge with the Math Emporium is an abundance of autonomy. Once established, the Emporium fit neatly enough on the organizational chart, existing within an academic unit. Yet over time it has become increasingly remote within Virginia Tech, including from even the mathematics department. Although it is an academic unit directly serving large numbers of students, structurally the unit is at the periphery of the university. The physical location of the Emporium in a former department store a few blocks from campus only increases its organizational distance from the rest of the institution. The university reaped considerable savings by not having to construct a new building, but it also fostered a structure where a few true believers who are personally committed to the project can operate essentially on their own, even apart from the core of their academic department. These include the Emporium director, the mathematics department chair (who is the former Emporium director), and a few faculty who design Emporium courses. The Math Emporium, as configured within Virginia Tech, can be easily overlooked, at least as long as it keeps operating relatively smoothly, continuing to serve the needs that led to its establishment.

Such distance and autonomy, as with centers and institutes, are common in a research university. It is only expanding as faculty, functioning as "academic capitalists," increasingly engage with their institutions as independent entrepreneurs in their research and consulting. The non-tenure-track instructors and the graduate assistants who provide much of the instruction at the Emporium can also be separate from the mainstream of the institution. The situation is similar elsewhere in American higher education, as universities and colleges move activities, including academic programs, to their peripheries and shift to temporary labor in providing instruction. The way in which the mathematics department chooses to array people to staff the Math Emporium contributes to protecting the research time of its tenure-track mathematics faculty, freeing them from teaching labor-intensive introductory courses. It also means that many of those who are on the floor of the Emporium working with students can easily be marginalized within the university—and even within the department. By focusing on introductory courses, the Emporium itself can similarly be marginalized within the mathematics department, existing so that "real work" can occur elsewhere.

These are structural issues. Where a unit is located within an organization certainly matters, but so does how people are configured within it. Strategic management defines structure broadly, encouraging leaders and senior managers to consider whether units and people are arrayed in the optimal fashion to realize the mission and aspirations of the institution. In shifting the instructional load away from faculty in tenure-significant roles, the Emporium serves purposes at Virginia Tech, enabling it to lower instructional costs while, it can contend, improving learning outcomes. Yet gaining an advantage by locating the Math Emporium at the periphery of the institution, and then staffing it with more transient instructors, influences matters other than structure, having a ripple effect across the other elements, especially culture.

Connecting with the Other Elements

One of these other elements is *governance*. A pronounced feature of the Math Emporium is its informal approach to management, conspicuously minimizing bureaucracy to the extent possible. Given its location in the Virginia Tech structure, as well as within the mathematics department, there is limited oversight of—and even attention to—the unit, making its less rigid approach to governance possible. Governance at the Emporium reflects its founding. The Emporium is as much the product of serendipity as it is of planning, contributing to its rapid implementation in 1997. There was no campus-wide committee involved in the conceptualization and launch of the initiative. Instead, a constellation of department-level advocates and senior administrative promoters moved the idea forward on a fairly ad hoc basis. A small group of mathematics department faculty were left to operate the Emporium as they saw fit, functioning essentially without outside influence. The Math Emporium drew considerable notice at its launch, as the effort had the provost, the arts and sciences dean, and the executive vice president working together with the mathematics department. When their work on the project was completed, the senior administrators moved on to the next major undertaking.

Where it sits within the institution (structure) contributes to the manner in which the Math Emporium is operated (governance). As a unit within a department within a school, governance questions at the Emporium are mostly local. It consciously flies under the radar, taking full advantage of its off-campus location within a decentralized university to operate as independently as possible. The faculty members involved understand that given its isolated setting, both physically and organizationally, there will be little direct involvement from the senior administration—and even their own department—unless the unit does something to draw attention to itself. To the extent possible, informality in governance fits with faculty culture at Virginia Tech, and those operating the Emporium view decentralization and minimalism as connected with autonomy.

There were governance issues in launching the Emporium. In asking the basic question of who needs to make what decisions, those planning the initiative rightly recognized the need to develop support from relevant units and individuals across the institution, recognizing the potential of obstruction from those believing themselves to have an interest. Such is the nature of governance at a research university. The senior administrators and those in the mathematics department working to launch the Math Emporium knew they needed to explain the project to those who might object to it, such communication, as well as supporting data, being an element in strategic management. They also recognized that the faculty across Virginia Tech, including those with institution-wide leadership roles, would likely defer to the mathematics faculty, especially if they were assured that the project was not being steamrolled by the administration.

As a matter of governance at a research university, the Math Emporium simply would not have worked had it not emerged from the mathematics faculty. An initiative like the Emporium could not realistically have been imposed by the central administration, given the influence that research university faculty members expect and exert over the curriculum. It is part of the division of labor between faculty and administrators that structures higher education institutions. Governance also connects with culture here, as there are symbolic reasons for an academic program needing to be viewed as a faculty initiative. Although the administration was supportive (and continues to be so), the mathematics department faculty drove the development of the project and continues to manage it.

Faculty governance, specifically departmental control over the curriculum, has been integral at the Math Emporium once it was established. The mathematics department chair and a small group of involved faculty make decisions at the Emporium, representing the interests of their colleagues and having their tacit endorsement. As long as the Emporium appears to be operating in intended ways, the remainder of the mathematics department, as well as the rest of the university, are content to have others tend to it. Not all processes involving faculty need to be collective at a research university, but colleagues do reserve the right to insert themselves when interested.

The simple and informal approach to managing the Math Emporium extends to *policies*. Virginia Tech launched the unit over a period of only a few months, so working through problems and developing rules on the fly—and establishing rules only as needed—became standard practice, and even formal policies often emerged in an informal manner. For instance, the rule for crediting on-the-floor hours for Emporium faculty arose when the issue materialized, with the ad hoc determination being sufficiently satisfactory that it became institutionalized. In principle, those involved with the Emporium project work within as few rules as possible, deviating from even those when possible and sensible. They have maintained the mentality of a startup organization, responding to operational issues as they emerge and recognizing that a distinctive venture, such as the Math Emporium, is going to require its own set of rules.

Such an approach can be advantageous, but it begs the question of whether the mature organization that the Math Emporium has become requires more formal rules. Are there sufficient formal protections for the instructors who do so much of the work at the Emporium? Or would formal rules damage the productive culture that has emerged at the Emporium and its ability to navigate institutional bureaucracies as an unusual unit, both of which have contributed to the success of the initiative for over a decade? In contrast, policies related to students are well defined—they know both the formal and the informal rules. Testing protocols, for example, are clearly established. Similarly, the Emporium exists in an administrative environment at Virginia Tech that is more formal, particularly its organization under the executive vice president, conforming to norms in interactions such as in financial accountability.

The Emporium has certain set *processes* for working with students on the floor, and others for interacting with the central administration through the EVP. Its informal approach to processes again has advantages and disadvantages. Developing processes only as needed contributes to the agility of the organization and can create a pleasing culture for its workers. Yet processes such as evaluation and assessment can require stricter attention. The Math Emporium evaluates its courses regularly, focusing on quantifiable measures and, where possible, compares its approach with that of traditional classes. It also measures student perceptions about their work with the Emporium. Its evaluation of its operations is limited, however. There is no formal process for adding, reworking, or eliminating courses. Similarly, processes related to faculty evaluation are minimal. The Math Emporium continues to act more like a startup venture than the mature organization it now is. Whether the continued success of the Emporium requires formalizing some of its processes is an open question—one that an approach to strategic management invites asking when diagnosing an organization. It is important to protect the productive culture that has emerged at the Emporium, and there is value in having the faculty control the enterprise, but it is also important to integrate processes such as evaluation into organizational life.

In addition, the structure of the Math Emporium can cause disconnects with policies and processes. For instance, promotion and tenure policies at Virginia Tech do not recognize the type of faculty work done at the Emporium. In addition, Virginia Tech organizes instruction by courses, but not into sections, and self-paced courses are unusual at the university. As a matter of process, Emporium courses do not always fit neatly into the overall university course schedule, such as with the Emporium's required orientation session conflicting with other courses. Even drawing on funding from across several academic divisions and using a rented building are potential differences that require a departure from the usual policies and processes at Virginia Tech.

The structure of the Math Emporium also influences *information*. For example, assessment and evaluation involve developing and disseminating a narrative explaining what a unit is about, including to sometimes skeptical outsiders. With units that are unusual both in activity and location, such as the Math Emporium, these narratives are likely to be even more crucial. Structural peculiarities can also complicate otherwise routine efforts in generating and communicating data to support decisions. For instance, the Math Emporium and those in finance at Virginia Tech have different ideas about how the Emporium contributes to—or takes from—the bottom line at the university. Such interpretations influence funding formulas across the institution. It may be that financial and budgeting processes at Virginia Tech may need to be more adaptable to accommodate unusual units—or perhaps there is too much flexibility.

Furthermore, the Math Emporium represents a significant initial and continuing investment in *infrastructure*, addressing shortages in facilities and reallocating staffing to realize budget advantages. Both would make the Emporium difficult to replace. The project illustrates how physical infrastructure can drive significant institutional change. Not only did the available empty space enable rapid implementation at minimal cost, but using the Mathematica software program also gave the faculty the technological capacity to write an online curriculum. Depth in information technology at the university was also a resource, providing the infrastructure needed to understand and support the initiative. Finally, Virginia Tech created a financial infrastructure that would support the Emporium as the initiative developed. Various academic divisions provided the appropriate startup funding and support of the initiative on an ongoing basis.

Would the Emporium have worked on a campus not dominated by the applied sciences, thus providing various economies, or one with a culture less accepting of technology? The *culture* at Virginia Tech supported an initiative such as the Math Emporium. The university had enough students who needed these courses to support the scale of the initiative, but such an initiative would have been impossible had the project not fit within the character of the institution. No significant opposition emerged to the idea of moving lower-level mathematics courses into an online setting, suggesting both respect for the judgment of the mathematics faculty and alignment between the initiative and the culture of the institution.

The research university culture at Virginia Tech readily accommodated an academic unit structured to operate relatively autonomously. The university also had experience with start-up ventures, as with its successful research park, increasing its comfort with a project such as the Emporium—and innovation, including the risk of failure, is part of the culture of the applied sciences. An additional cultural advantage was trust across the campus sufficient to allow academic and administrative leaders to move quickly to launch the Math Emporium when the opportunity to do so presented itself. Even an ideal culture is not enough without ancillary factors such as timing. Statewide budget cuts created a crisis that required some response; the university had an administration willing to make a large initial investment and mathematics faculty willing to explore a different way to teach calculus; and there was infrastructure-related serendipity with the availability of an off-campus building.

Finally, the Math Emporium itself has become an aspect of the culture at Virginia Tech. The facility has become part of the overall character of the university, becoming a touchstone of sorts—something graduates remember about their Virginia Tech experience.

➤STRUCTURE AND ALIGNING THE OTHER ELEMENTS: A CHECKLIST

In structuring an initiative such as the Math Emporium, those leading and managing institutions might consider the following related to structure:

☐ Does the initiative advance the mission and the aspirations of the institution? At Virginia Tech, faculty and others understood the need to improve both instruction and efficiency. Could a selective liberal arts college, even one seeking savings, tolerate such an approach, given the expectations associated with it as an institutional type?

☐ Is the approach to arraying people to do their work sensible? Launching the Math Emporium involved a division of labor across various functional areas at Virginia Tech, enlisting the people that it needed and keeping others across campus informed. Developing the facility itself required the involvement, on different matters, of those in finance and administration in startup capital; of the provost and relevant deans in operating funds; and of the mathematics faculty in curriculum development and implementation. Once the facility was operational, it could function with minimal oversight from the mathematics faculty. In an institutional setting with less faculty autonomy, such as a community college, more administrative oversight may prove to be a better governance approach.

☐ Are the people making decisions related to the initiative aligned with how it is structured? The structure of the Math Emporium project suggested its governance, with those in the mathematics department responsible for academic decisions, and with determinations related to the construction of the facility made by those in finance and administration. At a more collegial institution, the faculty as a whole might have been more involved in such an initiative, and at a community college there may have been more administrative direction. Also, an academic department at a less research-intensive institution might be less willing to delegate management to a group of interested colleagues.

☐ Are there rules in place to support the project, as it is structured? At Virginia Tech, the relevant deans determined a formula, constituting a set of policies, for allocating funds to operate the facility. They concentrated less on developing mechanisms for formal oversight, given the decentralized nature and local autonomy expected within a research university, but deans might have done more at a different type of institution.

☐ Is the way things get done through formal and informal processes logical and clear to those involved, given the structure of the project? As with policies at Virginia Tech, each relevant functional area—the executive vice president, the provost and deans, and the mathematics department—determined its own approaches to operations related to its particular responsibilities associated with launching the Math Emporium. Once established, the mathematics department instituted those processes it viewed as being necessary to operate the facility. A more bureaucratic institution might have had more formalized procedures, ones more connected with the broader institution.

☐ Do those involved in the project have the information they require to make good decisions—and are they communicating with each other in an effective manner? Given the delegation of responsibilities with the Math Emporium project, there may have been less need for communication, but a less decentralized project at a different type of institution might have benefited from sustained and broader interaction.

☐ Are those involved in the project, as it is organized, sufficient in number and abilities for it to be successful—and are other infrastructure needs met? In launching and operating the Math Emporium, Virginia Tech had (or could attract) sufficient staffing, as well as having allocated the requisite physical, technological, and financial resources to realize its goals with the initiative. When these are deficient, even the most elegant structure is likely to be doomed.

☐ Does the initiative, as structured, align with the culture of the institution—and the subcultures of the units involved? At Virginia Tech, the decentralized and entrepreneurial character of the institution fit nicely with how the Math Emporium project began and continued. A culture associated with a more hierarchical or collegial institution may have required another structure.

Applying the Framework

Leaders and managers can consider several questions in applying BOC at a research university like Virginia Tech toward realizing an initiative such as the Math Emporium.

Who should be responsible for managing, and monitoring progress toward realizing, the initiative, given its nature and scope? Because local faculty involvement is essential in any matter related to the curriculum, it was imperative to include the mathematics department in planning the Math Emporium. Given the scope of the initiative, it was also important to consult the faculty senate, especially at an institution like a research university, where some degree of shared governance is expected. Yet the faculty senate need not become involved in the details of the project, more properly providing broader input associated with the idea itself. Once the Emporium became established, leaving its management to the mathematics department (and even just a few faculty within it) was logical, but the institution could have implemented an oversight committee to consider how the unit was serving changing needs across the university.

Because launching the project involved significant infrastructure and financing issues, it was also crucial to have the executive vice president manage those aspects of the project. The scope of the initiative required the provost and the president to endorse the basic idea, briefing the board of trustees, major legislators, and perhaps even major donors to the institution. The deans who would ultimately contribute to funding the operation of the Math Emporium also needed to be involved at the outset, especially in setting policies related to annual financing. Launching a project such as the Math Emporium was best accomplished with a project team, primarily consisting of personnel from the office of the EVP and representatives of the mathematics department, with the work divided into academic and administrative tasks. The team could then consult with other relevant units and individuals across the institution, as appropriate. The Math Emporium illustrates the utility of a project team approach. The team was sufficiently agile to enable the university to develop the initiative within a relatively short period to take advantage of several factors that created an open window of opportunity.

Involving representatives of the mathematics faculty and senior administration offered the benefit of those launching the Math Emporium having a clear sense not only of the institutional purposes that the initiative was intended to advance, but also of core academic values. Such clarity is another important factor in providing the most leverage possible toward realizing an initiative. The purposes element in strategic management involves both mission and aspirations, with the Math Emporium intended to improve instruction and reduce the costs associated with it. By inclination and position, the faculty involved considered the more mission-related question of how the initiative could improve teaching. The administrators could concentrate on infrastructure issues apart from academic concerns, including in advancing the aspirations of the institution by increasing its efficiency. Through their work together, each side could appreciate the purview of the other, with the faculty realizing the challenges associated with financing and otherwise developing a significant infrastructure project. and the administrators aware of the need to maintain academic integrity. Had the Math Emporium team been concerned with either mission or ambitions alone, the project would probably not have succeeded.

To employ strategic management in designing and implementing a project such as the Math Emporium, those involved need not only a complete appreciation of purposes, but also a clear understanding of the elements and how they align relative to the initiative. What could too easily be seen as only an infrastructure project must be considered more completely. The Virginia Tech initiative depended on those involved with the Math Emporium developing it in ways that were consistent with the culture of the institution, which included being comfortable with the decentralized structure that enabled the faculty within the mathematics department to manage the facility once it was launched. Those involved with initiating the project also recognized the importance of communication. The mathematics faculty who subsequently managed it also understood how it could sometimes serve their purposes to operate under the radar. Applying a strategic-management framework also suggests the potential benefit from increased attention to policies and processes.

The Math Emporium, structured as it was, illustrates how leaders and senior managers can leverage clarity in purposes and alignment with culture. Virginia Tech had a strong sense of its mission and aspirations, and individuals throughout the institution could see how these were advanced by the Math Emporium, especially once the necessary people signaled their commitment to the project. Such clarity makes measuring progress and, ultimately, impact relatively straightforward, assuming one can assess quality and efficiencies related to teaching. The institution also had a culture that could accept such an academic initiative, situating it more at the periphery of the institution and having it operate much like an auxiliary unit. With such clarity and alignment, it was not much of a stretch for those across the university to consider the other elements in ways that were necessary to advance the initiative.

Finally, the advantages at Virginia Tech that allowed the Math Emporium to develop very rapidly and continue to operate with limited formality and in relative isolation also allow possible breakdowns to occur. For instance, the decentralized and informal approach to structure and governance that characterize the Math Emporium have led it to overlook potentially necessary internal policies and processes. It is possible that the "don't fix what isn't broke" culture at the

Emporium, while often productive, can discourage change or innovation; that the information needed to inform decision making is not always generated or disseminated; and that the massive infrastructure investments in the Math Emporium may make it difficult to end or significantly change the project, even if the institution wanted to. The relative success of the initiative for over a decade suggests that various strengths, particularly in how well the Math Emporium aligns with the purposes and culture of the institution and fits with the possibilities for structure and governance there, have generally compensated for potential problems.

CHAPTER FIVE

Governance

*Enterprise Resource Planning Implementation
at Valley City State University*

In October 2002, Valley City State University (VCSU), as one of three pilot sites, began implementing ConnectND, a statewide PeopleSoft enterprise resource planning (ERP) software system for academic and administrative functions. The new platform replaced legacy systems from the late 1980s, offering greater self-service, more and quicker information, Web-based access, personalized portals, and streamlined processes. ConnectND included both the North Dakota University System (NDUS) and the state government. Higher education in North Dakota is noted for being decentralized, with nearly 40,000 full- and part-time students spread across 11 campuses. The university system has 5800 full-time employees and the state government has just over 9000 permanent and temporary employees, so the implementation of an enterprise resource planning system was a significant undertaking.

In implementing ConnectND, VCSU needed to determine whether its approach was consistent with the purposes of not only the institution, but also of the state higher education system. It also had to consider the project in terms of the structure and governance of both the university and the state system, in addition to looking at various operational questions: rules to be established, means to accomplish them, information needed, and infrastructure required. In its planning and execution, VCSU had to accommodate the cultures of the campus, the system, and even the state. It also had to determine who needed to be involved in the implementation. For instance, did faculty and students care enough to merit their day-to-day involvement, or was this essentially and appropriately an administrative project? In deciding that the ERP implementation should involve just the latter, the VCSU case illustrates governance on the administrative side of higher education, as opposed to faculty governance, which is typically less hierarchical and more inclusive. It also features an administrative effort at a small, public comprehensive institution.[1]

Governance as an Element

Governance involves who makes what decisions within an organization, with mission and aspirations guiding these. What might be a simple construct, particularly when viewed only as a structural question, as is more typical in administrative units, is complicated by how power and influence is imprecisely decided at universities and colleges. The tradition of shared governance in higher education balances the interests of faculty, particularly on academic questions, with those of administrators. External influences, especially when funding is involved, are also important. " 'Governance' is the term we give to the structures and processes that academic institutions invent to achieve an effective balance between the claims of two different, but equally valid, systems for organizational control and influence," writes Robert Birnbaum (2004). "One system, based on legal authority, is the basis for the role of trustees and administration; the other system, based on professional authority, justifies the role of the faculty" (p. 1).

At institutions with a tradition of shared governance, decision making occurs at multiple levels, with specific entities claiming influence or authority over certain issues at public institutions: the faculty make curricular decisions, particularly within academic units; administrations set institution-wide budget priorities for academic programs; and states consider the distribution of academic programs across institutions (Kezar and Eckel 2004). Rosovsky (1991) frames governance as the competition for power involving the three most influential groups at a university—the trustees, the administration, and the faculty—"who is in charge; who makes decisions; who has a voice, and how loud is that voice?" (p. 261). Given the ambiguity in respective authority and responsibility among faculty, administrators, and trustees, "conflicts over the appropriate locations for making various kinds of decisions have occurred since tribal times" (Schmidtlein and Berdahl 2005, p. 77; see also Duderstadt 2004 and Gayle, Tewarie, and White 2003). Gayle, Tewarie, and White (2003) identify the multiple actors involved in governance more broadly, representing it as concentric circles: presidents, faculty, administrators, and trustees at the core; then community, students, and alumni; then state governors, legislators, departments, and boards; then the U.S. Congress, state systems, accreditation agencies, and the federal Department of Education; then national higher educational associations and funding organizations.[2]

The ultimate challenge in governance is how to share it. Duderstadt (2004) centers faculty governance at the unit level, deciding on such questions there as who is hired and promoted, what gets taught, and how funds are allocated. Complicating matters, even at the local level, is the incompatibility between the culture of the faculty and management needs, especially with corporate ideas seemingly ascendant within higher education (Gayle, Tewarie, and White 2003). Efficiency and accountability in an environment increasingly influenced by markets can conflict with adherence to the values and autonomy that are of greatest consequence to the faculty (Duderstadt 2004). The significant expansion of activity, including academic programs, at the periphery of institutions—and its tendency to be more influenced by managers—has shifted the equation there, with traditional conceptions of shared governance offering ever less guidance (Toma 2007). Burgan (2006) suggests that faculty influence is waning as competition between and among, as well as within, institutions increases, as in faculty hiring or research ventures (Slaughter and Rhoades 2004; Wilson 2004; Kirp 2003; Ehrenberg 2002). She also considers how even core faculty functions, such as teaching and the curriculum, are drifting away from faculty authority, both in traditional settings and through distance education. Drawing on empirical data, Michael Miller (2003) writes about the challenges to what he terms "academic democracy" in the increasingly corporate university, including questions associated with a growing reliance on temporary faculty. He also explores the decline in trust and respect between the faculty and administrators, as does Pope (2004). There is also writing on dysfunction in faculty governance, such as Twale and DeLuca's (2007) research on incivility.

Tierney (2004) argues that different conceptions of governance are inevitable and that improvement comes through focusing not on structure, but instead on shared culture and communication, as between faculty and administrators (see also G. Kaplan 2004a, 2004b; Kezar 2004; Tierney and Minor 2004). Faculty perspectives remain crucial, including in various peripheral activities that are seemingly more administrative in nature, such as athletics, medical centers, or conference facilities (Keller 2004a; Birnbaum 2004). Gabriel Kaplan (2004a, 2004b) concludes that faculty members continue to have an influence on governance, particularly in their areas of expertise—as with academic programs or faculty hiring—while administrators have more authority over budgets, strategy, and facilities. Most writing about governance in higher education focuses on the former, notably at institutions with strong traditions of shared governance, such as research universities and more selective liberal arts colleges. The VCSU case illustrates the latter, involving a more purely administrative issue.

What exactly is governance in higher education—and in strategic management? In discussing corporations, but in a statement that applies equally to universities and colleges, Pound (2000) notes that "governance is not about power but about ensuring that decisions are made effectively . . . [with] better accountability" (p. 79). A slightly different definition of governance, one drawn from political science, is that governance is the way a group, once gathered, goes about approaching its affairs, operating at multiple levels. In the context of strategic management, determining the group is structure and how it chooses to act is governance. Policies are the resulting rules that guide future decisions, and processes implement these policies. Governance and processes are active nouns; structure and policies are static ones. Governance is different from structure. Structure gets an appropriate set of individuals around the table—a faculty senate, for example—and governance is having those gathered there make a set of decisions in areas in which they are deemed responsible. Because there is such a human element to making decisions, and organizational culture is so idiosyncratic, two organizations can have the same structure and very different governance.

Governance in strategic management is certainly broader than oversight by a board of trustees or the involvement of faculty members in academic decision making—its two usual conceptions in higher education. The question of who makes what decisions arises at all levels of the organization, involves input from both internal and external stakeholders, happens in both formal and informal ways, and inherently involves oversight. For instance, state systems impose oversight over institutional governing boards, and boards do the same over administrations, but there is also an oversight function within governance at other levels of a university or college—administrations over bureaucracies, faculty over academic standards, and even students over their own organizations.

Mortimer and McConnell (1978) frame governance in academe as the "distribution of authority" and the "legitimacy of shared authority." For them, governance occurs in the context of academic senates, collective bargaining, stakeholder interactions, trustee-faculty interactions, administrative leadership, external accountabilities, statewide coordination, and decentralization versus centralization. They conclude that "a number of factors are important in the distribution of authority— among them the organizational level at which decisions are made; the constituents who are, or claim a right to be, involved in decisions; the issues under consideration; and the historical-cultural traditions under which the institution operates" (p. 266). Even though views on the balance of power differ, there is broad agreement that appropriate constituents should influence decisions— governance should be shared. Governance should take advantage of a natural division of labor among groups with different areas of expertise—the faculty on curriculum and administrators on financing, for instance. It should also recognize the need for decisions not to run afoul of academic culture, as with a decision by trustees conflicting with traditional academic norms, Finally, governance should integrate the advantages of broad consultation and participation in promoting consensus around a particular idea, which is essential in realizing change within an organization (Kezar and Eckel 2004; Hartley 2002b).

Even when there is agreement in the appropriateness of shared governance, concerns tend to arise with both boards and faculty. Balancing institutional autonomy with oversight by boards requires considering concepts such as authority, control, responsibility, and accountability. As the *Harvard Business Review* editors (2000) note, "most directors and managers agree that the board should be a more effective watchdog without undermining management's ability to run the business. They also say boards need to decide how to distance themselves more from their CEOs without turning a constructive relationship into an adversarial one" (p. 187). Trow (1989) extends the point to state higher educational systems, arguing that the central function of governance at that level is resistance to external pressures and the exclusion of partisan politics from internal functioning, resulting in the preservation of autonomy and the retention of self-governance.[3]

The involvement of faculty members in institutional decision making raises another set of issues. Given its rather imprecise nature, shared governance can frustrate those inclined toward rationality and efficiency, and it is commonly criticized as limiting agility within institutions, creating obstructions to rapid decision making (Birnbaum 2004; Kezar and Eckel 2004). Such critiques are more common at the macro level, as opposed to faculty governance within units (Bergan 2004). Faculty slowing change within institutions may be occasionally useful, however, as with providing a check on the administration when it fails to take the long view or rushes to adopt the latest management fads (Lohmann 2004). Kezar (2005) argues that institutional decision-making mechanisms are not prepared to handle increasingly complex challenges, particularly those related to a continually more competitive environment. While there may be consensus that some degree of change is needed, she cautions against either reinstalling bureaucratic approaches or simply adopting corporate models at the expense of decentralization and participation. Collis (2004) explains challenges in governance at universities and colleges in terms of there being nothing akin to the unidimensional goal of maximizing shareholder value. Higher education institutions have no clear measure of their outputs; have multiple constituencies with conflicting agendas, some with what amounts to veto power; and lack both effective means of hierarchical control and strong incentives to use with the faculty.

Although such challenges cut across institutional types, governance tends to differ in various sectors of U.S. higher education, particularly as it involves faculty. At research universities and selective liberal arts colleges, the academic core of the institution is likely to be the most predominant and the faculty role in governance the richest. These are the institutions that Rosovsky (1991), writing from Harvard, had in mind in framing his concept of shared governance (Toma 2007). According to Birnbaum (1988), faculty members at research universities exist in an anarchical environment characterized by individual autonomy, while those at liberal arts colleges work within a collegial model based on consensus.

At both, governance is more naturally influenced by the faculty. In contrast, faculty members at institutions with fewer resources are more likely to exist in more bureaucratic and political environments, those more defined by hierarchy, negotiation, and accountability (Birnbaum 1988). These faculty are less likely to have influence sufficient to balance administrators. The VCSU case resides in such an environment, as do most institutions in the United States, concentrating on preparing students for the workforce (Keller 2004a). They are reputation based, focused on serving student needs as opposed to being more interested in prestige, and are more responsive to market forces (Dill 2003; Brewer, Gates and Goldman 2002).

Governance: A Perspective on the Research Literature

Adrianna Kezar

University of Southern California

Scholarship about governance has focused extensively on structural theories, with more limited attention paid to political and cultural ones. Those drawing upon structural theories suggest that the most important aspect in understanding governance is to examine organizational structures, such as lines of authority, and themes, such as centralization versus decentralization. These theories assume that there is a structural solution for any governance challenge and an ideal result that organizations can reach through sound management.

During the 1960s and into the 1970s, researchers generally attempted to delineate which units or individuals were making decisions—boards, presidents, colleges and schools, departments and programs—and how much authority each entity possessed (Duryea 1973; Gross and Gramback 1968). These studies identified the salient features of the bureaucratic qualities of institutions, such as chains of command and role differentiation (Mintzberg 1979; Stroup 1966). Others described the legal environment of governance, such as charters or legislation from states (Birnbaum 1988; McGee 1971). Open systems theory emerged in the 1980s, but it continued to focus on structure, as did Mortimer and McConnell (1978) in identifying the growth of external forces on internal campus governance. Mortimer and McConnell (1978) also studied the distribution of authority (or delegated authority) across institutional decision-making structures, but they were concerned that not enough mechanisms existed to ensure accountability.

Birnbaum (1989, 1988) conducted the most extensive study into governance in the past 30 years, also using an open systems approach. He introduced the importance of cybernetics, the notion of recognizing the linkages between governance subunits and the significance of complex systems in making choices at institutions of all types. He asserted that governance is not efficient—with overlapping authority common at institutions, for instance—but it is effective, especially given its ability to accommodate both faculty values and administrative responsiveness (Birnbaum 1992; Berdahl 1991). Influencing Birnbaum, Baldridge (1971) focused on individuals within the organization, as opposed to structure, underscoring the importance of political influence and informal processes in making decisions and developing policy (G. Riley and Baldridge 1977). In the political model, conflict and

(continued)

bargaining between and among interest groups driven by values is paramount, as opposed to the logic of structure being the prime mover. Accordingly, governance is idiosyncratic from campus to campus—and even from issue to issue.

The impetus for much of the work in the 1990s came from external criticism, including that from activist trustees, that campuses were inefficient and ineffective, and thus insufficiently responsive (Benjamin and Carroll 1998). Trustees assumed greater decision-making authority, becoming involved in areas that were previously the domain of faculty and administrators. In addition, the Association of Governing Boards (1996) issued a new statement related to campus governance, focusing on the need to temper shared governance and have more external influences on internal functions. Others critics cited earlier findings that few campuses actually practiced shared governance, especially at community colleges and comprehensive institutions, but also even at most research universities and liberal arts colleges (Baldridge 1982; Mortimer and McConnell 1978).

In addition, some politicians, higher educational associations, and trustees argue that shared governance limits agility and flexibility within institutions, creating obstructions and sluggishness and fostering a predisposition toward the status quo (Association of Governing Boards of Universities and Colleges 1996; Schuster, Smith, Corak, and Yamada 1994). There is also the challenge of a diminished interest by faculty members in the work of shared governance. Some institutions have compensated by adopting increasingly bureaucratic approaches to making decisions (Rhoades 1995). Such administrative prerogative is characterized by more centralized, hierarchical administrative oversight, where quality is measured by the efficiency of decision making and not what results from it (Hardy 1990).

After 40 years of exploring governance, what do we know? First, complexity reduces the efficiency of the governance process. The composition of the bodies making decisions has a similar influence, with such characteristics as clarity of roles, redundancy of function, and expertise among participants leading to greater effectiveness (Schuster, Smith, Corak, and Yamada 1994; Berdahl 1991; B. Lee 1991; Birnbaum 1988; Dill and Helm 1988; Mortimer and McConnell 1978; Cohen and March 1974). In addition, consultation contributes to effective governance, as well as to an increased awareness across the institution, which in turn develops the ownership thought to facilitate smooth implementation (Dill and Helm 1988; Mortimer and McConnell 1978). Participation in the governance process leads to satisfaction among those involved and to more inclusive processes that can improve decisions (Birnbaum 1988; Williams, Gore, Broches, and Lostski 1987). Finally, leadership is important both in shaping governance and in its effectiveness (Schuster, Smith, Corak, and Yamada 1994;

B. Lee 1991), although presidents may have a lesser role than is commonly believed (Birnbaum 1988).

Moving forward, too few have followed Birnbaum in acknowledging the influence of politics and symbolism in governance. Barbara Lee (1991) and Williams, Gore, Broches, and Lostski (1987) are exceptions, as is Gumport (2000) in examining cultural and political conflicts in governance. Several theoretical frameworks centered on the human dynamics of organizations remain underutilized in the study of governance. Human relations theories emphasize how people within organizations affect organizational processes, featuring concepts such as motivation, training, and rewards. Cultural theories examine how symbolism, values, and beliefs affect institutional operations, focusing on institutional climate and culture. Social cognition theories explore how learning occurs within organizations or how people make sense of their environments.

Valley City State University and ConnectND

Valley City State University is located in the southeastern part of North Dakota in Valley City, a community of approximately 8000 people. Chartered in the original state constitution, VCSU began in 1890 as a normal school, became a state teachers college in 1921, and evolved into Valley City State College in 1963. In 1987, the North Dakota Legislative Assembly designated the institution as Valley City State University, a regional baccalaureate university within the state's higher educational system. VCSU is accredited by the North Central Association of Colleges and Schools, the National Council for the Accreditation of Teacher Education, and the National Association of Schools of Music. In January 2005, the State Board of Higher Education authorized VCSU to offer a master of education degree, its first graduate program.

VCSU enrolls just over 1000 students and has a student-faculty ratio of about 13:1. The university offers undergraduate programs distributed among five divisions: (1) business and information technology; (2) communication arts and social sciences; (3) education and graduate studies; (4) fine arts; and (5) mathematics, science, and health and physical education. In 1996, North Dakota designated VCSU as a technology-intensive campus, distinguishing it within the state and elsewhere. The university frames the role as delivering a technology-enhanced, communication- and collaboration-focused learning experience in which every student has direct access to the latest multimedia and networking technology.

VCSU issues a laptop computer to each full-time student and faculty member. As part of their graduation requirements, all students must also develop a digital portfolio illustrating the abilities and skills acquired in their general education and major coursework.

In 2007, in-state tuition was approximately $5000 per year ($12,000 for out-of-state students), and over 80 percent of VCSU students received some form of financial assistance, including numerous scholarships. Surveys conducted by Noel-Levitz, a national consulting firm, suggest that VCSU students are significantly more satisfied than the average for students at four-year colleges, both in North Dakota and nationally. In addition, a survey of employers of VCSU graduates found an overall satisfaction rate of 98.8 percent. The VCSU Vikings compete in the Dakota Athletic Conference in the National Association of Intercollegiate Athletics (NAIA).

The implementation of ConnectND at VCSU provides an uncommon illustration of governance, given that it was driven by administrators and did not particularly involve faculty—or even the information technology staff. In accordance with the direction set by the university system, VCSU organized the implementation of Connect ND to facilitate making disciplined decisions within a formal structure. An executive steering committee drawn from across the statewide system developed the several guiding principles for the configuration of ConnectND. The principles limited customization by individual campuses and encouraged collaboration among them, with the ultimate goal of having the implementation be a statewide system that recognizes the "unique missions and needs of each campus." The steering committee also developed clear lines of authority for those involved with the project. In addition to the steering committee itself, there was a project director for ConnectND and project managers for the four major areas on the higher educational side of the project: financial, human resources, student, and technical. Within these areas, the project was organized into modules—functional areas such as accounts payable or student records—with a team and team leader responsible for each.

Each campus also selected an implementation team, with Ellen Earle Chaffee, the president at VCSU, chairing theirs, thus underscoring the institution's commitment to the project. Chaffee, a noted scholar on strategy and management in higher education, in addition to being a long-serving president, was able to stress information flow and businesslike efficiency, but she was also available to hold hands when people became frustrated. In addition, subject matter experts on each campus participated in the implementation, and Maximus, a consulting firm, assisted the various teams. As a pilot site, VCSU also benefited from having a large number of people involved in setting policy and developing processes statewide.

ConnectND provides not only an example of business-style governance in higher education, with the question of who makes what decisions determined in an orderly, hierarchical manner, but it also illustrates the influence states can have on institutional governance. ConnectND also exemplifies the trend within higher education toward seeking efficiencies, often involving the use of technology. Although North Dakota was deliberate in deciding to invest in the ERP system, institutions commonly commit to such investments without considering various, even foundational, questions and concerns, sometimes telling horror stories for years afterward. VCSU, in contrast, was ready for the implementation of ConnectND, within the controlled manner in which the state system set it up to unfold.

Purposes and Governance at Valley City State University

The ERP system implementation went smoothly at VCSU, in large part because it fit so neatly within the purposes of the institution. Beginning with the laptop initiative in 1996, the university has claimed technology as a significant part of its formal identity—not only in how it emphasizes its distinctiveness, but also in its mission and aspirations. Accordingly, people at VCSU expect a certain amount of experimentation with technology, given that it is so central to the essence of the institution, and take justifiable pride in their technological savvy and willingness to step out front in this area. Technology is both an aspect of institutional purposes and ingrained in the VCSU culture—and connecting these two strategic management elements is essential. When VCSU became a pilot institution for Connect ND, the campus community knew from experience that the university possessed the necessary flexibility and adaptability to pull off a major technology initiative. Those at VCSU were proud that the university was chosen as a pilot site, seeing it as an opportunity to continue to be at the cutting edge within the state.

In addition, the university understood that statewide connectivity is important in a rural state like North Dakota, so ConnectND aligned with the service mission associated with any public institution. Although they advocated for the needs of their own campus in planning ConnectND in conjunction with other institutions in the system, people at VCSU recognized the advantages associated with implementing a common system statewide. They also supported ConnectND as part of the economic development of the state and the local community, an acknowl-edged and increasingly important part of the institutional mission at VCSU, as it is across public higher education. Indeed, institutions across types—especially those without ready sources of other income, such as private giving or funded research—are more likely to feature their commitment to local economic develop-ment in justifying their state appropriations and other forms of support. VCSU had recently demonstrated its commitment when it developed a regional technology center and reworked its curriculum to attract a major technology firm to the Val-ley City community. ConnectND served the overall economic development effort, providing necessary infrastructure.

Those at VCSU also recognized that its legacy system was too fragile, having undergone too many patches and fixes, to continue to provide for the needs and ambitions of the state and their institution. The system also could not handle vari-ous emerging needs, such as the reporting requirements related to federal man-dates. Furthermore, the university was clear about its student-centered mission—and ConnectND supported this. Students also expected the most up-to-date technology, given what VCSU professed to be, and the legacy system lacked a suit-able interface for students when applying online, sending a poor symbolic message.

In determining who would make what decisions involving the implementa-tion of ConnectND, the administration decided at the outset that faculty would not be interested in the project—a determination with clear governance implica-tions. Contributing to the decision that faculty participation would be unnecessary was a concern that, even had the administration thought it relevant, their involve-ment might have needlessly slowed progress. Although faculty were involved with technology in their teaching, formal faculty governance at the institution tended to be dysfunctional. Even with VCSU's small size—which should have diminished bureaucracy and enhanced collegiality, at least to some degree—initiatives still bogged down over minor issues, too often having to come before the faculty senate. Some committees, such as the curriculum committee, were more effective, as was the group of academic division chairs that could have been employed to get faculty input into ConnectND.

The VCSU faculty in general were ultimately not concerned about being ex-cluded from the process, assuming that others had appropriate expertise. Perhaps a lesson here is that even when valuing faculty involvement in governance, there are simply some areas where their direct participation is neither meaningful nor productive—nor especially desired by them. Had ConnectND involved instruction, as opposed to tracking students, faculty involvement would have been essential, even at the most managed institutions.

Some faculty did complain that the implementation did not adequately address faculty needs and interests. Additionally, specific deficiencies emerged in ConnectND, particularly in relation to the needs of division chairs, who were unable to easily run particular types of useful reports, such as lists of how many students major in a given area. There was also ongoing frustration about not giving certain users, such as chairs, access to parts of systems that they deemed necessary in completing their work. Consequently, another lesson in strategic management may be that short-term inconvenience in involving a group such as the faculty in a project like ConnectND might lead to a more productive result, even if merely at the level of symbolism.

Connecting with the Other Elements

A pronounced feature of the ERP initiative at VCSU was its meticulous *structure*, which was mostly attributable to the state-level coordination of ConnectND and aligned with the approach to governance defined for the project. ConnectND coupled explicitness about who was to make what decisions with a mandate for a rational, modular structure. The structure had a clear hierarchy and carefully defined work groups, the latter comprised primarily of future users. Having decided on such a careful approach to governance within the project, ConnectND needed a formal structure to complement it. As with governance, particularly within the flatter parts of the organizational chart, structure at universities and colleges is not always so tidy. Nonetheless, there are regular occasions when institutions, sometimes by necessity, arrange people quite carefully. For instance, promotion and tenure committees not only must follow policies and processes carefully, but the structure of the groups of faculty involved at various levels is prescribed. Approaching decisions in such a manner contributes to the integrity of the process and desired perceptions by outsiders. The same is true of the governance that the structure of promotion and tenure supports, as it matters that faculty are the ones making such decisions. Those without a direct interest are excluded by the structure of the group. Another illustration concerns task forces commonly convened at universities and colleges. Leaders and senior managers select participants purposefully, typically seeking appropriate representation of various interests. Meanwhile, such committees, once structured, tend to have a clear charge, so those involved know what decisions they have been gathered to make.

The approach to ConnectND maximized order, which also excluded some from the process. The state viewed the project as being about back-office operations, not substantive concerns, structuring it accordingly. Its organizers envisioned the implementation of ConnectND as an orderly process, dividing work among teams who would then execute tasks, making decisions only within their purview. A more diffuse structure that accommodated more voices might have had the advantage of inviting a richer discussion of basic assumptions and operational possibilities, as might an open meeting to consider a hot-button issue on campus, but it would have been less tidy and expeditious. These are tradeoffs that leaders and senior managers make in determining structure and governance related to an initiative. ConnectND illustrates that an entire campus may not always need or want to have a full discussion of absolutely every issue. Some decisions can probably be left to smaller groups of colleagues who are directly concerned with a given matter.

The structure of the ERP system implementation in North Dakota, including at VCSU, was notable, as much as anything, for whom it excluded: not only faculty, but also information technology (IT) personnel. The thought was that the system needed be owned by the people in the units who would use it, with the overall implementation team structured accordingly. ConnectND was neither framed nor ultimately structured as an IT project, but instead as a means to improve various management information systems. Where ConnectND prompted the hiring of new staff, the positions were generally in the units, not in the IT division. However, there was some need for IT expertise in launching the new platform, as in the example of IT people becoming involved when an encryption issue arose. In addition, students were consulted and involved to some extent, which was thought to be appropriate, considering that a portion of the technology fee they paid was directed toward ConnectND. Nonetheless, their interest in the project as an operational matter was minimal, so there was no need to include them in the day-to-day work of the planning committee. Instead, those students involved with the initiative added their voices at appropriate junctures, essentially symbolically.

With governance and structure being so rigid, it followed that the statewide project team tended to reference the original plan for ConnectND when setting policies and making decisions. The implementation process was logical and disciplined, as intended, with people expected to stick to the plan. The idea was for ConnectND to be uniform across the system once it was set in place, avoiding individual adaptations that might later cause complications. When patches and updates are eventually needed, they can be done statewide. Such an approach, with anyone's problem becoming everyone's problem, aligns with the closely knit culture of the state. Furthermore, standardizing its management information systems enabled higher education in North Dakota to function even more as a system, which was one of the goals of ConnectND. For example, students can now more readily enroll across multiple campuses. There were frustrations, as with local staff having to wait for problems to be fixed by state-level colleagues, but people viewed these as part of the tradeoff for having statewide coherence.

In implementing ConnectND, VCSU needed to change various *policies* and *processes* toward achieving system-wide consistency. Certain decisions were a part of the formal implementation process, but other questions arose during it. For instance, the project team knew from the outset that grade point averages at the institution needed to become cumulative and include transfer courses, in order to be in line with policies across the state. Even the most systematic implementation plan cannot anticipate all contingencies and requires various work-arounds.

The new ERP system transformed processes, It streamlined some, as with staff not having to enter admissions applications into the system twice, as was previously required. Everyone can, in theory, enter information into ConnectND, not just one trained staff person, so the new system, once operational, encouraged units to reallocate personnel. Moving to ConnectND also illustrates that changing familiar processes that have evolved over many years can prove challenging, as it was for the lower-level staff on the processes' front lines. Finally, Connect ND made self-service options available to students, allowing them direct access to their records, The new system also enabled VCSU to run more detailed reports and readily access a greater depth of information about its students.

The ready exchange of *information* across the VCSU campus proved to be advantageous in approaching ConnectND. Being inclined to talk through problems as they occurred was part of the culture at the university. With Connect ND, the governance and structure of the project further encouraged such regular communication, as with localizing decision making, when possible, to within the various project teams. For example, an informal list serve emerged at VCSU, allowing easy questions about the installation to be answered and avoiding the requirement of a formal "ticket" for a fix. Governance and structure within the project required more formal communication up and down the hierarchy within the state, but informal means were also important, as always. The same is true across the elements in strategic management. There are always informal approaches that coincide with formal ones. Even in the most rigid formal environments have accompanying informal aspects that those within organizations adapt as they shift from planning to implementation.

The user groups formed during the implementation process also provided additional communication channels within VCSU. The teams involved in the process knew what the other local teams were doing, through both formal and less formal means. They also had a good sense of how the project was emerging across the state. The ERP installation facilitated needed communication across campuses in the North Dakota system. Because the initiative mostly concerned process, not strategy and tactics, there was little, if any, cause for holding back information due to rivalry or competition. The information flows developed for the implementation also proved useful in getting the message out about what was becoming available through ConnectND and how those at VCSU could access it. Having users involved in the implementation encouraged the kind of informal communication about possibilities related to the system that generated support. Finally, ConnectND itself strengthened the exchange of information within the institution and across the state system. With its eventual launch, certain communications simply became easier. Understanding what others are doing is a necessary condition in strategic management and systems thinking.

Infrastructure was both another advantage and perhaps the main shortcoming of the project. VCSU had constructed a sound IT infrastructure well before ConnectND, possessing what was arguably the finest computing and communications system in the state. Even given its modest size, VCSU had established a chief information officer position. The real challenge related to ConnectND was how rapidly the implementation would occur, given the complexity of the initiative. VCSU could have avoided significant confusion and frustration had the state allocated sufficient resources for implementation—a common-enough infrastructure challenge. ConnectND devoted insufficient attention and resources to training, which proved to be a significant weakness in the project. ConnectND adopted a just-in-time approach to training, with mixed results, particularly given the lack of manuals and documentation for the project that would have allowed for some degree of self-instruction. "Just in time," those on campus came to joke, was really not "in time." The technical infrastructure being added required supporting data and communication, but such information tended to lag behind.

Training for eventual users was often more ad hoc than systematic, presenting a disconnect with the more formal approach to governance and structure. For instance, there was no training on how to conduct searches for information, which is especially important in a system that is not always intuitive and sometimes lacks documentation. However, there were examples of effective local training, such as e-mail instructions from the registrar to faculty as they used ConnectND for the first time to enter grades. The training offered to students, including during first-year orientation, was more successful, but it was also a more straightforward task, as the interfaces students used were more basic. Lastly, akin to people having relevant skills, staff time is also a resource—and the implementation process did not always adequately account for it. Even though some staff members had a portion of their time formally devoted to the project, they still needed to tend to their regular duties while working on the implementation, ending up stretched and exhausted. No amount of structure or formality in governance could compensate for a lack of investment in infrastructure, as with investing the resources needed to properly train personnel.

Finally, the *culture* of VCSU was such that implementing an ERP system was less disruptive than might otherwise have been the case. Its laptop program and its subsequent initiatives, including implementing the Blackboard software program and switching e-mail systems, enhanced the comfort level with technology across the institution. People were accustomed to being at the cutting edge in technology and highly tolerant of change in that area. Faculty, staff, and students understood that problems with new technology are inevitable and must be worked through—such is part of being innovators. There is also a small-town, can-do culture at VCSU, People are generally willing to do whatever it takes and hesitant to say "no." The VCSU president, Ellen Chaffee, was influential here. Her symbolic act of chairing the ConnectND implementation committee at VCSU emphasized the importance of the initiative to the mission and aspirations of the university. Chaffee was comfortable with business approaches to planning and strategy, such as those that accompanied the ConnectND implementation. For over a decade, she had imbued the entire Valley City community with a similar level of ease during her decade as president. She also had developed a significant degree of trust with the VCSU community, affording her the goodwill needed to get the campus behind such a significant undertaking as ConnectND.

➤GOVERNANCE AND ALIGNING THE OTHER ELEMENTS: A CHECKLIST
In organizing a project such as the implementation of a statewide enterprise resource planning system on a small campus, those leading and managing institutions might consider the following related to governance:

☐   How does the resulting capacity from the implementation advance the
    mission and aspirations of the institution? At VCSU, the new manage-
    ment information system enabled the university to be more effective in
    serving students, as well as being more efficient. Being among the pilot
    sites for ConnectND enabled VCSU to emphasize the leadership role in
    technology within North Dakota that it had claimed.

☐   Who is best situated to make decisions related to such an implementa-
    tion? VCSU assigned the implementation to a team of administrators,
    only including those who could make directly relevant contributions and
    featuring those who would ultimately use the system. Given that the state
    was coordinating ConnectND, the VCSU president led the project herself,
    in recognition of her responsibility over the external affairs of the
    university. In the interest of consistency across institutions, those at the
    state level dictated the structure of the project, and this shaped gover-
    nance to a large extent.

☐   Who should be involved in an implementation—and who does not need to
    be? As structured, the implementation of ConnectND excluded various
    end users, such as faculty and did not emphasize IT staff. These people
    may have offered useful insights, but the approach adopted emphasized
    efficiency over inclusiveness, recognizing the short timeline involved. An
    initiative that was more academic in nature would have needed to involve
    faculty members, both for practical and symbolic reasons.

☐   What rules should guide an implementation, and how should it unfold?
    The ConnectND project was akin to construction management, with a
    sequence established at the outset and specific tasks delegated to various
    groups. New policies and processes were required, with limited flexibility
    available, given the statewide nature of the implementation. The approach
    in North Dakota was efficient, but less responsive to unanticipated needs
    related to policies and processes.

☐   What data and communications are required, both for those within the
    group directly involved and for others, for the approach to be successful?
    Information did not always support decision making within the VCSU

project team, as well as for those coordinating ConnectND at the state level, as the project somewhat neglected training needs. However, the informal exchange of information was a strength of the initiative.

☐ What infrastructure is necessary, whether human, physical, technological, and financial? Implementing ConnectND was a significant undertaking, requiring infrastructure investments in order to be successful, as with making sure there are enough people assigned to the project.

☐ How must an approach align with the culture of an institution? VCSU had a can-do culture and was comfortable with being out in front on technology initiatives, the latter trait having been developed over several earlier projects. The extra work required to navigate a complicated process was within the grasp of those involved, given the character of the university.

Applying the Framework

When applying strategic management in the context of an operational project, such as an ERP implementation at a small, comprehensive institution, leaders and senior managers may wish to consider several questions.

The VCSU case illustrates that faculty—and even many IT staff—do not need to be involved in a project such as ConnectND. Teams of lower-level administrators with relevant operational responsibilities can manage the daily aspects of the project, especially given its prescribed decision points. There does, however, need to be broader responsibility for monitoring progress, ensuring accountability, and measuring impact. Especially at a smaller institution, it is sensible for the president to opt to direct the project. Perhaps the chief information officer or chief financial officer could serve that function, but given the links between ConnectND and the statewide interests of the institution, the president probably needed to be personally involved, if only for symbolic reasons. The project also had a sufficiently direct connection with mission and aspirations at VCSU to merit her involvement. The statewide oversight of the project and its orderly nature enabled the president to be involved without being consumed by the initiative.

Those with broader responsibilities, such as the president, have the clear understanding of the big picture necessary to be able to identify the elements and how they align and clarify these for those with more local responsibilities. For example, some individuals involved in the project may be primarily concerned with policies and processes, and the president can remind them of the other elements, especially purposes, that must align with these to implement a large project like the ERP system. The broader university community, as with faculty members, also needs to have some understanding of the project—and its importance to the institution—but they do not have to enter into it in any detail. Basic communication and symbolic acts may serve their requirements. Those not involved will likely have only a vague notion about a project such as ConnectND, and will really only need to know that it is good for VCSU.

In addition, having the president direct the project ensures that it will align with the institutional purposes that the initiative is intended to advance—the essential question that leaders and managers need to ask in applying strategic management. VCSU had the advantage, going into the implementation, of having a sufficiently clear understanding of institutional mission and aspirations among the lower-level administrators involved in the ConnectND project team. They appreciated, as did those across the university, that since VCSU had claimed technology as being central in its identity statewide, piloting the ERP initiative furthered its institutional ambitions. Also, the entire university community tended to understand VCSU's mission to serve the interests of the state. The challenge is that the aspirations of an institution—and even its mission—may be broader or more nuanced than what those in operational roles readily understand, thus requiring leaders and senior managers to clarify and emphasize purposes. Here is where a president can best step in. Another advantage at VCSU was that the culture across the institution aligned with the bases needed to implement ConnectND. The alignment of an initiative with institutional culture addresses another important question for leaders and senior managers to ask: how might understanding differ in various parts of the university, and what are the possibilities for alignment between and among the strategic management elements, especially purposes and culture, to connect to the institution?

Who else needs to be involved, both internally and externally, so that each of the elements is considered and aligned with the others? An ERP implementation is likely to interest only those directly involved, with others probably being comfortable just knowing the project is moving forward and will ultimately benefit the institution. There may be merit in consulting with those who may perceive themselves to have a general interest in such a project such as ConnectND, including faculty members and IT staff. Their insights might have improved the implementation and actual product, and framing their involvement as consultative can minimize the potential for distraction. Consultation also has symbolic value, insulating somewhat against later complaints. ConnectND is probably not a project that would concern outside constituents, such as legislators or donors, but it is always important to keep them appraised of larger undertakings.

Finally, it is essential for leaders and senior managers to ask where breakdowns are likely to occur. The primary breakdown in the implementation of the ERP system was because of insufficient attention to certain infrastructure concerns, such as training. Because the governance of the project was so confined, some useful voices that could have been included with minimal effort were excluded, as the implementation emphasized efficiency and sacrificed inclusion. In addition, the aggressive time frame for planning and implementing ConnectND—another governance matter—seemed reasonable, but it exacted a price from those involved, as it overburdened them. There were other connections that were more easily addressed, such as changing routine policies and processes to conform to the new system. Communicating the broad advantages of the project to the VCSU community was not particularly complicated. However, at another institutional type, or with another project, doing so might be more challenging.

CHAPTER SIX

Policies

*Enhancing Faculty Scholarship and Integrating Student Research
into the Curriculum at LaGrange College*

Consistent with the approach to faculty work at the most noted liberal arts colleges nationally, LaGrange College identified enhancing faculty scholarship and integrating student research into the curriculum as strategic initiatives. LaGrange sought to transform itself into the leading liberal arts college in the state of Georgia. In addition to realizing the benefits of enhanced prestige, as in more readily attracting resources, the college anticipated that the teacher-scholar approach would "foster a more rigorous and challenging academic community," enhancing the achievement and satisfaction of its students in measurable ways. As LaGrange considered how to enable its faculty to advance the teacher-scholar initiative, it addressed critical questions of institutional policy, first considering reducing teaching load to 21 credit hours, having previously lowered it from 27 hours to 24 in 2000. There was also a need to develop policies related to tenure and promotion and approaches to faculty evaluation consistent with the teacher-scholar orientation. A premise in strategic management is that if policies such as these are neglected or misguided, it is unlikely that an initiative will flower.

At any institution, determining such policies is closely connected with mission and aspirations. LaGrange began its initiative with the advantage of having expressed these purposes clearly, including in its strategic plan. Nonetheless, the faculty scholarship and student research initiatives were not simply a question of determining a vision for the institution and formulating a set of policies to advance it. For instance, there were various infrastructure needs. LaGrange had been attracting more accomplished students and increasing enrollments. The college was adding new faculty positions in targeted areas, recognizing the need to have faculty members available to teach its core curriculum "cornerstone" courses. It was also constructing a new library capable of supporting emerging needs. In addition to these infrastructure investments, the college needed to change the expectations of both its faculty and students embedded in its culture, as well as reshape its governance and structure to be more consistent with a teacher-scholar orientation. This new approach to faculty roles required faculty members to work, and even think, differently—and they were skeptical. Allaying these concerns was crucial to LaGrange realizing its ambitions. The case study examines the period when the institution was just getting started in moving toward its vision of being a more selective liberal arts college, so it is less about implementation than about the earlier stages of an initiative, including developing policies as part of planning.[1]

Policies as an Element

There are both formal and informal rules within any organization, with the latter broadly understood, even if not always expressly articulated. (These informal rules might be termed *practices*, but I include them with formal rules as *policies*, given that they tend to have the same effect.) For instance, a set of formal rules associated with promotion and tenure are captured in documents. One such rule could be a requirement that only articles in peer-reviewed journals are considered in assessing faculty research. There is also an informal set of understandings that those involved have internalized, such as which journals in their field are acceptable as publication venues for a faculty member up for promotion and tenure at a given type of institution—and even which journals are more esteemed. Another example is a policy within an institution that allows no "comp time" for staff members—for instance, they cannot take Monday morning off in exchange for working on Saturday afternoon. However, units within institutions often come up with their own informal arrangements to circumvent these policies. These informal understandings are often the product of culture and tradition within the organization, producing unwritten, yet quite meaningful, expectations and practices.

Policies should further the purposes of the institution, such as the ones setting the teaching load or determining tenure and promotion at LaGrange. They should also align with the culture of the institution. Formal policies are a product of governance and are thus imbued with legitimacy, while informal ones simply become institutionalized over time, with their source being less relevant. Policies might then result expressly from actions by trustees or administrators, or through faculty committees—or might simply be informal understandings or agreements. For example, assigning various faculty members to teach in a particular semester, a department chair refers to the teaching-load policies at the institution. The chair also knows whether unwritten rules followed at the university or college allow him or her to reduce the teaching load for a given faculty member through devices such as counting dissertation or practicum advising as a course.

Policies are distinct from the processes that implement them. Policies are standards; processes are actions. As rules, policies put boundaries around and set limits upon various functions, whereas processes determine how these functions transpire. Attention to developing appropriate, comprehensive, and unambiguous policies can enhance efficiency and effectiveness within an institution, particularly when coupled with processes of the same quality. (Similarly, well-bounded and sharp research questions tend to yield more effective research studies.) In addition, as the values upon which institutions and individuals once solely relied are increasingly challenged by entrepreneurial impulses and external influences, rules thus assume a greater importance in a more diffused and complex environment.

Unlike the discussion of governance in the previous chapter, or even purposes or structure before that, there is little written about policies in higher education. There is a rich body of literature on higher educational policy, but that is different. It is more macro, and thus more likely to be external in origin, unlike distinct institutional policies such as on teaching loads or tenure and promotion. Few writers concentrate on how institutions actually develop policies, although more focus on how universities and colleges respond to various externally generated rules. Nevertheless, policies are crucial, especially as institutions remake themselves, as at LaGrange with its faculty scholarship and student research initiatives. Policies offer a measure of clarity, and thus reassurance, in what can be a changing and sometimes confusing environment.

Policies: A Perspective on the Research Literature

Kathleen Shaw
Temple University

In the research literature on higher education, there is scant attention paid to the rules under which institutions proceed. In a rare article on policies at the institutional level, Olivas (1992) focuses on the legal aspects of three policies in higher education: the residency status of foreign students, faculty rights to their inventions and discoveries, and racial harassment on campus. Specific policies, such as tenure and promotion, are covered more regularly by researchers, but not the actual concept of policies within organizations. In addition, certain of the "management fads" that Birnbaum (2001) describes, such as zero-based budgeting, have become policies within an institution.

It is important to remember that strategic management addresses institutional policy, as distinct from policies emanating from external sources, such as federal or state governments, that are the focus of most writing. Indeed, the research literature usually examines institutional policy only in the context of universities or colleges reacting to rules and regulations imposed upon them from the outside. In reviewing the relevant literature on institutional policies in higher education, it is easier to summarize limitations than to identify insights. In fact, there is seldom even a clear definition of policy, whether it be practical or theoretical, especially in distinguishing the concept from implementation.

There is a robust body of literature on public policy and higher education that can be instructive, however. Policy issues in higher education are attracting increasing attention, as on federal issues such as affirmative action (Rhoads, Saenz, and Carducci 2005). There are also concerns at the state level, as with admissions policies and student access (Olivas, 2005; Perna, Steele, Woda, and Hibbert 2005; Rendon, Novack, and Dowell 2005) and performance assessment (McLendon, Hearn, and Deaton 2006). McLendon, Heller, and Young (2005) discuss the interstate migration of policy ideas. Such state-level analyses have become common, as federal policy increasingly provides states with more autonomy (McLendon 2003; Shaw and Rab 2003). Also, Hossler, Kuh, and Olsen (2001) focus on how higher educational policy research can improve institutional effectiveness, but they do not define policies, per se, as an institutional matter.

Analyses of the impact of state-level policy on institutions are rare. When addressed, as in Shaw and Rab (2003), the focus is on institutions reacting to policies, rather than formulating them. As a result, there is relatively little insight into how institutions proactively generate policies to serve their

(continued)

strategic ends—or simply to advance their routine operations. For instance, Rendon, Novak, and Dowell (2005) examine how California State University–Long Beach responded to state affirmative action policies. They describe particular and often complex policies designed by the university in response to the disorder resulting from state dictates, including curtailing the admission of transfer students and developing more intricate admissions standards. However, these policies reacted to external pressures, as opposed to ideally advancing the mission and aspirations of the university—or even just furthering its institutional effectiveness.

In writing about policies, the risk always lies in confusing rules with implementation—not sufficiently separating setting policies with operationalizing them. Writing about higher education policy commonly assumes a popular understanding of the term "policy," not distinguishing it from implementation (as through processes)—or really even defining the term. Those writing outside of higher education tend to pay more attention to distinguishing between policies and their implementation—and BOC characterizes processes as a separate element. Policies are legislation or regulations subsequently implemented through responses by actors, such as caseworkers or bureaucrats (Mintrom 1997). These actors can resist policies by simply refusing to implement them. Alternatively, they can amend or adjust the policies to suit either political or practical circumstances, such as when there are insufficient resources to fully implement a policy or a disagreement with a policy for ideological or pragmatic reasons.

Defining policy, as distinct from implementation, enables leaders and managers to identify factors such as structure, information, or culture that influence outcomes. The transition from making policies to implementing them is less straightforward than it was once thought to be. The ideology or culture that underlies policies may not be shared among those responsible for enacting it—a situation as common at universities and colleges as it is in governments (Hasenfeld 2002). Such distance between policy and practice is termed "slippage" (Marshall 1997). Policy slippage can occur for a number of reasons, many of them captured by the BOC elements. For example, new policies may not be implemented consistently or effectively because of discord between them and the traditional purposes or culture of the institution. Similarly, there may be insufficient resources (infrastructure) or poor communications (information). Or, in the case of faculty getting around a teaching-load policy, it might be mere resourcefulness, given an insufficiently prescriptive policy, instead of oppositional or subversive behavior. It is thus crucial to understand both how and why policies emerge and how those within institutions respond (Mazzeo, Rab, and Eachus 2003).

LaGrange College and the Teacher-Scholar Approach

LaGrange is a private, four-year liberal arts college and the oldest independent institution of higher learning in Georgia. It embraces its relationship with the North Georgia Conference of the United Methodist Church, as in its mission statement: "LaGrange College is called through the United Methodist Church to challenge the minds and inspire the souls of students by improving their creative, critical, and communicative abilities in a caring and ethical community." Located about an hour by highway southwest of Atlanta, near the Alabama border, the college sits on 120 acres atop the highest point in the town of LaGrange, which has a population of nearly 30,000. The institution opened in 1831 as a women's academy. In 1851 it changed its name to LaGrange Female College, and then to La-Grange College in 1934. The school officially became coeducational in 1953 and integrated in 1968.

LaGrange offers 50 academic programs for traditional undergraduates and highlights its prominence in drama, music, and art. It also has a master of arts in teaching degree. LaGrange offers programs to what it terms "adult learners," with full-time or part-time courses of study leading to a bachelor of arts degree in business administration or human development, as well as an associate of arts degree in liberal studies. In 2002, the college began an extension site in southwest Georgia, LaGrange College at Albany, offering an interdisciplinary curriculum in organizational leadership developed especially for nontraditional students.

For several years, *U.S. News and World Report* has ranked LaGrange among the top ten in its category for both reputation and "best value." In 2008 the magazine identified it as one of 70 "up-and-coming" schools. The college enrolls about 1100 students, representing 29 states and 15 countries. In 2004, when we visited the college as it was launching its faculty scholarship and student research initiatives, the average SAT score at LaGrange was 1035, up from 960 in 1996. Approximately 80 percent of LaGrange's students receive financial assistance, and the college awards more than $8 million in financial aid yearly to offset its annual tuition of approximately $15,000, representing itself as one of the most affordable private colleges in the Southeast. Georgia students with a B average in high school are eligible for annual support from the state HOPE scholarship program, and LaGrange offers the same award to out-of-state students. The college has a nearly $70 million endowment, an annual budget of $30 million, and a $22 million unrestricted gift that it has used for initiatives such as building capacity in enrollment management.

At its core, LaGrange remains a teaching-focused institution in the liberal arts tradition. Its student-faculty ratio is 11:1. (The college has considered adjusting that ratio, believing that it is lower than is needed, thus creating excess capacity.) Nearly all of the over 60 full-time LaGrange faculty have earned the highest degree available in their fields, and there are 40 or so part-time faculty members. Faculty members act as academic advisors for students and the college does not use graduate-student teaching assistants. LaGrange has structured its curriculum on a 4-1-4 model, offering a January interim term aimed at providing students with the opportunity to explore a given topic in depth. Students may use the time to study abroad, complete an internship, pursue an independent project, research a subject of interest, or take a "Jan Term" course. All first-year students participate in a freshmen cornerstone course as part of their general education requirements. Cornerstone courses employ teaching teams of faculty from different disciplines.

The stated vision of the college under F. Stuart Gulley, who became LaGrange's 24th president in 1996, is to become the premier college of liberal arts and sciences in Georgia. To achieve its vision, LaGrange has set various goals, termed "vision indicators," to be achieved by 2012. These include enrolling 1000 students in its traditional undergraduate day program and housing 800 of them, increasing the SAT scores of entering students to at least 1100, and maintaining a first-year-to-sophomore retention rate of at least 80 percent and a six-year graduation rate at or above 60 percent. Other indicators are having over 50 percent of students major in a traditional liberal-arts-degree program, employing a faculty with 10 or more members in Phi Beta Kappa, and having an undergraduate-degree-holder giving rate of 30 percent. In 2004, the board of trustees voted to add a football team, which is a strategy pursued by other institutions of LaGrange's type nationally. Aside from enhancing enrollment through the men participating, the college believes that a football team will advance student life and external relations. The LaGrange Panthers compete in 14 sports (seven each for men and women) in the Division III Great South Athletic Conference.

In a strategic move toward its institutional aspirations, LaGrange planned to enhance faculty scholarship and undergraduate research opportunities, including a proposal to reduce the faculty's teaching load. Based on its initial study of faculty workload and potential enrollment increases, LaGrange administrators believed that a reduction in the teaching load was feasible, even with the prospect of adding 100 students to its 2005 entering class, increasing its day-program enrollment to approximately 950 students. The college determined it would need to add

2.5 full-time-equivalent faculty to teach its other lower-division courses, based on both the enrollment increase and reduced workload. Some departments, such as Spanish and biology, as well as the cornerstone courses, would require additional faculty to accommodate the changes, which would shift the student-faculty ratio from 11:1 to a more sustainable 12:1. Lastly, the administration predicted that with a workload decrease, more faculty members would be able to participate in the cornerstone, humanities, and American experience courses common to all LaGrange students. It presented these calculations in introducing the faculty scholarship and student research initiative to the faculty, soliciting their comments. The case study here concentrates on that moment, as the institution was planning for what promised to be significant change.

LaGrange is not unlike other institutions nationally in its aspirations. Institutions across types in American higher education have essentially defined their vision as getting to the next level. Even though universities and colleges across sectors are vastly different in their orientations, the markets they serve, and their available resources, they are all seeking the same end in positioning themselves for greater prestige, having framed their aspirations in a similar manner. They are also employing a rather generic set of strategies toward that end, primarily attracting more accomplished students, investing heavily in infrastructure (namely, facilities, but also faculty), and launching appealing academic and related programs (Toma 2008). For LaGrange, the next level is moving the ranks of the leading liberal arts colleges in the Southeast, such as Sewanee, Rhodes, and Rollins, all members of the Associated Colleges of the South (ACS). (Those institutions, in turn, are aspiring to be more like Williams, Grinnell, and Pomona—and there are four-year independent institutions in Georgia and elsewhere looking to replicate what LaGrange has achieved.) Having begun to position itself for greater prestige, as through the faculty scholarship and student research initiative, LaGrange now must align policies, and the other elements, with its mission and aspirations.

Purposes and Policies at LaGrange College

Clarity of intention and an ambition to improve as an organization imbues work with a sense of uniqueness and importance as it informs day-to-day decision making (Hartley 2002a). That LaGrange had such a sense of direction as it launched its faculty scholarship and student research initiatives was a significant advantage for the institution. Those in the LaGrange community readily understood its mission in providing instruction, as well as its aspiration to emerge as the best liberal arts college in Georgia. Becoming more like the members of the ACS was both easy to grasp and broadly appealing.

Gulley was effective in the first step, articulating his vision and underscoring its attractiveness. LaGrange trustees, faculty, and administrators became invested, believing themselves to have a significant role in putting the college on what they have come to view as the right track. The adjustment may prove most challenging for the faculty, whose orientation probably must change the most as LaGrange advances. Most were acculturated at a higher-prestige institution, so the strategic direction that Gulley defined tends to resonate with them. The necessary next step was to align policies with purposes, as with those associated with realizing the teacher-scholar model. Changed expectations can require new rules.

A challenge at the college was making sure that its aspirations were not higher than its capacity, whether in conceptual or practical terms. LaGrange identified enhancing faculty scholarship and developing student research as a goal—a reasonable means toward the end of joining the most selective liberal arts institutions in the region. Beyond the initial question of teaching load, LaGrange had several other policies to consider, such as what constitutes faculty scholarship, how it will be measured and valued, and how much is enough. The college will have to continue to align purposes and policies if it wants to retain the support of its faculty as it attempts to realize its ambitions. As the college launched these initiatives, the LaGrange faculty was unclear about these questions, having different understandings of what the institution meant by them. Some have viewed the effort as changing faculty norms—and thus rewards—about publishing. Others understand it as simply engaging in research with undergraduates. With such confusion can come anxiety and discord, threatening the success of an initiative and ultimately the purposes it is intended to advance.

Policies can provided needed clarity—and solace through increased certainty. LaGrange appreciates that it will need new policies, both formal and informal, to accommodate a faculty of teacher-scholars. For example, will faculty members be able to decide not to engage in scholarship and research without eliciting negative consequences, say in the determination of merit pay? Promotion and tenure standards must also change. Also to better align with its evolution as a college, LaGrange addressed professionalizing its administrative operations by implementing various formal policies in areas such as purchasing, human resources, and financial systems. For instance, there are now written job descriptions for most positions at the institution.

Developing the sensibilities that are likely to be the source of informal policies related to faculty scholarship and student research will be more challenging than writing new policies. Promotion and tenure policies provide an illustration. A formal policy reducing the teaching load to encourage faculty scholarship and student research is concrete enough—and the college can simply implement it. Developing a sufficient understanding among faculty members about what should count under a teacher-scholar conception of faculty work is more nebulous—and can only happen over time. Such policies must align with culture. There may be formal rules in place, but there also must be informal ones, shaped by shared institutional norms and consistent with the selective liberal arts college model. Understanding what, specifically, the college will value as it stresses scholarship is embedded as much in a set of informal practices as it is in a set of formal rules. Meanwhile, the culture of the institution cannot evolve so rapidly or so appreciably that scholarship and research compete with and potentially undermine, instead of complementing, the teaching mission at the core of the institution. LaGrange must frame scholarship and research not only in terms of its aspirations, but also its mission.

Connecting with the Other Elements

As with its policies, LaGrange began aligning its *governance* with its aspirations, developing a model more akin to the collegial approach common at the leading liberal arts colleges in the region that it has in it sights. Under Gulley, the college has attempted to flatten decision making, especially in encouraging its faculty to assume greater responsibility. LaGrange faculty members had not been involved in governance. Gulley sought change here early on in his tenure, forming committees with cross-constituent representation and chaired by faculty members to address mission, student life, ethics, and athletics. From these committees came a mini-strategic plan—and the work provided the foundation for more of a partnership between the administration and the faculty. As a faculty member suggested, "faculty have begun to take a sense of ownership for the academic side of the campus, which is a culture shift, and it would be hard to go back the other way." Developing trust was particularly important at LaGrange, as a 1977 settlement agreement, related to an attempt by the faculty to organize under the American Association of University Professors (AAUP), formalized relations between the administration and the affected faculty. The agreement (which constitutes a policy, of course) still influenced relations over two decades later, creating more of a legalistic climate than is optimal on a liberal arts campus that should depend on collegial governance. On the administrative side, Gulley restructured to broaden his cabinet and enabled senior staff to develop relationships with the board of trustees, so everything did not funnel through the president. The college also created a staff council as a step toward more collegial decision making campus wide.

Although the college has worked on encouraging faculty participation in making decisions and setting policy, the LaGrange faculty is still adapting to its expanded influence. The college had advanced significantly and rapidly under Gulley on several fronts—and some on campus are still not entirely caught up. People took to calling the college "LaChange," due to the pace and scope of the alterations Gulley has implemented. The senior administration is concerned, for instance, about faculty members still seeming hesitant to express their views in meetings and appearing surprised at being consulted on matters such as strategic planning. The faculty has needed time to absorb what a teacher-scholar model really entails, including their role in shared governance. Like policies, governance (and structure, or any of the other elements, really) is easier to reshape than culture—and the LaGrange faculty has had to assimilate how to assert themselves in ways consistent with the governance norms of the type of institution the college aspires to become.

In a change in *structure* to better align itself with the selective liberal arts college model, LaGrange reduced the number of its academic divisions from seven to four. The new structure at the college streamlined communication among division heads, making their interactions more efficient, and shifted more responsibility and accountability onto faculty chairing divisions. An institutional planning council also became part of the structure of the college, linking planning and budgeting. Its approximately 17 members span various responsibilities: the cabinet, institutional research director, registrar, financial aid director, comptroller, student government association president, director of evening studies, and faculty. Yet, in strategic management, there is always the question of whether there is sufficient clarity about governance within the new structure. Over time, the faculty members and others at LaGrange are likely to work through the challenges associated with who makes what decisions within the new structure, especially as the culture of the institution adapts. The college will also have occasion to address additional structural issues that remain, such as the role of the faculty assembly within its formal decision-making structure.

Faculty members seem to have initially concluded that they have an opportunity for input, but limited formal power.

Operational concerns also matter in developing a teacher-scholar approach at LaGrange. Whereas policies are rules, *processes* implement them. LaGrange instituted a formal faculty evaluation process—a self-evaluation linked with faculty development—to better align with its emerging approach to faculty work. LaGrange also initiated a merit-raise policy—with 1.5 percent of a 2.5 percent increase going to everyone, and the balance accruing to those who are leading performers—and an appropriate process to implement it. Both new processes were intended to develop the type of faculty that LaGrange will need in order to realize its vision.

The college employed *information* more effectively in making decisions and establishing rules. Gulley was credited with being a strong communicator, using multiple forums to connect with the various constituents of the college. The college community viewed him as a good listener who regularly sought input and feedback, important traits in a setting increasingly influenced by shared governance. The new faculty evaluation process promised to be an example of effective use of information at the college, as it included feedback loops connected with other instruments, such as the strategic plan. The college began regularly evaluating its financial processes. It also expanded its institutional-research function, hiring a full-time person in that role, enabling the development of a more robust assessment program and creating more available data to support its decisions. Both promise to allow LaGrange to know whether enhancing faculty scholarship and student research actually improves student outcomes—and where the institution might make adjustments.

LaGrange also began developing needed *infrastructure* to support its faculty scholarship and student research initiative, linking a building program to its curricular and other goals. The college connected fund raising for the construction of a new library with the initiative, which also advances the cause of enrolling more accomplished students. The same is true of its plans for a new residence hall, which also supports its goals of increasing enrollment and having more students live on campus. Early on in his tenure, Gulley devoted $30 million to upgrading facilities related to his vision for the institution. LaGrange renovated its student center and added two new residence halls that housed 248 students, bringing the total on-campus enrollment to 539. This new space was intended to contribute to changing the student culture away from LaGrange being a "suitcase campus."

However, the college delayed constructing a new science building until the next capital campaign, using the project to prompt the revamping of its science curriculum. LaGrange will have to consider some generic facilities concerns, such as the physical infrastructure needed for faculty and students to undertake research, particularly in the sciences, where laboratory space is required. There will also be needs related to research infrastructure, such as providing for conference travel and grants administration. In addition, as it seeks to increase class sizes, the college will have to address the shortage of larger-sized classrooms on campus.

Similarly, LaGrange has hired faculty—the human component of infrastructure—with the purposes of the institution firmly in mind. In furthering change at the college, it helped that one-third of the faculty turned over under Gulley, with the new faculty being generally more oriented toward scholarly work. The college has also built infrastructure related to finance almost from scratch over the past few years, establishing a reserve account and implementing the Banner records system. It has enhanced its admissions capacity, adding a vice president for enrollment management and establishing processes, such as a Web-based admissions form, that have increased applications.

Finally, LaGrange illustrates that institutional *culture* can evolve, but that the norms, values, and beliefs of an organization do not readily change, as with faculty only slowly accepting their new role in governance.

➢ POLICIES AND ALIGNING THE OTHER ELEMENTS: A CHECKLIST
In an initiative such as enhancing faculty scholarship and integrating student research into the curriculum at a liberal arts college, those leading and managing institutions might consider the following related to policies:

☐ Have people come to understand the kind of institution the college is becoming? In moving toward the approach common across the most selective liberal arts colleges, which includes faculty as teacher-scholars and undergraduate students active in research, LaGrange initially had to find ways for those on campus to appreciate what doing so really meant. Particularly for those without direct experience at a leading liberal arts college or who are established in a different kind of faculty career, the model can be threatening. Without clarity across the institution about what LaGrange was becoming—and, ultimately, acceptance of it—change associated with the other elements can lack a necessary focus.

☐ Are policies aligned with the purposes that the college defined for itself? For instance, LaGrange needed to realign its faculty evaluation policies, including promotion and tenure, to the teacher-scholar model. In the same way, aspiring research universities need to change both their formal and informal rules as practices and culture evolve. A common challenge is that even with new policies, some senior faculty members charged with applying the rules in situations such as tenure and promotion are unlikely to really understand norms at the kind of institution their campus has developing into.

☐ Is the college structured in a way that is consistent with its mission and aspirations? As with changing policies, restructuring is relatively straight-forward, especially in comparison with reorienting purposes or culture. There is likely to be a structure common among institutions of the type that a college is aspiring toward.

☐ Does how decisions are being made fit with the type of institution the college is becoming? LaGrange moved toward an institutional type in which the faculty has influence in governance. As the college clarified its purposes and changed elements such as policies, it also decentralized decision making wherever possible, especially in empowering the faculty.

☐ Are there processes that would aid in moving the college toward its purposes? LaGrange found that it required new processes to implement the faculty evaluation policies it implemented.

☐ What information related to decision support and improvements in communication would assist the college in realizing its mission and aspirations? As LaGrange becomes more complex, as in its governance, it will require better decision-support data. Moreover, communication in the more collegial environment that typically marks a selective liberal arts college is different from that in a more bureaucratic setting.

☐ Does the college have the infrastructure in place to support faculty scholarship and student research? LaGrange must build a faculty ready to engage in the kind of work that advances its new conception of itself. There will also be facility needs, such as laboratories to support research. Both require resources, as developing infrastructure always does.

☐ Does the culture of the college align with its purposes? Articulating purposes is easier than changing the norms, values, and beliefs at an institution so as to be in accord with them. Members of the LaGrange community will need to adjust how they view both the institution as a whole and their roles within it. Various symbolic and practical efforts, especially by the president, can offer guidance in doing so.

Applying the Framework

What provides the most leverage possible toward realizing initiatives such as the one at LaGrange? The essence of the intended evolution at LaGrange involves reshaping its culture to better align with its aspirations, and only its president has the stature to lead such change. As the vision is his, he is not only best positioned to sell it, but is also expected to do so. The ultimate ambition at LaGrange is so significant that almost everything the president does needs to be associated with advancing it. There need to be measures of progress, perhaps involving the institutional-research function. More qualitative means are also important, such as communicating with the extended university community about accomplishments and framing the challenges that remain. Benchmarking can be useful here, both to indicate advancement relative to "peer" and "aspirational" institutions, but also in planning for the infrastructure a college or university will require to realize its aspirations.

Because Gulley is seeking to sharpen understanding of his aspirations for the institution and change its culture to be in accord with these, symbolic acts assume particular importance. Clarifying purposes and developing culture also makes it easier for those across the institution to understand strategic management—identifying the elements and how they relate. Once someone comprehends the purposes of an institution, addressing such issues as how people should be configured to do their work (structure), how things get done (processes), and what needs to inform decision making (information) is done more readily and effectively. It also enables the president to delegate, as with senior managers and faculty committees being responsible for developing policies and processes. The president is best positioned in delivering big picture messages, however, with symbolic measures being particularly powerful. For instance, reducing the faculty's teaching load is, in essence, a basic change in rules, but it also sends a strong message that LaGrange is serious about enhancing faculty scholarship and undergraduate research, especially when it is accompanied by related policies and other messages. One of these is a change in governance, moving toward a model that is more consistent with the one at leading liberal arts colleges.

The president also needs to remember that individuals' understandings of elements such as purposes and culture—and even of a more tangible area like policies—are likely to differ across various parts of the institution. Leaders and senior managers obviously must comprehend the strategic direction of a college or university, but for it to truly transform, everyone needs a relatively sophisticated understanding of purposes. Culture is embedded across organizations, so not only must faculty realize what is involved with working with more accomplished students, but so must the staff members who interact with those students. In addition, leading institutional change is likely to require both creativity and patience, as with helping those who may never have experienced the collegial approach to governance understand what it entails. The same is true in developing informal practices to correspond with the new formal policies established in areas such as tenure and promotion. LaGrange also illustrates that leverage came from having addressed some of its operational challenges, such as establishing formal policies for human resources and instituting processes for employee evaluation, clearing the way for discussion of more strategic issues and evolution in less tangible areas, such as culture.

There is also the question of who needs to be involved in a given initiative. When shifting the direction of an organization, internal accord must be combined with understanding and support from important external constituents, especially trustees. Significant change thus requires a considerable investment in external affairs, with the president being the necessary agent here. Change also has to be paced, so that people can become comfortable with it and not burn out because of it. Reserving some initiatives, such as the new science building at LaGrange, for a time when the vision for the institution has more fully developed is helpful both in underscoring what change will entail and in calibrating its pace.

Finally, where are breakdowns likely to occur—and how strong are the connections—between and among the elements? Developing policies and processes, as well as restructuring—and even articulating purposes and building infrastructure—may prove easiest in an initiative as at LaGrange. The more significant challenges are in changing the culture of the institution. There may also be some difficulties in communicating messages internally and externally in an environment marked not only by enthusiasm, but also by uncertainly, and even apprehension. The LaGrange case suggests that changing governance, like developing culture, involves more than simply restructuring, as with teaching a faculty how to assert itself in making decisions. At an institution with existing collegial norms, such as a liberal arts college similar to primarily what LaGrange aspires to be, the challenge of moving up a level would be likely to involve another element, such as infrastructure—finding the resources to support what is needed to compete with the wealthiest institutions at the very top of the hierarchy.

CHAPTER SEVEN

Processes

*Improving Student Retention at Paul D. Camp
Community College*

I n Virginia, the State Board for Community Colleges has defined an ambitious set of goals for its institutions that includes increasing retention, linking it with access, the paramount mission of any community college. Like most community colleges, Paul D. Camp Community College (PDCCC), in rural Virginia, has significant challenges related to retention. Some of these at PDCCC are external in cause, driven by the overall low socioeconomic status of its students, while other problems are more internal. The faculty and administration at PDCCC understand the mission of the college, but considering and aligning other elements are also required toward advancing purposes related to improved retention. One of these is processes.[1]

Processes as an Element

Processes, whether written or unwritten, connote action, operationalizing various rules. They are connected with implementation, bridging policies and outcomes—the means by which institutions actually achieve their ends. They are thus outputs, and not inputs, as are policies. For instance, a job posting is essentially a policy, while the steps in deciding whom to hire and then the formalities associated with employing him or her is a process. These steps are mostly formal, but they can also be informal. It may become an informal part of any job interview to include a walk around campus, even though mentioning this in a human resources manual as a stage in the hiring process would be unlikely. As with policies, the units within institutions often arrive at their own informal arrangements to accomplish various tasks. Again resembling policies, processes are more effective when they are transparent and understandable, even when they are informal and thus unwritten. Whether on the academic or administrative side of an institution, processes are usually systematic and include several steps— and there are simple and complex processes, as well as regular and ad hoc ones.

Processes should ultimately advance institutional missions and aspirations, working best when aligned with the other elements. Even the most elegant structure and most coherent set of policies will not be effective if various processes do not align with the culture of an institution. At PDCCC, people understand and embrace the mission of the college, working to make postsecondary education available for local students, especially those from challenging circumstances. There is also a culture across the institution that is supportive of these ends. The PDCCC case illustrates the need for processes related to retention to improve and better align with purposes and culture. As with policies, there is little empirical research on processes in higher education, although there is a body of literature on specific processes within universities and colleges, such as accreditation and admissions.

Paul D. Camp Community College and Improving Retention

Paul D. Camp Community College is one of 23 community colleges, each serving a given region, that comprise the Virginia Community College System (VCCS), which includes a total of 40 primary and branch campuses. Both its own board and the State Board for Community Colleges govern PDCCC, which is financed primarily with state funds, supplemented by student tuition revenue. The Commission on Colleges of the Southern Association of Colleges and Schools (SACS) accredits the college. PDCCC offers occupational and technical programs leading to certificates or associate of applied science degrees; programs in the arts and sciences and in certain preprofessional areas to facilitate transfer to four-year institutions; developmental studies programs; and credit and noncredit adult education courses, as well as cultural events, for the local community.

Processes: A Perspective on the Research Literature
Christopher C. Morphew
University of Iowa

The research literature on higher education does not explicitly delineate processes from policies, yet writings on organizations can be useful in doing so. In particular, Weick (1995, 1979) contributes at least two key concepts to understanding how policies and processes connect in organizations such as universities and colleges: the "loosely coupled" organization and "sensemaking."

Weick (1979) describes how some organizations consist of units that are loosely coupled, and he examines the behavioral consequences of their relatively inelastic relationship with one another. In essence, a unit that is not really connected to others may not be affected by actions by, or changes in, them. For instance, if the athletics department at a large university is found to be using ineligible basketball players in its pursuit of an NCAA championship, the repercussions will have virtually no effect on the faculty and students in the history department. In other words, the interdependence of, and interactions between, athletics and history is negligible. The same disconnect can occur between and among the purposes of an organization, the policies it develops, and the outcomes it desires. The institution still needs to get things done, however. Thus processes (sometime informal ones) intervene both to connect an institution's purposes, policies, and outcomes and to mediate differences between and among them. Birnbaum (1988) amplifies the concept of the loosely coupled organization with the "perverse black box" that he uses to illustrate the improbable and unpredictable relationship between units in a typical university or college, even those in a hierarchical relationship with one another. Birnbaum argues that what goes on in this perverse black box—the process that occurs within it—is largely undecipherable, save that it is not predictable from one action to the next.

Weick (1995) discusses sensemaking, contending that organizations are oriented toward process rather than structure. (The discussion in the sidebar in chapter 8 also considers sensemaking.) From this perspective, organizations behave as they do because those within them must find ways to manage the ambiguous, equivocal information they experience, continually asking "what kind of organization is this?" (Albert and Whetten 1985). Structure in an organization may be clear, but sensemaking is an ongoing process, especially in organizations with relatively unclear goals, such as universities and colleges. For instance, faculty members can be equivocal toward their institutions, given that their connections to their discipline may be as (or more) important

(continued)

to them. Similarly, higher education institutions lack the bottom line that a corporation would have to use in judging behaviors or results associated with the organization (Meyer, Scott, and Deal 1981; Cohen and March 1974).

An institution can clarify purposes and update policies, but real change within an organization only occurs with sensemaking, which Weick (1995) portrays as a three-step process of enactment, selection, and retention. Apart from purposes and policies, accomplishing organizational goals depends on the ability of those within the organization (or institution) to define situations, select important information, and identify the meaning of these data. They must do so in a manner consistent with the mission and aspirations of the institution, but inputs are usually ambiguous in their meaning. Sensemaking— the essential process within an organization—is thus subjective, requires deciphering a vague environment, and is perverse in its irrationality. It *is* a black box.

PDCCC was established in 1970, opening in Franklin, Virginia, the following year. It is named for a member of the family who donated the land for the college and long operated the major employer in Franklin, a large paper-processing facility. The college serves the cities of Franklin and Suffolk, and Southampton and Isle of Wight counties, in southeastern Virginia, to the west of the Tidewater area. The original PDCCC campus is in rural Franklin, located 40 miles west of Norfolk. A campus in suburban Suffolk, located between Norfolk and Franklin, dates to 1982, and there is a center in Smithfield, located 30 miles northeast of Franklin, established in 1993.

PDCCC is modest in size, with the second-lowest enrollment among community colleges in Virginia. Among its roughly 1500 students, the proportion of those attending full-time in 2004, when we visited the campus, was about 24 percent, lower than the 31 percent average across the system. Over two-thirds of the students at the college were women and 37 percent of its students were African American, both higher proportions than the Virginia average. The proportion of students in transfer (42%) and technical (22%) programs, as well as those taking developmental courses (18%), were similar to statewide numbers. Over one-half of the PDCCC students (775 of 1468 in 2004) received $1.68 million in financial aid, averaging $2171 per student.

The fall-into-spring-semester retention rate at PDCCC was 64 percent during the 2003-2004 academic year, which is similar to other VCCS institutions, but the fall-into-fall rate was 33 percent, compared with 40 percent for the system. For the fall 1997 cohort at PDCCC, the combined retention rate for students who ultimately completed, transferred, and remained enrolled was 43.8 percent (as reported in the 2000 Integrated Postsecondary Education Data System [IPEDS] survey), similar to the figure across the VCCS. The VCCS strategic plan, entitled *Dateline 2009: A Strategic Direction*, has ambitious goals in increasing enrollment and transfer to four-year institutions, as well as "ranking, as a system, in the top ten percent nationally with respect to graduation rates, retention, and job placement." The semester-to-semester retention goal is 90 percent, significantly higher than the present 65 to 70 percent range at the college.

Given its mission, PDCCC inevitably confronts multiple challenges related to retention. Some are external to the institution, as the region served by the college is in the midst of an economic transition. Even when unemployment is officially low, there are significant pockets of poverty and large numbers of discouraged workers, with the available social services stretched. (The college itself assumes, by default, certain social-service functions.) Students regularly have to leave college based on an interruption in income—or they might be evicted or have to care for an ailing relative. They also frequently have transportation problems, as public transportation in the service region is severely limited. As of 2004, many did not have home computers, making communication between the college and its students more difficult. Students often lack support from their families and commonly have significant family obligations, with many single mothers enrolled, causing childcare to be a common concern. (If PDCCC could find the funding needed to underwrite it, the college could provide childcare, thus lowering a significant barrier to retention for many students.) Over two-thirds of its students work while attending PDCCC, providing another distraction.

Other contributors to attrition at PDCCC are also more structural in nature. PDCCC students have choices in the local postsecondary education marketplace and can readily leave the institution for another. Sometimes they only need a course or two to prepare for a given job, thus appearing to have dropped out in the retention statistics when they have, in fact, used the college to fulfill their needs. In addition, someone who starts and then returns to the college a decade later is nonetheless counted as "lost" in the retention figures. The definition of retention itself is thus problematic, as is common within the community college sector nationally.

Furthermore, numerous PDCCC students tend to have an unclear sense of purpose. Those in developmental courses view them as irrelevant, lowering their motivation and engagement. (The college addresses this problem by having these students enroll in basic substantive courses concurrently, as possible.) Many students do not fully understand why they are in college and what is expected of them—and are thus easily distracted. Others have a clearer sense, but they either lack confidence in their abilities, have limited actual ability, or experience too many outside distractions to be successful in college. Many at PDCCC are first-generation students with little of the cultural capital that is so helpful in navigating college, or are at the institution because of low high school grades (whether due to modest effort or ability). Retention at PDCCC—an output—thus suffers because of weaker inputs.

Retention is a critical challenge across American community colleges, which educate more than one-half (over 11.5 million) of all undergraduate students in the United States. These 1200 institutions instruct particularly high proportions of under-served students, as with low income, first-generation, and minority students, including approximately one-half of all African Americans, Hispanics, and Native Americans enrolled nationally. Among students seeking an associate's degree or higher, only 53 percent earned a degree or transferred to a four-year institution within eight years, with underrepresented groups doing so at even lower levels (Lumina Foundation 2004). Retention across higher education has accordingly drawn significant attention from researchers, foundations, and policy makers. The issue is connected with other concerns, such as recruiting and access, advising and mentoring, assessment and evaluation, preparation and remediation, and academic support and personal development, making increased retention a complex proposition. Success within and across these areas of concern involves not only improving policies, but also instituting sound processes to implement them. The PDCCC case study is not about retention per se, but it uses this issue at a small, rural community college to emphasize the importance of developing and refining the processes needed to realize the ambitions of any institution. The difficulty in retention is often not in clarity of purposes, but in operationalizing them within an organization through various behaviors and means.

Purposes and Processes at Paul D. Camp Community College

While many of its students may lack understanding of their own ambitions, the institution is clear about its purposes, embracing its mission and aspiring to improve its service to the region. Access is not a particular problem at PDCCC. Under Douglas W. Boyce, who became the sixth PDCCC president in 2002, the college has emphasized on recruitment. It has concentrated less systematically on retention. For instance, as a structural matter, PDCCC does not have an administrator charged with addressing the issue. Particularly for the business community, retention is less of a concern than is producing good employees. Retention at PDCCC, however, is still important—and not just because of the VCSS *Dateline 2009* goals and the national attention the issue receives. Increasing retention would put less pressure on recruiting, allowing efforts to focus on building enrollment instead of simply maintaining it. The business axiom of it being easier to keep a customer than to attract one also applies within higher education. The college could address retention statistics by emphasizing the recruitment of students who intend to earn a two-year degree and aspire to a four-year degree. Similarly, it could focus on more selective programs like prenursing, in which motivation among students is high and attrition naturally lower. Doing either, however, would be contrary to the college's purposes.

The student advising that is thought to promote retention is a relatively simple process—and involves an even more straightforward set of *policies*. (I include the discussion of policies here, as opposed to in the section on alignment that follows, given that processes implement rules.) One challenge at PDCCC is grounded in the structural decision that faculty members ones charged with advising, as opposed to having an advising center staffed with professionals. Implementation difficulties associated with faculty advising, may be somewhat attributable to it not being emphasized in PDCCC's institutional policies on faculty evaluation, and thus is not valued in promotion and compensation decisions. (The same is true of faculty work in recruiting.) Accordingly, faculty members who are active participants in the advising process can become discouraged, especially given that many colleagues are not sharing the load. The college may be losing a significant advantage here, as breakdowns in advising are an important process related to retention. A change in advising policies may at least partially address problems, as policies can be readily reformulated, as to more clearly include advising in faculty evaluations. At a typical community college, administrators have more discretion in setting such policies, as faculty governance is less robust. This does not mean that faculty members will not have either opinions or even influence, but instead that such decisions in this type of institutional setting generally reside with the administration.

The primary challenge here is not necessarily defining rules or even developing formal processes to implement them—and eventually informal ones as people work through day-to-day problems. It is whether the individual faculty members charged with implementing student advising, as a process, will actually execute the rules as intended. Just because a policy or process is on the books does not mean that those within an organization will implement it as intended. For some, faculty evaluation policies—and the annual process of implementing them—may provide limited motivation or recede as a means to shape behavior amidst the din of other demands on their time and attention.

There is also the challenge of getting all the PDCCC faculty members to understand the policies and processes related to advising such that they can be more effective in following them. For instance, faculty members do not always act upon the various clarifications and reminders related to advising that are communicated at in-service days and delivered via e-mail. Part-time faculty members are even more disconnected, essentially engaging with the institution only when they are in the classroom, and sometimes not knowing how to shepherd students into the advising process.

In addition, misconceptions about what constitutes advising remain, even among full-time faculty. Some view it largely as enrollment, guiding the student into the institution but not necessarily through it. These mistaken beliefs reside primarily with the least effective faculty, commonly those who rarely answer e-mail messages or return telephone calls. Having a contingent of faculty members who do not grasp expectations and consequences related to advising presents challenges in both policies and processes—they are bound to fail in implementation, given that they do not understand the rules they are to apply. Misconceptions by general studies and developmental students, who are the most likely candidates for attrition, only add to the problem. These students have little, if any, understanding of either their own responsibilities or those of their faculty advisors.

Some polices associated with retention, such as taking attendance, are established, but the processes to implement them are not fully developed. For instance, the early-alert feature on the PeopleSoft management information system at the college identifies enrolled students who are not attending courses, but if faculty members are, as a group, inconsistent in taking attendance, the process has limited impact. Some faculty even object to the attendance policy outright. There is also an implementation problem related to the technical competence of many faculty members in using PeopleSoft. Similarly, PeopleSoft affords opportunities for students to manage their own programs, but few students appreciate what is available and do not use the system.

A failure to take attendance has implications beyond retention. It can be an issue in financial aid, for instance, as that office needs to know about walkaways. Some students at PDCCC depart a month or so into the semester, right after receiving their financial aid disbursements (the amount in excess of tuition and books). There is an inevitable tradeoff between providing students with the funds that they need and holding back these funds to minimize the risk that they will depart during the semester. The former requires actually taking attendance—individual faculty members implementing institutional policies through processes. Establishing or clarifying rules here only goes so far toward effective implementation. Issues like breakdowns in advising may appear to be addressed most effectively through better rules, when instead they are often related to problems with processes.

Connecting with the Other Elements

Because the college has such a clear sense of its purposes, solving various internal difficulties, including those related to processes, is a more realistic prospect. The college is also more likely, where possible, to mitigate problems associated with the outside environment.

These internal challenges include *structure*. In order to improve retention at PDCCC, some faculty and staff members have raised the possibility of shifting academic advising from being a faculty responsibility to one housed in an advising center staffed by student-services personnel. They suggest that students seemed to favor continuing to work with the counselor who introduced them to the college during recruitment and enrollment. A relatively small number of students—among the most capable at the college—prefer to use the new Internet-based enrollment system, which increases efficiency but can distance both faculty and staff from advising. The most active faculty, meanwhile, emphasize the importance of their remaining central in the academic-advising process, preferably with a single advisor staying with the student throughout his or her program. A structural advantage that PDCCC should not risk losing is that some faculty are outstanding advisors, with advising viewed as a strength within those programs with more accomplished and motivated students, such as nursing, police science, or information systems technology. Developmental students and general studies, the most challenging areas in the institution, also have the most difficulties associated with advising, however, which may suggest a structural problem addressed by an advising center rather than a problem in processes. There are also financial consequences associated with the structure of advising at PDCCC, as with adding staff or other infrastructure.

An equally difficult structural problem related to retention is the presence of large (and expanding) numbers of part-time faculty at the college. While they are valued members of the college community, they are thought to diminish the ability of the college to improve retention. These adjunct faculty are not expected to advise students, but some degree of informal advising occurs within the classroom. However, adjuncts are known to sometimes share incomplete or mistaken information with students; they do not always know where on campus and to whom to direct students in order to address problems; and they do not always use student information systems, Blackboard, or even e-mail. Given their minimal degree of contact with the campus—perhaps just a couple of hours one evening a week—it may be unfair to ask adjuncts for the level of engagement needed to keep as current on policies and processes as are most regular faculty members. The college has taken the step of developing templates for course syllabi to keep adjuncts in sync with full-time faculty, and perhaps there are similar means to address advising-related problems.

There is also the structural difficulty of placing increased expectations related to advising on those who already feeling stretched in their work. The first group is full-time faculty members, who are not only declining in number, but also have added responsibilities, such as administrative duties in recruiting students, finding adjunct faculty, and fulfilling various reporting requirements. Because there are shortages in student-services staffing, the faculty can also end up doing nonacademic counseling, even though they are not necessarily trained to do so, further cutting into the time they have available for academic advising. There is also the problem of some faculty members advising many students, while others work with only a few, if any. Those in student services note that when faculty members fail to meet their advising responsibilities, the work falls on them.

Academic advising is thus seen as extra work assumed by the most engaged faculty on campus, rather than a core responsibility of the entire faculty, for which it will be held accountable. Perhaps advising should be addressed as less of an institutional problem and more of one in some specific areas or units. It is a pressing issue, however. When students self-advise, problems tend to emerge at the ends of programs, when options for fixing them are limited. Advising is decentralized and sometime marked by inconsistency at PDCCC, its quality depending on the individual involved. One indicator of capacity, particularly as it relates to processes, is whether an organization can produce the same product every time.

Retention at PDCCC also raises *governance* questions. In addressing the retention issue at PDCCC, it is vital for leaders and senior managers to emphasize it as an institutional priority. The college has recently named two campus deans to whom the faculty report, with measures thought to increase retention as part of their portfolio. Additionally, the president is crucial in setting the agenda on the retention issue, as in allocating resources and providing symbolic leadership. Boyce has signaled that improving retention at PDCCC is essential to the institution realizing its purposes, which is an important first step. The deans can be helpful in providing sustained attention to the retention issue, but having the president designate a senior manager to be accountable for retention could also prove useful. There is presently no such person—nor is there a standing committee on retention. The college has worked to reduce the governance fatigue among faculty and staff members that comes with having too many meetings, but retention is likely a significant enough issue to merit an exception.

Another governance issue is the perception among faculty and staff members that, while their input is generally solicited, the past senior administration has not always expected them to actually fix problems and has not necessarily heeded their suggestions. These are governance issues, but they can also be problems related to *information*. In response, the new dean of the Franklin campus has launched an internal Web site, using Blackboard, for faculty to visit to post documents and discuss matters, including those that pertain to retention. Communicating information related to advising and retention remains an issue at PDCCC, however. Faculty members often do not have accurate lists of their advisees, so they do not know who has been assigned to them or with how many students they are expected to work. Lists for a given program or faculty member regularly include students who have transferred or withdrawn, or omit students whom a faculty member should be advising. Better employing various functions in the PeopleSoft system the college recently implemented should provide some relief, perhaps accompanied by purchasing some related consulting services. Getting students coded within the right program is a fixable data-management problem, albeit a significant one. These problems, which PDCCC has been addressing, make even calculating statistics such as retention rates more difficult, weakening the ability of the college to benchmark within the Virginia system and elsewhere and provide mandated accountability data.

These problems with processes and information relate directly to *infrastructure*. An advising center, a childcare facility, or a faculty-development center—each of which would likely aid retention—all would require significant investments in personnel and other infrastructure. The same would be true of reducing the number of adjunct faculty at PDCCC, which is unlikely, given national trends and probable resources at the college, even with enhanced private support. Shortages in personnel tend to force those at PDCCC to decide between attending to recruitment and financial aid or tackling advising and retention, as the former leave little time available for the latter. Those faculty members who *are* involved and effective advisors feel stretched. Because PDCCC is small, its personnel have overlapping responsibilities, often by necessity, but this can be an advantage, as change does not necessarily mean navigating through a large bureaucracy. Nevertheless, problems at the college are almost always due to insufficient staffing. Under these circumstances, even though PDCCC has framed retention as a priority, it may not have the capacity, as an infrastructure issue, to make desired improvements. Finally, a less-apparent need in infrastructure is related to faculty development. Established teaching approaches can become dated, especially as enrollments grow more diverse, and efforts toward more effective teaching can help address challenges such as retention. Funding required for training can be difficult to come by, however.

A final potential reform associated with strengthening the advising process and advancing retention at PDCCC is related to the *culture* of the institution. Several faculty and staff members indicated that instituting an obligatory first-semester orientation meeting would provide a means to disseminate needed information about policies and processes in a structured manner. Orientation might also contribute to instilling a needed sense of purpose in students, providing them with a better idea of why they are in college. Given the deficiencies in motivation and abilities among many PDCCC students, holding students' hands through various orientation processes, such as advising, might improve retention. Although there are practical barriers to instituting orientation, there are ways to accomplish at least some of its goals, such as program-by-program mini-orientations. Another suggestion is to involve the students' family members in orientation, similarly acculturating them to college life.

Finally, the desire among faculty and staff to build the capacity at the institution needed to tackle retention underscores the loyalty and investment among its faculty and staff that are perhaps PDCCC's greatest advantages. The faculty and staff tend to take responsibility for what they view as "their" students, both in formal and informal ways. PDCCC is a small college, so people know and care about each other. The culture at the college is informal and familiar, so attrition is more apparent—when someone leaves, it tends to be noticed. There is also an overall belief at PDCCC that rapport, particularly between students and faculty, and a customer-service ethos lead to student success. Challenges remain in building a productive overall student culture, as many are not serious about their work. Morale among faculty and staff who feel overworked can sometimes be low, including for front-line administrators still experiencing frustrations related to the PeopleSoft system. There are also differences among the faculty in their core beliefs about the appropriate role of a community college and what signifies quality instruction. Nevertheless, the personal, small-town culture at PDCCC makes much possible, even with limited resources.

➤PROCESSES AND ALIGNING THE OTHER ELEMENTS: A CHECKLIST
In considering an effort such as improving student retention at a rural community college, those leading and managing different types of institutions might consider the following related to processes:

☐ Do people understand how important retention is, given the mission and aspirations of the college? PDCCC had the advantage of those across the college community appreciating that retention is a meaningful issue— and that there is, realistically, some natural attrition at any community college. The president did not need to explain why the college had to take certain steps toward improvement, including revising various processes. Retention is also a priority at the statewide level, with the possibility of state and private resources (as with those from the Lumina Foundation for Education) being tied to improvements in the area.

☐ Are there changes in processes that will aid in the retention of students? PDCCC could make various adjustments rather easily, although certain process problems sometimes defy straightforward solutions. When there are barriers, ones involving processes are usually simpler to overcome than those involving a needed change in culture.

☐ Are there structural barriers the college can remove to reach its goal of improving retention? Instituting an advising center might prove beneficial, but there are expenses and tradeoffs associated with moving from the present faculty-based approach.

☐ Does governance at the college maximize possibilities for improving retention? As with structure, there are fundamental questions about where to assign responsibility in terms of retention, whether at the local level or more centrally.

☐ Are there policy changes that may improve retention? It is important to ask whether new rules, which are relatively simple to implement, are necessary, as with integrating advising into faculty evaluation at PDCCC.

☐ Is there sufficient data to support decisions related to improving retention, and is communication at the college a limitation in the effort? An issue at PDCCC is whether people are fully employing the information systems available at the college underscoring that implementation is often the most persistent challenge at institutions.

☐ Would investments in infrastructure contribute to addressing the retention challenge? PDCCC could probably hire the personnel needed improve retention, but resources are unlikely to permit retaining additional faculty and staff.

☐ Is the culture of the college supportive of improving retention? PDCCC has the advantage of people wanting to help its students succeed and favorably viewing reasonable and sincere attempts to address the retention problem. They likely are even willing to sacrifice time and volunteer efforts, knowing how important retention is in realizing the purposes of the college.

Applying the Framework

Leaders and senior managers facing a challenge such as improving retention at a small community college may wish to initially consider who needs to be responsible for managing and monitoring its progress. The problem is not necessarily one that needs to directly involve the president, even at a small institution, although the president does need to indicate and demonstrate his or her support. He or she also has the usual responsibilities for sending signals and employing symbols. Perhaps those best positioned to lead such efforts, including attempts to improve processes, are the campus deans, who have the most direct influence over those faculty and administrators who are on the front lines of the problem. Given that there are administrative aspects to the retention problem, in addition to challenges related to academic advising, involving the chief financial officer and the head of student affairs, when relevant, may also be productive.

Although faculty governance is typically not very developed at community colleges, except in unionized environments, finding ways to integrate faculty into the search for solutions may yield positive results. Even in more bureaucratic and managed environments, it is usually sensible to involve faculty in matters involving academic concerns such as retention. Convening an ad hoc committee of faculty and administrators to address the overall problem—or even various committees to consider different components of the problem—could prove effective. Naming a "czar" responsible for retention is another possible solution, but even more-bureaucratic institutions tend to value collaboration enough to make such an approach less desirable and workable. The difficulty with a committee is placing boundaries, including timing, around such work, so that committee fatigue does not set in or a group does not reach beyond its jurisdiction. The president can contribute to the effectiveness of any ad hoc committee, defining the problem, indicating deadlines related to moving forward, and empowering those involved. He or she might also emphasize that those who are involved need to develop means to measure the progress and, ultimately, the impact of their efforts. Finally, the president can make sure that the defined goals challenge the institution while remaining realistic. For instance, an open-access institution in an economically stressed area is not going to have full retention, but some improvement is possible, with the college knowing it is doing all that is reasonable to expect of itself in the area.

One difficulty in so directly involving faculty and lower-level administrators is that they may not have a sense of the whole institution. Leaders and senior managers might make an investment in various means required for those across the institution to have a clear understanding of the elements and how they align. Doing so could simply involve holding a workshop to introduce strategic management as its potential uses, building appreciation of both possibilities and complications in confronting such a complex issue as retention. There is rarely consensus among various groups within an institution about how to address any problem. For instance, engaged faculty and front-line support staff tend to view potential solutions differently. The president and others in senior positions may need to offer broader perspectives. Those directly managing the retention issue might also provide a forum to discuss it, using both online and in-person means. They can build on the advantage of people at PDCCC generally having a clear sense of the mission of the institution and the importance of retention in achieving it. Another advantage at PDCCC is that having so many people involved in considering the retention issue makes communication somewhat more immediate, with those across the college needing to be a part of the conversation already included in it.

Finally, given the initiative and the type of institution involved, breakdowns in infrastructure are the most likely ones among the elements to occur. There are possible solutions to the retention problem at PDCCC that are simply outside of the reach of the institution, with the college only able to hire so many people or develop so many programs—if any, really. There are also structural tradeoffs, such as launching an advising center—if there were even the resources to do so— but thereby diminishing the benefits of faculty involvement with students. Both approaches limit the effectiveness of various policies and processes related to retention, however seemingly well-conceived they might be. The most important advantage at PDCCC is that people tend to agree on its purposes—and that, given these, the retention issue is important. There is also a productive culture at the college, so solutions to the retention problem can generally be confined to more operational matters, such as processes.

CHAPTER EIGHT

Information

Tuition Discounting at the University of Redlands

The University of Redlands, located in Southern California, has taken a purposeful approach to tuition discounting, maximizing its net tuition revenue
through careful attention to its financial aid policy. A working group on the issue
meets regularly throughout the year and includes senior managers from financial
aid, admissions, finance and administration, arts and sciences, and institutional
research, in addition to an outside consultant. Institutions commonly make tuition-
policy decisions ad hoc or by default. At Redlands, the contrary is true, with these
decisions carefully managed and driven by data.

Redlands considers what actually influences, and what should influence, the
discount rate—and how effective the annual rate is in advancing the mission and
aspirations of the institution. The goal each year is to find the point at which tuition policy can bring Redlands the most impressive class of students it can attract, maximizing its net tuition by arriving at the optimal discount rate. In doing
so, Redlands benchmarks against a set of similar institutions, using data from
consultants and consortia. The university embeds an examine how effective its
tuition-discounting policy was that year in its annual process and determines
what fixes may be needed.

Beyond employing information, there are also structural and governance components to the Redlands working group. It includes various units, and those individuals within them, that should be involved with formulating policy and developing strategy related to tuition discounting. The Redlands group also appreciates that tuition policy is instrumental in realizing institutional purposes. As at other selective universities and colleges, these ambitions relate to increasing institutional prestige and thus available resources, as the most prestigious U.S. universities are also the wealthiest. The profile of its entering undergraduate students is the main available means to enhance its standing, heightening the stakes in setting the discount rate. Furthermore, the working group itself is a process, meeting regularly across the year. Finally, the institution has developed an open and inclusive culture that allows the approach they have adopted to work. Those not directly involved trust those who are to make good decisions, such delegation being a necessary aspect in governance, even at the most collegial institution. In doing so, Redlands has enlarged the capacity within the organization that is needed to support its ambitions.[1]

Information as an Element

Information, in strategic management, is the generation, dissemination, and assimilation of facts and figures needed to inform and support decision making within an organization. Communication, an aspect of information, can serve a linking function within organizations, especially loosely coupled ones such as universities and colleges, in which the units do not always completely connect with one another. At a macro level, information flows assure that those across any institution understand its mission and aspirations—and progress toward these. For instance, disseminating data about the composition of the students enrolled at a university or college provides both external and internal audiences with evidence of what it has become and where it is headed. Information also supports governance, providing evidence for decisions, including those related to optimizing structure, policies, processes, and infrastructure. Communication also tends to enhance institutional culture, whether the setting is more collegial, as at Redheads, or bureaucratic, political, or even anarchic.

Recognizing that the demands on universities are ever greater and margins for error are increasingly slim, institutions are emphasizing decision support, not only in management, but also in planning and strategy. Benchmarking, both within a university or college and relative to comparable institutions, has never been more crucial, encouraging standardizing data both across institutions and units within them. The data warehousing necessary in decision support, including in benchmarking, involves collecting and organizing data from multiple sources for easy extraction, analysis, and use. When analyzed—as within institutional research offices—these data can inform both short-term tactical decisions and long-term strategic ones. Managers can use warehoused data to draw meaningful correlations and discover trends and patterns toward making projections, generating "what if" scenarios and indicating conformity with performance metrics. Doing so contributes to positioning institutions relative to competitors, as well as translating broader aspirations and more specific goals in strategic plans into day-to-day management. Without the management capacity grounded in data-based decisions, strategic plans tend to languish, their ideals and promise failing to become reality. Benchmarking strengthens strategic planning itself, encouraging the development of more realistic goals and more robust means of assessing progress toward them.

Information generated and communicated within decision-support mechanisms suggests the available tactics leaders and senior manager can use to address a given situation. For instance, a dean who senses an increase in students leaving the institution between semesters during their second year would have the option of considering different kinds of data as he or she develops a response. The dean might (1) view historical data such as attrition rates in past years (which may suggest a trend) and when students are departing (which may suggest a pattern); (2) readily draw upon academic data, including the programs and courses enrolling the departing students, perhaps suggesting a correlation; (3) access specific student data, such as the characteristics of those departing, including their entering characteristics, whether they are tuition paying, their grades to date, and so on; or (4) make projections about the impact of student attrition on staffing and facility use, as well as its impact on anticipated revenue for his or her unit. In each circumstance, the dean could make comparisons with other units and even similar institutions. He or she would also be able to run much more comprehensive reports for accountability and related purposes with far greater efficiency. Perhaps more importantly, as competition between and among institutions is only likely to increase, these data are critical in positioning the institution through various strategies.

Information: A Perspective on the Research Literature
Kevin Kinser
State University of New York at Albany

Information, as applicable to the BOC strategic-management approach, is elucidated by research related to higher education, including: (1) Senge's description of the learning organization and systems thinking; (2) Weick's sensemaking (as discussed in chapter 7); (3) the concept of data-driven decision making embedded in the federal No Child Left Behind legislation; and (4) Petrides's recent writings on knowledge management.

Senge's (1990) "fifth discipline," the learning organization (discussed in more detail in chapter 1), is useful in understanding information as an element. The concept involves understanding the whole of the organization through identifying the patterns that influence individual parts and appreciating how they come together to create the greater sum. Organizations become more understandable and "learn" from feedback, whether it is immediate or delayed. The learning organization is therefore intimately concerned with identifying proximate information that illegitimately reinforces behavior and locating the more distal information sources that provide a more accurate long-term view of a changing situation.

According to Weick (1995), sensemaking allows organizations to evolve by means of individuals interpreting ambiguous (what he terms "equivocal") information, providing both the necessary prerequisites to decision making and assistance in rationalizing the results of decisions once made. Sensemaking is particularly important when organizations encounter new and unusual events, as Weick (1993) portrays in his case study of U.S. Forest Service firefighters caught in the deadly Mann Gulch disaster. It is at these times, when the regular processes and structure of an organization collapse, that sensemaking provides the means to overcome various obstacles and challenges. Weick refers to this as "organizational resilience" and identifies four sources from which resilient solutions may be found:

- The first source is through improvisation and bricolage—the ability to develop creative responses under pressure using whatever tools are at one's disposal. Rather than seeing only confusion and chaos, the sensemaking organization is able to take stock and improvise a new order when the old one fails.
- The second source comes from the broad understanding of information that is needed to operate under what Weick calls "virtual role systems." When change renders existing organizational structures ineffective, sensemaking allows members, as individuals, to recognize vacated roles,

reconstitute the group as a mental construct, and reproduce the functions necessary to respond to new challenges.

- The third source is the attitude of wisdom, described by Weick as understanding that in novel situations, one's knowledge is always incomplete. Curiosity and openness to new ideas are the hallmarks of an attitude of wisdom in sensemaking organizations.
- The fourth source is the importance of respectful interaction: communicating with honesty (telling what you know), trust (believing what you are told), and self-respect (creating a new understanding by integrating what you know and what you are told). Without respectful interaction among participants in an organization, each person is alone and cannot draw on the resources of others in a crisis.

Organizational resilience can be seen as roughly equivalent to organizational capacity, with the four sources of resilience offering specific examples of the value of understanding and using information in an environment suggestive of organizational change.

The federal No Child Left Behind Act focused the attention of those involved with K–12 education on accountability, and with it the importance of using data to understand student performance. "Data-driven decision making" is a phrase in current vogue, used to describe the gamut of activities undertaken under this accountability rubric. The emphasis is on improvement and reform—fixing the problem rather than fixing the blame—through the systematic application of information technology to collect and analyze data to be used by decision makers. Bernhardt (2005), one of the key commentators promoting the use of data in schools, identifies "data-smart" schools as those that employ data tools to help students learn, helping, by extension, school districts as a whole become more efficient and effective. Information in the data-driven decision-making model is quantitative and digital, and it is specifically collected and organized to be useful to the front-line teacher as well as to the district superintendent.

Bernhardt (2005) and others (Education Commission of the States 2002) provide practical advice on how to collect information, what information is important, what to do with the information, and even specific technologies available for organizing and disseminating information to decision makers and stakeholders. In short, information is understood to be explanatory and useful to decision makers. The data-driven decision-making model provides concrete examples of how information can be used, and it identifies technological issues that should be considered by users of that data. At the same time, it presents a rather narrow view of information, seeing only quantitative,

(continued)

digitalized information as being relevant, and discounting information sources that involve qualitative, communicative, and intuitive strategies or approaches.

While "data-driven decision making" is the term of art in the K–12 world, in higher education a similar concept is described more fully by the term "knowledge management." Petrides and her colleagues (Petrides, Nguyen, and Doty 2005; Petrides 2004; Petrides and Nodine 2003) have written extensively about how information is used on campuses and how these applications can be improved. While suffering somewhat from the same quantitative/ digital biases that encumber data-driven decision making, knowledge management encompasses fewer prescriptions regarding technology and a greater emphasis on user needs. Petrides employs the phrase "the democratization of data" to suggest that information should be widely available throughout an organization. Her research suggests that centralized databases are not always the most effective ways of providing information to users and that adapting available information to specific purposes often requires "work-arounds"—inventive data-collection techniques that bypass standardized and digitalized resources—by local users who best understand their own needs. Petrides argues that work-arounds offer opportunities for organizations to better understand and take advantage of information that is typically not collected. Yet they also represent wasted effort and resources when they occur because of centralized procedures that are flawed. Like data-driven decision making, knowledge management provides key examples of the use of information in educational organizations. As such, it emphasizes how much information is available, as well as how much is wasted due to underestimating its importance.

The University of Redlands and Tuition Discounting

Situated in Redlands, California, about 65 miles east of Los Angeles, and enrolling about 4000 students, the University of Redlands describes itself as an independent, coeducational, liberal arts and sciences university. Founded in 1907 by the American Baptists, Redlands maintains an informal association with that denomination. The university offers 42 undergraduate programs in its College of Arts and Sciences, which includes the School of Music and the Johnston Center for Integrative Studies. In addition, Redlands offers graduate programs in business, communication disorders, education, geographic information systems, and music. The university is accredited by the Western Association of Schools and Colleges and governed by a 35-member board of trustees. James R. Appleton, appointed in 1987, led the institution before his retirement in 2005, which is when we visited the campus.

The academic profile of the Redlands student body reflects that of other reasonably selective liberal arts colleges. The middle half of its freshman class in 2007 had SAT scores between 1080 and 1260, and the average high school grade-point average for the class was almost 3.6. In 2007, U.S. News and World Report ranked the university within the top 10 master's degree universities in the West. Redlands draws roughly one-third of its students from outside of California. More than half of its undergraduates are enrolled in the College of Arts and Sciences, and over 80 percent live on campus in one of its 11 residence halls. The Johnston Center allows students to design their own majors in consultation with faculty advisors. It has received national acclaim for its innovative approaches, as with students writing contracts for their courses and receiving narrative evaluations in lieu of traditional grades. Redlands also offers programs for working adults at regional centers and corporate locations throughout Southern California that are associated with its schools of business and education.

The tuition sticker price at Redlands is roughly $32,000 per year, with room and board an additional $10,000 annually. Over 85 percent of the students at Redlands receive financial aid through scholarships, grants, loans, and work-study programs, which is consistent with the national average for institutions of its type (National Association of College and University Business Officers 2006). For the 2005 academic year, the Redlands working group recommended a discount rate in the 45 percent range for freshmen (plus a modest amount of discretionary funds allocated by the financial aid director), in the 40 percent range for transfer students, and an aggregate institutional discount range between these two figures. The five-year trend at Redlands had been to set the discount rate at roughly the same percentage. With the discount, the effective tuition rate for undergraduates in arts and sciences was about $19,000 in 2005. (In 2003, it was about $14,000, given that the sticker price was considerably lower.) Also, to keep pace with tuition increases and offset declining Cal Grant awards, grants at Redlands have increased annually by about 10 percent. The average financial aid package, which includes funding other than from scholarships, covered 71 percent of the total cost of attendance in 2005. Redlands generally only discounts tuition for its 2500 arts and sciences students, not those in education and business.

NACUBO, in its annual tuition-discounting study, defines the discount rate as institutionally funded financial aid divided by gross tuition and fee revenue. In

2005, the average discount rate for freshmen at high-tuition small colleges was 37.9 percent, with the rate only slightly lower for all students (National Association of College and University Business Officers 2006; see also Baum and Lapovsky 2006). Once again, the rate for freshmen at Redlands was about five percent higher. Among institutions in the high-tuition small college category, about 75 percent have a discount rate between 31 and 50 percent—with roughly one-third of institutions in the 40 percent range, such as Redlands (National Association of College and University Business Officers 2006). Also, NACUBO reports that the average discount rate for freshman has increased about 5 percent across institutional types over the past decade or so, as has the percentage of freshmen receiving aid. Meanwhile, gross tuition rates at all institutions have skyrocketed during the period, from just below $15,000 in 1996 to closer to $24,000 in 2005—but net tuition rates have remained more constant (although still increasing), from just below $10,000 to just below $15,000, based on NACUBO data.

Redlands operates on a 4-4-1 academic calendar, consisting of two 15-week semesters and a one-month intensive May term designed to allow concentration on a single course, study abroad, community service, or research. The student-faculty ratio at Redlands is 12:1, with class sizes generally small and faculty involved with students outside of class, as mentors and advisors. Redlands offers a value-centered education, challenging assumptions and stressing moral concerns in both its classes and its activities. The full-time faculty at Redlands is comprised of 213 teaching faculty, librarians, and coaches, with 91 percent having earned a Ph.D. or another terminal degree. Redlands also accentuates athletics. Over 450 student-athletes compete on 20 sports teams for the Redlands Bulldogs in the Division III (nonscholarship) Southern California Intercollegiate Athletic Conference, earning eight league championships in 2002. The women's water polo team has six national championships, and the men's soccer team finished second in the nation in 2002.

In the decade before 2005, Redlands invested nearly $100 million in capital improvements and added 125,000 square feet in new facilities, increasing total square footage by 12.5 percent. In doing so, the university has vastly improved its curb appeal to prospective students and others, while acting in accord with national trends, the arms race in constructing and remodeling facilities being a defining feature of contemporary higher education in the United States. Endowment at Redlands grew steadily in the decade before 2005, increasing from $46 million to $78 million, with its operating budget almost doubling to reach $36.3 million between 1992 and 2002. The university has taken care to minimize the percentage of endowment funds used to support its operating budget, with its spending rate having averaged 4.4 percent between 1994 and 2004, with a low of 2.7 percent in 1994.

Tuition discounting is critical across all institutional types in attracting the more accomplished students that are so important to institutions realizing their aspiration of advancing in the prestige hierarchy within American higher education (Geiger 2004; Ehrenberg 2002; McPherson and Schapiro 1998). Selectivity is an important variable in reputational rankings, in addition to factors such as endowments (and funded research at research universities)—and it is the one most easily manipulated by institutions such as Redlands. Institutions have made significant investments in attracting students, commonly using discounting to seal the deal. In addition to lowering price, institutions have invested in facilities such as student residences, dining commons, fitness centers, and commercial districts. They have also developed various academic initiatives intended to appeal to students—popular undergraduate majors, graduate programs, faculty scholarship and student research, honors programs, study abroad, and the like (Geiger 2004; Kirp 2003). Enhancing intercollegiate athletics has been another common strategy (Toma 2008).

Such practices have been strongly criticized, both for reducing access for lower-income students and for not achieving desired results for institutions. In a Lumina Foundation report, Jerry Davis (2003) contends that institutions are allocating more of their financial aid budgets to students whose families can afford their higher tuitions, with less remaining for lower-income students (see also Redd 2000). In the latter 1990s, grants from private institutions increased by 145 percent for those with family incomes over $100,000 and around 15 percent for those making less than $40,000—with similar percentages at public universities and colleges. In the decade before 1995, the trend was in the opposite direction, as aid to lower-income students grew faster than that for higher-income students (McPherson and Shapiro 2002). Also, lower-income students are paying a greater proportion of what have been significant tuition increases, which is only exacerbated by the shift from need-based to merit-based aid over the past two decades (J. S. Davis 2003; Heller 2002). Higher tuition also drives lower-income students away from private institutions, according to Davis. The same is true of students across income levels, so private colleges and universities appear to be losing market share and not realizing desired gains, whether in student quality or net revenue—all of which are inconsistent with what tuition discounting seeks to accomplish. Redd (2000) found that upping tuition discounting does not necessarily increase average SAT scores, and it can result in meaningful losses in tuition revenue. Finally, there are questions about whether discounting draws funds away from efforts that would contribute to improving institutions, such as initiatives to improve teaching quality.

Purposes and Information at the University of Redlands

Carefully managing tuition discounting maximizes the contribution financial aid makes to institutions being able to realize their aspirations. It can also advance values, allocating resources as efficiently as possible, so as to reserve the maximum amount of funds to support less-affluent students. The process that determines discounting decisions at Redlands begins with clarity about the purposes of the institution. Redlands understands that with a relatively low endowment, tuition decisions come with higher stakes, especially if the university wants to raise its stature while maintaining its principles. It has responded by imposing a significant degree of discipline on tuition discounting, building a policy around a set of core principles and instituting a rigorous process. For instance, Redlands has eschewed bidding for certain highly valued prospective students, such as National Merit scholars, believing that it can attract the caliber of students it desires without having to enter into bidding wars. Similarly, the university no longer provides financial assistance to lower-achieving students simply because they are admitted to the institution, targeting these funds instead to advance objectives related to enhancing the academic profile of the overall entering class. Such policies are consistent with its strategy to be at the midpoint in net price among a group of competitors.

Redlands has attracted growing numbers of more accomplished and more diverse students into the arts and sciences, where it focuses its tuition-discounting efforts, taking advantage of opportunities in the marketplace for California students. As its main competitor, the University of California system, has become less able to accommodate many accomplished students, Redlands has been successful in attracting them. It has also taken advantage of opportunities, such as the Cal Grants program, to lower its price to be more competitive, as with the University of California institutions. Coupled with establishing a competitive price, the university has enhanced its profile by improving its physical plant, building its faculty and maintaining a low student-faculty ratio, and intentionally increasing diversity. The institution has taken advantage of debt financing options, a buyers' market for full-time faculty, and the impressive diversity of prospective California students. Redlands has deliberately increased enrollments from 1400 to 2500 traditional students, while maintaining or improving the academic quality of its students.

Its tuition-discounting policy has been central to improvements and expansion at Redlands—the realization of its aspirations. Before adopting its present approach to tuition discounting in the early 1990s, the university had a need-based financial aid policy. Redlands intended its shift to a merit-based policy to enhance its admission profile—and thus the reputation of the institution. The university used the same amount of financial aid as before, but came to focus its commitments on stronger students and away from weaker ones, while making certain that there was no negative effect on priorities such as recruiting a diverse class. Redlands determined where it could be most strategic in financial aid decisions, while still allocating funds in a manner congruent with its values by continuing to provide opportunities for lower-income and underrepresented students.

In its deliberations, the working group at Redlands relies upon data. Bill Hall, the consultant retained by Redlands, brought a more sophisticated way of looking at numbers, maximizing the data available for decision support in setting net tuition price for various types of students. He encouraged a strategy that targeted the second and third quintiles of admitted students for aid, as well as enrolling lower-achievers who were more able to afford the full cost of tuition. His approach caused an immediate and lasting increase in the admissions profile of the university—and was reflected in its ranking.

Since the establishment of the working group, information dissemination related to financial aid at Redlands has been purposeful, both through formal approaches and informal channels. Having convincing data to actively communicate to interested colleagues has proved important in building the credibility of the working group, enlisting support across the university for its approach. Having voluminous and relevant data has proven preferable to relying on intuition alone, especially to the Redlands board and senior administrators.

In addition, the data is sufficiently nimble so that when Cal Grant awards change, for instance, Hall can predict the impact on Redlands quintile by quintile—and the institution can work on alternative approaches to filling gaps. The data is predictive, while also enabling the university to see the financial bottom line and the impact of various strategies across the institution. It can examine what is working and what is not—and then make appropriate adjustments. In its planning, Redlands can explore the impact different pricing will have on various types of applicants and what the opportunities are for more meritocracy in financial aid

decisions. An upgraded institutional research office assists in the decision support effort, as with drawing data from comparable institutions. Redlands has also
enhanced sharing data across different units, enabling them to better understand
one another and contributing to breaking down "silos" within the university.

Pricing in a more systematic manner through an intensely data-driven process
has come to be viewed across campus as essential to the success of the institution
toward realizing its aspirations. The strategy has required the support of the entire campus community. Appleton, the Redlands president, has been effective in
communicating the mission and aspirations of the institution. Phillip Doolittle,
the senior vice president for administration, who oversees financial aid, has clarified over time the benefits of the information-driven financial aid strategy that
supports these. Appleton and Doolittle initially needed the faculty to appreciate
that Redlands, given its limited endowment, had to be disciplined in its approach
to tuition discounting—more so than Pomona College or a University of California campus, both of which have greater available resources and can take a broader
approach. Had these leaders not paid attention to communicating the idea in
terms of institutional purposes, skeptics would have become opponents, representing the strategy as "ignoring needy students and buying affluent ones." Those
across campus at Redlands have instead come to accept the approach, broadly viewing it as keeping the university's mission alive and advancing its aspirations.

Connecting with the Other Elements

While information provides the fuel for the tuition-discounting approach at Redlands, the working group organized to coordinate the process is its engine. With
the establishment of the working group, Redlands moved enrollment management from academic affairs to being under the senior vice president for finance
and administration. Although the usual *structure* is to house financial aid and
enrollment management elsewhere, Redlands recognized the utility of integrating them into finance. Before it restructured, the institution had established a
cap on discounting at an arbitrary 50 percent figure, which did not accommodate
differences in wealth among students and resulted in smaller enrollments than
were desirable. The financial aid director had departed, but the vice president for
finance and administration, Doolittle, who would oversee the financial aid unit,
had experience in this area. Because he was credible to those in admissions and
across academic affairs, moving enrollment management under finance proved
palatable.

In addition, given the smaller size of the institution, the administration, as structured at Redlands, is also sufficiently permeable to afford the necessary informal communication between and among units that inspires needed mutual trust, especially those in academic affairs, who might view enrollment management as properly within their purview. The generally collegial approach to organizing people and making decisions at Redlands encourages needed communication across functions. While a relationship-based approach tends to work within the culture at a traditional liberal arts college, it is an open question whether the same would have been true at a more bureaucratic, political, or anarchical institution (Birnbaum 1988). It also helped that Redlands had an admissions director who "understood numbers" and could operate comfortably within finance and administration. Finally, many of the leaders and senior managers responsible for the restructuring remained in their positions when the working group was formed, viewing it as a step in the maturation of the approach.

With its working-group approach to tuition discounting, Redlands not only developed a structure, but also clarified *governance*, making decisions and setting policies by regularly convening those representing interested units. (The group included the president during its first three years.) The working group, which has ten members, is not a committee, as it does not work through problems in an iterative manner. It instead operates on an annual cycle, within carefully set boundaries and through an established five-phase process. The group thus tackles its work each year more as a project team would. Having all those with expertise relevant to tuition discounting around a single table lends credibility to decisions; has led to better judgments than simply having the financial aid director make them; and spreads the risk of failure (and praise for successes) among those in the group. The working group concept, a flat as opposed to a hierarchical approach, invites consensus through debate among those with different perspectives and interests. It also emphasizes connections across units and functions, avoiding the silos that are a common governance challenge at universities and colleges.

The working group does not include an academic affairs administrator or representatives from the faculty, but it is purposeful in informing these groups and relevant others across campus of its functions, which has proven to be satisfactory over the years. The precept at Redlands is that academic affairs should determine the substance of admissions decisions—the actual students the university admits—but that financial aid is more properly a budget decision residing with finance and administration. Those across campus are confident, as they generally have been from the outset, that issues that the faculty and academic administrators might suggest are adequately covered within the working group, such as concerns related to student diversity, intercollegiate athletics, and institutional profile. This group is careful to consult regularly with colleagues elsewhere within the university, especially in areas where issues tend to cross over with their tuition-discounting work, including the faculty committee working on retention and the faculty review committee involved with admissions.

The academic affairs side of Redlands considers itself to have a checks and balances function relative to the working group, recognizing that it does not have a need for direct involvement with what has come to have been seen as a financial decision. It is doubtful that faculty members understand—or even care to—most of the details related to tuition decisions, but they do know that the process exists and are aware of the results associated with the approach. Some discussion occurs about whether the institution should have different priorities in areas where discounting can have an impact. However, the working group approach is not questioned, as those across the university recognize it not as a forum to debate policy, but more as a vehicle for analyzing the impact of potential strategies and outcomes. For example, if the institution decided to pursue a new enrollment profile, the working group would act from that basis, analyzing decisions related to the overarching strategy in terms of institutional finances and other operational concerns. The working group defers to the faculty on policy, and the faculty defers to the working group on managing the bottom line of the institution, which has proven to be a satisfying and productive approach to structure and governance related to tuition discounting at Redlands.

In addition, the working group connects with governance at Redlands through the finance committee of the board of trustees, which is involved with matters such as the targeted size of incoming classes. The board reviews considerable amounts of data related to discounting, but it does not micromanage the process, consistent with its proper role of working at the level of *policies*. Foremost among these policies is that the dependent variable at Redlands is always net tuition revenue, while keeping priorities such as its academic profile and student diversity firmly in mind.

Tuition discounting at Redlands is a five-phase *process* that has been fine-tuned, as needed, for over a decade, becoming institutionalized within the university. In December, the group develops awarding strategies, with a different plan for each of its prospective student populations, and shapes policy in response to Cal Grant changes. It then monitors its decisions, reviewing the data generated by its consultant, Hall, each week and adjusting policies as needed, as in response

to receiving too few applications for admission. Redlands maintains a commitment to data integrity—having good data to use—and takes advantage of the
relevance and timeliness of that information. In May, Redlands begins looking at
its yield, already having collected data on student financial need, waiting until
then to offer financial aid packages. The university can then analyze its annual
results, plugging data into both long- and short-term budget scenarios. Each fall
it plans for the coming year, building on recommendations from relevant constituents. There are also informal processes at Redlands related to the working
group. For instance, those in admissions know that they often need to operate
outside of normal deadlines to accommodate music students and student-athletes
who require various exceptions. Similarly, the financial aid director commonly
holds some applications in reserve until the admissions staff has made certain
decisions.

Integrating Hall and his firm into decision making related to financial aid at
Redlands can be framed in terms of *infrastructure*. The university has come to view
consultants as augmenting its internal resources, eagerly and openly working with
them as needed and as appropriate. Hall is perceived as adding an articulate and
credible voice to the discussion on tuition discounting. In short, Redlands has come
to appreciate that consultants can build capacity within an organization, supplying
depth and breadth without making additions to staff. Without external consultants,
Redlands could not have reached the level of complexity and sophistication that
it has, using such a large number of variables in such creative ways in its financial
aid process. Several administrators at Redlands noted that without these outside
voices, such a significant change in tuition discounting might not have been possible at the university.

Redlands also encourages those who use data to improve their facility with it
through training, with professional development having become integrated into
the culture of the campus, building its human infrastructure. In addition, enhance-
ments to its administrative infrastructure accompanied the increased rigor in
tuition-discounting decisions at Redlands. The university has developed an effective management information system that integrates financial aid, admissions,
the registrar, student life, and other functions. Furthermore, as it addressed tuition discounting, Redlands began spending more on capital projects and human
resources, aligning campus infrastructure with the expectations of the students
it was now recruiting and enrolling.

Finally, accountability and responsiveness is expected of members of the working group. It has become part of the *culture* of the group. While each member owns

each decision made by the group, he or she is individually responsible for contributing certain information and for coming to the meetings prepared. The working group has also developed the norm of meeting when it must, canceling scheduled meetings, as a rule, where there is no urgency, in the interest of preserving the engagement of those involved. The fact that the president and senior vice president commonly adopt the recommendations of the group also encourages high morale.

The culture of Redlands strongly influences the culture of the working group. Trust, as generated through relationships and communication, is a clear aspect of the culture at Redlands, particularly between the senior administration and the faculty, with information shared openly and decisions paced so that no one is surprised. For instance, the president commonly brings issues before the faculty, who feel free to reject ideas they object to strongly enough, with the president reserving the same right relative to faculty proposals. The working group operates in a manner aligned with these norms. The extensive use of data in decision making related to discounting has yielded results and won the admiration and support of those across campus, itself becoming part of the institutional culture.

➤INFORMATION AND ALIGNING THE OTHER ELEMENTS: A CHECKLIST
In considering an effort such as the rigorous use of data to support tuition-discounting decisions, those leading and managing institutions might consider the following related to information:

☐ What is the institution attempting to accomplish through tuition discounting—and what values does it want reflected in these decisions? Redlands was interested in enrolling as many of the most accomplished students as it could, given its available resources and consistent with its desire to increase its prestige—one that is common across selective universities and colleges. Working with an outside consultant, Redlands attempted to maximize the impact of its tuition discounting, offering packages to students who would improve the profile of the university and for whom reduced tuition was necessary to convince them to attend. Yet no university wants to be mercenary in such decisions. Mission at any institution cannot simply be to improve its enrollment statistics and increase its reputational ranking, so values such as diversity and access mattered in setting policies and making decisions.

☐ How can those responsible for allocating limited tuition-discounting resources best employ data to maximize leverage in advancing the institution's values and ambitions? Redlands imposed discipline on its discounting decisions, supporting them with data it collected and analyzed for that purpose. Doing so inspired confidence across the institution in the approach, particularly given the propensity of the working group to regularly communicate with those interested in the process. Institutions are not always so successful in decision support. They regularly collect data, but rarely employ it to full effect. For instance, decisions to reduce budgets in times of financial crisis are commonly to make across-the-board cuts, even though institutional effectiveness efforts have, in theory, identified specific areas where targeted reductions may make more sense.

☐ In what functional area should tuition-discounting policy reside? Redlands chose to locate discounting in finance and administration, recognizing it to be more of a financial decision than an academic one. It did so even in the most collegial of institutional settings—one in which faculty influence is pronounced. A research university, where delegation is more the norm, would certainly be able to do the same—as would generally more bureaucratic institutions, such as community colleges. Given the information needs associated with the Redlands approach, structuring it as they did was sensible, since those across finance and administration could spend the time needed to understand and accomplish what the institution intended with discounting.

☐ Who should be involved in making tuition-discounting decisions? The yearly working group represents the various functional areas relevant to discounting. It does not require the active involvement of the president or representatives of the faculty, although they are kept informed, with the vice president for finance and administration assuming responsibility. Other institutions could take such an approach to discounting. Where Redlands is not willing to delegate is in its admissions decisions, which require more involvement by the faculty and those across academic affairs. Yet even these would be administrative decisions in more centralized or managed institutional environments.

☐ What set of principles should guide discounting decisions in each admissions cycle? The working group at Redlands developed several policies to help direct its work in using the data it was generating. Doing

so contributed to keeping its approach disciplined. The working group
also included evaluation into their annual cycle, making improvements as
indicated.

☐ How should the actual process of determining discounting operate each
year? The working group put discounting on an annual cycle, with certain
activities occurring and decisions being made at specific times of the year.
The process aligns with the admissions calendar, which is necessary,
given the link between financial aid and student recruitment. The process
is disciplined, which is consistent with the data-driven nature of the
decisions being made.

☐ What infrastructure is required to pursue a given approach to discounting? Redlands invested in the information systems and outside consultant
needed to perform the sophisticated data analysis required to pursue its
chosen approach to discounting. Using data to the extent that the university does requires such investments.

☐ How does the approach to discounting at an institution fit with its
culture? Redlands found a means to integrate decision support into the
culture of the institution, which is collegial in nature, as is typical of a
liberal arts college. Again, such a culture might seem to be especially at
odds with its approach, but the combination of effective communication
and positive results has made it work at Redlands.

Applying the Framework

Given the technical nature of the overall task of managing tuition discounting to
maximize net revenue at a selective liberal arts college, assigning responsibility
to a working group operating on a regular cycle appears to be a good option. Both
the senior administration and the faculty need to be involved in establishing policies for the institution that advance its purposes, including how managing its
student profile contributes to these. Such individuals are less relevant in implementing these policies, as in generating the data needed for decision support.

The distinction between establishing policy and producing information to inform an annual process is critical, as with the careful division of labor at Redlands. The university assigned the working group a specific set of decisions related to generating, analyzing, and communicating data to maximize the impact
of its discounting decisions. The faculty and others responsible for academic matters will rightly take issue if the group's work is perceived to be more substantive,

drifting into determining who is admitted. In structuring the working group, Redlands involves representatives from the relevant units, which are mostly associated with finance and administration. The group is then purposeful in relaying information to others on campus with an interest in tuition discounting as a strategy, but not directly including them in the actual process of determining rates. In doing so, Redlands is thus gaining leverage from both the decision support and communication components of the information element in strategic management.

A challenge commonly associated with administrators who are more focused on technical matters is ensuring that they have a sufficiently nuanced sense of institutional purposes. Responsibility here begins with the president, in articulating, and then reinforcing through a variety of symbolic illustrations and practical means, the mission and aspirations of the institution. Perhaps the working group at Redlands could function in an effective manner just by understanding its technical responsibility, crunching numbers and making recommendations. Nonetheless, understanding *why* Redlands is seeking the most accomplished set of students possible each year imbues its work with a sense of purpose. Such context is also likely to make the group more effective in framing and answering questions related to their analyses. Sustained investments by universities and colleges in creating a deep understanding of purposes across the institution tend to produce such dividends, as at Redlands, which has developed a culture—including acceptance of delegating a set of enrollment management decisions to a particular group under the auspices of finance and administration—that aligns with its purposes.

A project team such as the working group also tends to be more effective when it understands where its work fits within the university as a whole. Strategic management can be useful here. For instance, the Redlands working group focuses on information. Yet the communication embedded within the element has an impact on culture within the university; the data it generates influences decisions on infrastructure; and policies and processes guide data collection and analysis. Perhaps it is less important for an entity such as the working group to have the same holistic appreciation of the institution as a president or provost, but a broader view tends to enhance their work. Even the composition of the group, made up of representatives from relevant units, fosters shared understandings across the university. It is important to consider what kinds of efforts tend to further understanding about the BOC elements and how they align, both within a project and across an institution. For instance, the working group reviews relevant policies and processes annually, as part of its regular cycle, by including an evaluation stage in its yearly work, the group also considers questions about structure and governance. It also regularly determines how it can improve upon its primary charge, the information that it generates and disseminates.

Having a strict annual cycle encourages measuring the progress and, ultimately, the impact associated with the work of the group, with proof in the annual numbers. Such regular evaluation enhances the credibility of the working-group approach, as those across the university can see that Redlands is making better decisions toward realizing its ambitions. Moving enrollment management and financial aid into finance and administration is sufficiently unusual that analyzing and communicating impacts provides useful reassurance, particularly to faculty and academic affairs administrators. At a larger institution, one less defined by collegial relationships, professionalizing what might be considered academic decisions may not draw much attention. For example, at a research university, the faculty are not particularly involved in admissions, even at the level of setting policy. At a liberal arts college, there are somewhat greater expectations.

The working group also illustrates an effective means of addressing the question of who needs to be involved, both internally and externally, in a particular set of administrative decisions. The delegation of responsibilities at Redlands is successful because the working group is disciplined about staying within its jurisdiction and effective at keeping others on campus informed. The same is true of other sectors within Redlands. The trustees review the results from the working group each year, but properly limit their efforts to broader policy concerns; the president focuses on clarifying purposes; and the faculty concentrate on admissions policy, which is more directly related to their oversight of academic issues. The working group has developed the necessary trust with those across the entire campus, which is especially important at a smaller institution operating within the collegial tradition, to enable Redlands to have a strategic advantage by maximizing efficiency in its tuition discounting.

The approach can break down in governance. For example, if the working group became involved in policy matters that are best considered by the faculty and others in academic affairs, or if those with academic responsibilities were to become directly engaged in decisions that should be delegated to finance and administration. The institution must also invest in the infrastructure needed to generate required data, including the institutional research office and management information systems. In addition, policies and processes need to support the effort and to evolve themselves, as necessary; infrastructure must be prepared for the more accomplished students attracted by more effective discounting; and the annual tuition-discounting effort at Redlands must have clarity of purposes, as well as the right culture, to allow the degree of delegation it demands. The working group can generate the data that the tuition-discounting initiative requires, but it will only be effective if those across the institution are receptive to it.

CHAPTER NINE

Infrastructure

Maintaining Quality with Static Resources at Seminole Community College

S eminole Community College (SCC), in suburban Orlando, Florida, reversed a six-year period of steep decline in its college-credit enrollment in spectacular fashion. SCC was losing students to the aggressive marketing of competitor community colleges and was not well perceived in its community. It was either the "sleepy little college across from the flea market" or the place that students with discipline problems in high school attended. In the late 1990s, its new president, E. Ann McGee, hired a fresh leadership team and charged them with raising the visibility of the college in the surrounding community. The college initiated a strategic marketing and recruitment plan, making a concerted effort to change its image in the community to one identified with individual student success. The plan focused not on changing, but instead on clarifying, its mission, while articulating values and defining aspirations, always keeping the interests of prospective students in mind. In realizing its ambitions, SCC transformed what was a challenge into a strategic advantage.

The plan not only reframed the identity of the college, but also involved structural changes, such as SCC developing community relations and marketing departments. There were also significant adjustments to its operations, clarifying rules (policies), improving implementation (processes), and enhancing communication and data for decision support (information). The college instituted online registration, revamped catalogs, systematized the advising process, placed more emphasis on admissions, and launched a student activities program. SCC also made a significant investment in technological infrastructure, switching to a PeopleSoft management information system. Following these changes (and most likely because of them), SCC enrollment increased to include one-third of the high school graduates in Seminole County in 2005, up from 20 percent in 1997. The college also added three new campuses and other facilities, significantly enlarging its physical infrastructure. SCC grew to become the tenth largest of the 28 community colleges in Florida, and was the 11th fastest-growing community college in the nation in 2003.

Such expansion is not necessarily rewarded in the Florida community college system, however. SCC became the community college in the state with the lowest funding per full-time-equivalent (FTE) student. The question at the college became one of maintaining the capacity and quality it has built, particularly within a context of static, or even declining, resources in relative terms under the formula Florida uses to fund community colleges. The impressive growth at SCC requires additional infrastructure, not only in the buildings that it has added to its several campuses and its investment in technology, but also in the personnel that are a necessary asset. SCC needs to enhance the instructional and administrative capacity of the institution. Strategic management might contribute to enabling the college to withstand the resource pressures and resulting infrastructure shortages that are increasingly common in higher education, especially at public institutions with state-appropriated funds in decline.[1]

Infrastructure as an Element

Few institutions avoid the challenges and frustrations associated with insufficient infrastructure, whether it is an inability to hire the necessary faculty and administrators (or even attract enough paying students at certain universities or colleges), construct or maintain needed buildings and other facilities, and keep pace with the demands in both instructional and information technology. Stagnation—or even reductions in infrastructure, sometimes over multiple years—is hardly uncommon across universities or colleges. Faculty retirements are increasingly filled not by other hires in tenure-significant positions, but instead by those on short-term contracts; deferred maintenance is a challenge on many campuses, as needed repairs and renovations to buildings are often the first items cut from budgets in difficult economic times; and keeping up with changes in technology and replacing outdated equipment is an ongoing problem. Few institutions have the resources that they require to maintain their current commitments while making investments toward realizing their aspirations not to mention having financial assets kept in reserve for a "rainy day."

The expansion of activities outside of the academic core that marks contemporary higher education has shifted the nature of human infrastructure within institutions and across institutional types, with more reliance on temporary faculty members and greater outsourcing of personnel elsewhere in the institution. Furthermore, research university faculty are increasingly involved in outside ventures, often as individual entrepreneurs, and institutions have come to expect auxiliary enterprises such as housing and dining to generate revenues in excess of expenses. A growing acceptance of professional management, even over academic programs, has accompanied these trends toward disposable faculty and academic capitalism, with the proportion of administrators to full-time faculty shifting dramatically in favor of the former (Toma 2007; Rhoades 2005; Collis 2004). As the way institutions are financed is changing, with an increasing reliance on fund raising, and universities and colleges are adding significant infrastructure in external affairs, both in people and in systems. External research funding has become more important, particularly at research universities, which also requires building a specialized administrative-support network.

In seeking to attract the desirable students that drive prestige while keeping up with the Joneses, selective institutions—and even some community colleges—have instead made significant investments in their physical infrastructure (Toma 2006). There is a trend toward building splashy academic buildings, such as science buildings at liberal arts colleges and business schools at research universities. Students increasingly expect institutions, including community colleges, to provide the latest technology—and these new or renovated building do not disappoint. Particularly at more selective, residential institutions, students and their parents, accustomed to increasingly luxurious lifestyles at home, can demand the same environment on campus. Americans have long had a propensity toward grand campuses, with institutions expressing their aspirations through buildings, so the current construction boom associated with privatization and commercialization

Infrastructure
A Perspective on the Research Literature
Lisa Wolf-Wendel
University of Kansas

Infrastructure consists of the capital assets of an institution and constitutes a significant investment for any university or college—one that requires periodic maintenance and upgrading (Balderston 1995; Winston 1993). The concept is usually narrowly defined, as facilities and perhaps as people (Balderston 1995). Bensimon and Neumann (1993) discuss infrastructure in terms of two cases involving new presidents: one who focuses on improving human resources and another who concentrates on the physical plant. The former is a common topic in organizational literature, while the latter is discussed in a discrete set of literature on higher education. There is a considerable amount of writing on technological infrastructure in higher education (Bates 2000). On this topic, Green (1996) reminds us to keep an institution's mission, strategic direction, and future in mind when changing its technology. Financial infrastructure is also significant in building organizational capacity, as Simpson (1991) notes when connecting financial and academic policy.

Institutions must have sufficient infrastructure in place to be successful in any endeavor, whether it be in delivering instruction, developing research, providing services, or otherwise. It is folly to attempt to transform a university or college without considering how its existing infrastructure will be employed, adapted, upgraded, or replaced. Crampton and Thompson (2003), drawing from the K–12 sector, caution that even the most promising reforms will fail without the proper physical environment. For instance, if an institution increases its enrollment, it must have the necessary capacity in its classrooms, residence halls, libraries, and other facilities. Classrooms also need to be the right mix between smaller seminar rooms and larger lecture halls for the curriculum being offered. Moreover, a university or college will also require the faculty needed to teach additional or different courses, adequate instructional technology and management information systems, and the necessary financial resources to pay for it all. An illustration of the latter might be the startup packages required by faculty engaged in laboratory research.

Institutions often postpone attention to their infrastructure needs (Fink 2005; Bensimon and Neumann 1993). Adding or replacing needed personnel is increasingly difficult as budgets tighten. Similarly, a lack of resources to maintain, upgrade, or construct facilities and technological infrastructure is increasingly common, particularly given ever-rising costs (Maltz and DeBlois

(continued)

2005). With technology, concurrent upgrades are often necessary in security and identity management, management information systems, instructional support, and distance learning, which require institutions to make difficult decisions in prioritizing their needs. Deferred maintenance is another problem (Manns and Opp 2005)—one that has long been identified as urgent, but that seems to defy being addressed through a comprehensive strategy (Rush and Johnson 1989).

in higher education is consistent with our history of attempting to impress with our campuses.

In addition, the strategy of moving functions to the periphery of universities or colleges has included the expansion of "convenience" academic programs, often part-time bachelor's and master's degree programs in professional fields that serve adult students off-site or through distance learning efforts. The latter requires significant investments in technological infrastructure, with instructional technology costs also increasing across institutions. Several universities and colleges are also concerned about whether legacy management information systems are sufficiently robust to meet campus needs—and about the expense and disruption associated with installing new systems.

Seminole Community College and Maintaining Quality with Static Resources

Established in 1965 as Seminole Community College, the institution provides instruction in a variety of settings: at its four campuses and two instructional centers; at businesses, high schools, and other facilities throughout Seminole County; and through its distance-learning programs and corporate college. The original Sanford–Lake Mary campus provides two-year college-credit degrees; specialized career certificates; continuing professional education; customized workplace training; adult education; and community, leisure, and youth programs. The University of Central Florida began offering five complete baccalaureate programs there in 2004, increasing it to 20 such programs in 2008. In 2009, the institution changed its name to Seminole State College of Florida, recognizing the addition of its first four-year degree, a bachelor of applied science in interior design. The move to offering the baccalaureate reflects a national trend among community colleges. In 1986, the college opened its Hunt Club facility, which evolved into its Altamonte Springs campus. In 1996, the Seminole board of trustees approved the purchase of a 161-acre site in Oviedo for the development of a third campus, opening SCC at Oviedo, located near the University of Central Florida, with a complement of college-credit, technical, continuing education, and personal-enrichment class offerings. SCC added its fourth campus, an economic development center at Heathrow, in 2007.

Seminole County includes the northern suburbs of Orlando and has a rapidly expanding and increasingly affluent population. The Florida High Tech Corridor includes Seminole County, fostering industrial growth in several forms. Most notable is the establishment of the corporate headquarters for the American Automobile Association (AAA) and the emergence of high-tech manufacturers such as Veritas, Siemens ICN, and InterVoice Brite. With the opening of an international complex and the enlargement of its domestic terminal, Sanford–Orlando Airport has become the third-busiest international port of entry in Florida.

SCC aspires "to serve the community by providing a learning-centered, high-quality educational institution that anticipates and meets the needs of the community by providing a comprehensive range of programs and services." To accompany its mission statement, SCC developed a set of promises, including faculty and administrators who "foster a caring and professional relationship with students and the community." The college also pledges exemplary academic programs providing the first two years of university studies, career and technical programs that lead directly to employment or career advancement, continuing education programs that offer opportunities for advancement or recertification, and adult education programs directed toward strengthening basic academic skills and earning a high school diploma. SCC has created needed student development services to support these programs. In addition, the college strives to advance business, industry, and educational partnerships to enhance the economic development of its service region. Finally, it is involved in offering leisure and personal development programs that "contribute to the enrichment of the community."

In February 1996, McGee became the second president since the founding of the college. She had previously served as a faculty member in English and speech and as dean of students at Florida Keys Community College, as provost for the South Campus of Broward Community College (BCC), and as the campus-wide vice president for development and the executive director of the BCC foundation. A five-member board of trustees governs SCC, and there are also advisory committees for several programs. Under McGee, SCC's vision is "to be renowned, first and foremost, for its enduring commitment to learning and focus on individual student success." The college seeks to fulfill its mission and aspirations by being, as it terms it, community-connected and future-focused. In doing so, it concentrates on developing a collaborative and technologically advanced learning environment where students are the first priority; championing diversity and inclusiveness, both in the hiring of faculty and staff and in its student body; ensuring excellent programs that prepare students for success, including those related to corporate, community, academic, and internal partnerships; and advancing institutional effectiveness through ongoing assessment.

In 2004, when we visited SCC, the college employed 161 full-time faculty members (that figure increased to over 200 in 2008 academic year), and about 1100 administrative and professional staff, career-services personnel, part-time faculty members, and other regular part-time employees. The college enrolled 31,995 students, roughly 46 percent in A.A. and A.S. degree programs. Women comprised 58 percent of its students; minority students were 38 percent of the student population—a figure that had been increasing—with slightly more Latinos than African Americans; and the college enrolled almost 1200 international students from 119 different countries. The average age of its total student population was 31 (28 for credit-seeking students).

The college projected steady growth, estimating (during 2004) a headcount of 37,000 students by 2010 and between 41,000 and 55,000 students by 2020. The population of Seminole County, then 350,000, was anticipated to increase by almost 10 percent during the decade beginning in 2000, with impressive increases expected to continue beyond 2010. In 2008, SCC tuition and fees for college-credit courses were about $2500 for full-time students, compared with over $3500 at the University of Central Florida, the University of Florida, and Florida State University. SCC charged approximately $81 per credit hour for Florida residents and $287 for non-Florida residents, increasing modestly (from $75 and $275) over the previous four years. In fiscal year (FY) 2003, SCC received 64 percent of its revenue from the state and 34 percent from tuition; the college had a $46.5 million budget that year.

In 2004, SCC faced challenges moving forward, not only to maintain what it had established, but also to build its capacity to accommodate needed expansion to serve a growing community in an environment characterized by the prospect of continuing insufficient resources, especially in instructional and administrative personnel. Faculty and staff were overextended, putting the student-service ethos at SCC at risk. Facilities issues were somewhat more readily addressed, given how Florida funds community colleges, with funding for buildings more accessible than for employees to work within them. By 2009, SCC was completing an $85 million makeover of its Sanford–Lake Mary campus, and it had already constructed multiple new campuses. Being able to afford enhancements in physical infrastructure can pose challenges. For instance, SCC was concerned about how to administratively and culturally remain "one college," even as it was becoming more physically decentralized, adding the new Altamonte Springs and Heathrow campuses and continuing its operations at Oviedo and Sanford–Lake Mary. SCC also had considerable success in developing its technological infrastructure, leveraging resources creatively, including in making advances in its mechanisms for decision support and communications through a new management information system. However, persistent and worsening shortages in full-time human resources threatened to eclipse progress in other infrastructure areas. Infrastructure at SCC thus provided advantages and challenges in strategy and management as the institution moved forward, particularly in the context of what are likely to be persistent resource pressures.

Florida confronts various difficulties in higher education, including a demand for higher education that exceeds its supply—especially in the community college sector, which serves proportionately more students in Florida than in other states—as its population continues to increase (although more slowly than before) relative to other regions of the United States. There are also lags in achievement among traditionally underrepresented groups, and Florida is well behind national averages in areas such as degree production (Pappas Consulting Group 2007). Public financing of public higher education in Florida has increased over time, as it has in other states, but not to the degree necessary to match escalating costs (McGuinness 2005). Like Florida, many states are appropriating a smaller proportion of their overall budgets for higher education, instead allocating their resources to pressing needs in health care (which consumes half of most state budgets), as well as to corrections, homeland security, infrastructure, and primary and secondary education (Toma 2006; Zusman 2005; J. Lee and Clery 2004; Longanecker 2004).

State funding as a proportion of the budgets of public institutions declined nationally from 46 percent in 1980 to 36 percent in 2004. The nine research universities in the University of California system offer a dramatic illustration, going from 37 percent in 1990 to 21 percent in 2004, with tuition increases comprising only two-thirds of what replaced the lost appropriated funds (Zusman 2005). Nevertheless, the contribution by states has continued to be significant, over $7500 per FTE student on average nationally (Markowitz 2006). Meanwhile, higher educational institutions themselves are spending more on basic services, such as health benefits, technology, energy, and maintenance and construction (Society for College and University Planning 2005; Zusman 2005; J. Lee and Clery 2004). Selective institutions are also continuing to discount tuition, thus reducing the price paid by the most desirable students, and investing in infrastructure thought to attract them.

Such problems are exacerbated in Florida, given its tradition of low tuition and the creation of the Bright Futures merit scholarship program, funded by the state lottery, which puts an effective limit on what the state is willing to allow in tuition increases (Pappas Consulting Group 2007). The state experienced significant budget reductions in 2007 and 2008 even in advance of the severe economic recession. In higher education, this resulted in faculty salaries stagnating and layoffs and enrollment reductions at four-year institutions coming under serious consideration, the latter putting increasing pressure on community colleges. With the budget surpluses of the late 1990s and early 2000s at the federal and state levels becoming deficits, forecasts are for these trends to continue, with no real expectation of a return to 1990s levels of taxation (McGuinness 2005; Longanecker 2004). Institutions are looking to control costs where they can. One approach has been to outsource various nonacademic functions, including bookstores, dining, security, facilities maintenance, technology support, financial operations (budgeting, purchasing, billing, payroll, etc.), and even fund raising (Collis 2004; J. Lee and Clery 2004). Universities and colleges are also looking to generate revenues by expanding activities with commercial potential, such as revenue-generating, part-time degree programs for working professionals, as well as by increasing their contracts for corporate training, reliance on revenues from auxiliary services, attempts at private fund raising, and quests for research funding.

Tuition has also increased across higher education, even in Florida, but not at a sufficient pace to cover increasing costs. Nationally, the poorest families spent 6 percent of their income in 1980 to pay community college tuition, and 12 percent in 2000, with a similar doubling from 13 to 25 percent for four-year public colleges and universities (J. Lee and Clery 2004). McGuinness (2005) notes that tuition at public institutions, while increasing markedly, was low to begin with, particularly when compared with the price charged by private institutions. Moreover, public institutions continue to charge less than what it costs to educate their students (Gayle, Tewarie, and White 2003). Meanwhile, both the states and the federal government have reduced their commitment to need-based aid, and there has been a shift from grants to loans, beginning in the early 1980s, with loans presently at 80 percent of the mix, as opposed to 25 percent in 1975 (Gladieux, King, and Corrigan 2005; Longanecker, 2004). Concerns about rapidly rising tuition prices and growing indebtedness have increasingly become the subject of political rhetoric. Also, some states have acted to limit tuition increases, often in essentially symbolic ways, such as announcing specific figures for the tuition that entering students will pay across their four years of attending a given public institution, calling it a "freeze" (Morphew 2007). Budget pressures on institutions such as SCC are unlikely to decrease in the near future, making investments in human, physical, technological, and financial infrastructure, as well as in other areas, increasingly difficult.

Purposes and Infrastructure at Seminole Community College

SCC clarified its purposes when McGee arrived, sharpening its identity as a student-, community-, and future-focused institution. The college engaged in planning more aggressively, which not only had promise in enhancing accountability, but also in underscoring aspirations—thus connecting the information and purposes elements in strategic management. Over the past decade, the reputation of the college has improved steadily and significantly, in part through achieving the important goal in enhancing enrollment. SCC will likely continue to be constrained by challenges associated with insufficient infrastructure, with no apparent answer to the question of how to attain needed expansion in personnel, technology, and facilities in the context of continued limited resources. Yet SCC has an essential advantage in knowing what it has become and where it wants to head as an institution.

Despite such clarity in its purposes, limited resources have frustrated SCC in realizing its mission and aspirations. SCC ranked 28th among 28 community colleges in Florida in funding per FTE student in 2004. Even were the state to adjust the funding formula, resources might well still not be available from Tallahassee to fund various needs. Most significantly, SCC has been unable to add full-time faculty or administrators to match its rapid growth in enrollment. It is relying heavily upon adjunct faculty—and it is coming close to exhausting the pool of those who are qualified and willing. Also, in stretching its staff it is nearing the breaking point in providing the student services that are so mission critical. SCC is constructing and renovating facilities using more readily available state funds, so its physical infrastructure is less of a concern. The main concern is whether the college will have the personnel to adequately staff these new facilities. The challenges related to human infrastructure thus not only threaten the realization of the mission and aspirations of the institution, but also the positive organizational culture it has developed over time.

Technology has become an advantage for SCC, providing enhanced administrative capacity. The college has had notable success in leveraging partnerships (that included significant discounts) with providers such as Dell, Microsoft, and Novell. The college recently implemented a PeopleSoft system, integrating financial, human resources, and student systems, impressively completing the task in 14 months. There were the usual frustrations associated with such a major overhaul, but improvements in the information technology infrastructure at SCC have enhanced institutional research, provided better data for decision support, and significantly improved administrative processes at the college. Ingenuity here has served SCC well, but even the exercise of great creativity is unlikely to solve other infrastructure problems at the college, particularly in staffing.

Connecting with the Other Elements

In determining its *structure* and *governance*, SCC is clear about its desire to be one college, as opposed to several separate campuses. Its lack of ambiguity about its desired direction is an institutional advantage, but actually arraying people to do their work (structure) and resolving who will make what decisions (governance) is still a challenge in any organization. The college has to resolve several issues, such as what decisions it should make at the campus and unit level; whether and how policies and processes can be determined at the institutional-wide; and where information should reside. These basic questions of structure and governance are hardly straightforward, particularly given how its culture of local means of getting things done is so important in the success of the college.

Such difficulties only become more pronounced when an institution is expanding as rapidly as SCC is, adding to its physical infrastructure through the establishment of multiple campuses. Illustrations from neighboring institutions suggested what to avoid to SCC—a structure where units compete for resources and where there are differing administrative philosophies and practices from campus to campus. Having one dean or chair per academic department across the institution reduces competition between and among campuses. However, there are disadvantages associated with having such dispersed units, including in developing and maintaining a productive campus culture. Physical proximity is important in making decisions collaboratively and through informal efforts, with technology a partial, imperfect substitute for physical presence.

Both faculty members and administrators at SCC recognize that some restructuring is needed to increase efficiency, both in the interests of squeezing more from existing resources and in launching new campuses. There is a governance component to restructuring, with some faculty concerned that the process will be from the top down, with decisions simply announced, given their negative perceptions about who presently makes what decisions at SCC. Also, there is an interest in protecting what is already working at SCC as the institution expands. For instance, the college has strong informal networks of midlevel administrators, especially chairs and those in student services, which enables effective decision making through both formal and informal means. Furthermore, the lack of depth in personnel puts pressure on governance at SCC, as there are not always people in place throughout the organization capable of making the necessary decisions. Restructuring will help here, but it alone cannot solve certain problems, particularly in an environment where decision making is commonly decentralized. Another governance challenge is that the administration is not noted for making quick decisions, instead preferring a consensus approach, which can prove frustrating.

The recent implementation of a PeopleSoft management information system promises to improve decision making at SCC, as with increasing the administrative consistency across the college that is needed to realize its one-college goal. This new infrastructure has prompted SCC to clarify various *policies* and consider the coherence between and among them. However, even the system cannot overcome the disincentive in Florida to commit things to writing, due to its broad open records laws. There are also difficulties related to enforcing the revised policies consistently from campus to campus at SCC, given the differences in subcultures and the other elements (although not purposes) at these disjunct sites.

SCC has developed new *processes* to accompany these rules, again building on the enhanced capacity provided by the PeopleSoft system. For instance, the registrar has used the more robust processes made available to put limits on exceptions and overrides, enhancing the equal treatment of all students in registering for courses. SCC has changed several business processes in response to thin staffing, with the college community taking pride in doing more with less, particularly in making such processes student-friendly, but there are always limits to how much an institution can expect and individuals can give. Restructuring at SCC will necessitate some changes in how various rules are implemented. For instance, staffing shortages may require flatter processes, since with fewer people there can be fewer levels. Scarcities in its human infrastructure already mean lower-level personnel at SCC have to perform multiple tasks and are charged with making more decisions at the college, which is both an advantage, as it empowers workers, and a disadvantage, as it can overextend them.

Even the best processes can still be slowed because of difficulties related to *information*, especially in having clean and accessible data, even with a good information technology platform. The PeopleSoft system at SCC has enriched the flow of information between units and expanded its internal audit capacities. Such capacity in information has the potential to change the administrative culture at SCC, enhancing not only communications, but also decision making and accountability. Nevertheless, richer flows of information for decision support can only accomplish so much when there is not an adequate human infrastructure to staff the college.

Shortages in infrastructure are also a challenge in maintaining the *culture* of the institution. The SCC community believes there is a can-do attitude characteristic of the institution—and that culture is a great advantage, in that faculty and administrators tend to work hard and care about students, providing a personal touch. However, faculty and staff are significantly overextended as enrollments have increased dramatically and personnel levels have remained static. A significant challenge for SCC related to its culture is that the entire campus community is tired. There is concern across the college about losing the ability to serve students in ways consistent with how it believes that it should. Expansion has also caused the SCC community to question how it will maintain the essential character of the college as it continues to decentralize further onto multiple campuses. As at any institution, the physical infrastructure of SCC influences its culture. SCC is committed to being one college, despite having its functions spread across several locations, and has made structural decisions accordingly. Having people disconnected spatially tends to work against having a coherent overall culture, however, even with other elements, such as structure or policies, emphasizing commonalities.

Another difficulty is that SCC possesses something of the disconnect standard in higher education between administrative and faculty cultures, with the latter not always certain about the motives of the former. There is occasional, but significant, dissatisfaction with how decisions are made. These challenges may be associated to some degree with structure—functions being arrayed across multiple campuses—and some with infrastructure shortages, causing people to be overextended. Restructuring might provide some relief, especially in response to concerns about the need to have decision making be more rapid and efficient, but it alone is not the solution. There is also a persistent danger of disrupting the informal means of influence, especially involving department chairs, that are so important in mediating the relationship between senior administrators and the SCC faculty.

➤INFRASTRUCTURE AND ALIGNING THE OTHER ELEMENTS:
A CHECKLIST

In confronting a situation where the infrastructure needs essential to maintaining quality are combined with static resources, those leading and managing institutions might consider the following related to infrastructure:

☐   What infrastructure is required for an institution to advance its mission and achieve its aspirations? Once it began to increase enrollments, SCC needed additional people, facilities, technology, and finances. Resources, especially those provided through state appropriations, given the effective limits on tuition and other local revenue sources, are crucial in securing these assets.

☐   Are deficiencies in infrastructure hindering the institution in advancing its purposes? The funding formula in Florida enabled SCC to construct new facilities, but did not always provide the resources needed for the institution to hire the necessary faculty and administrators to adequately populate them. SCC used corporate partnerships to support instructional technology improvements, but, as with facilities, until it had the people it needed, serving its mission meant those already employed there had to stretch themselves beyond a sustainable point. It is also important to have the right kinds of human, physical, technological, and financial assets. For instance, community colleges need faculty who embrace their teaching and access missions, while research universities require faculty members with a different orientation.

☐   Can restructuring contribute to addressing shortcomings in infrastructure? Sometimes there are efficiencies to be found in reassigning people, but doing so can be disruptive and may only have a modest impact. At SCC, the challenge was not necessarily how it arrayed its people, but simply in having enough of them to serve its students. In making the decision to be one college, having single units work across its various campus, SCC may realize some structural efficiencies, but these are challenges associated with fragmentation.

☐ Are inefficiencies in who is making what decisions adding to the problem of having an inadequate infrastructure? As with structure, there were some inefficiencies related to governance at SCC. Some of these were attributable to shortages in faculty and administrators, as well as to the structure associated with operating academic programs and service functions across multiple campuses. The management information system implemented at the college provided possibilities for increasing SCC's efficiency, including enabling those at more local levels within the institution to make more and better decisions.

☐ Would better policies and processes contribute to getting more out of less? As with restructuring, there is only so much that can be accomplished by improving the rules the institution operates under and the means by which it gets things done, especially when there are infrastructure shortages. Nonetheless, institutions can readily address such problems without always needing to invest resources. Solving other difficulties, as with changing a culture or even with restructuring units, are a more significant undertaking.

☐ Would better data to support decision making and more robust communication across functions increase efficiency, thus somewhat alleviating infrastructure shortages? Once again, doing so can help, but it cannot overcome simply not having enough people. At some point, an institution is going to need to hire personnel, but information is critical in maximizing where it allocates these faculty and administrators, and in enhancing their effectiveness in making decisions once employed.

☐ How can infrastructure change, either strengthening or weakening, the essential character of an institution? Shortages in personnel at SCC stretched its faculty and administrators to nearly the breaking point, putting at risk the positive culture of institution perceived itself to have. Also, having facilities on multiple campuses has made coherence in culture across the institution more of a challenge. As at other institution types, enrolling more or different types of students can mean adding facilities, personnel, or technology that require the culture of the institution to adapt.

Applying the Framework

The struggle to attract the human resources needed to adequately staff a booming community college, as well as the desire to remain one college amid expansion onto multiple campuses, illustrates various actions leaders and senior managers can consider in pursuing strategic management. At a public community college, such challenges tend to be the responsibility of the president, in his or her capacity in securing resources, as through work at the state capitol. At a private institution, building infrastructure would involve considerable attention to private fund raising. For facilities projects, the vice president responsible for finance and administration is likely to be deeply involved, as is the chief information officer with technology investments and the provost and academic deans in hiring faculty. These individuals can devote the time needed to plan and develop an undertaking, but the president is primarily responsible for finding the resources that make it possible. He or she is also the one who will need to emphasize the positive impacts of previous investments, so as to justify future ones.

Because the president is likely to have the clearest sense of the institutional purposes that various infrastructure initiatives are intended to advance, he or she is best positioned to mobilize the entire university or college community. The same is true of ensuring—across a given initiative—the understanding of the other elements relative to the initiative and how they must align for a project to be successful. The kinds of efforts that are likely to advance appreciation of such institutional priorities and emphasize the contours of strategic management, both among those responsible for a project and across a university or college, tend to differ in various areas within an institution. Given the more hierarchical nature of community colleges, the president is again crucial here, employing both symbolic measures to accentuate important messages and allocating discretionary resources to emphasize priorities. While operational concerns relative to an infrastructure initiative can be the responsibility of senior managers, the president is instrumental in clarifying purposes and developing culture.

Even for a president focused on and effective in doing so, serendipity is sometimes a factor when infrastructure is involved, such as unexpected funds becoming available for construction, hiring, or purchases. External constituents over whom the president has no real control—such as legislatures, state boards and agencies, banks, and donors—can drive infrastructure initiatives. Funding is typically the most uncertain aspect of most infrastructure projects, even in a healthy economy. A strategic plan may justify an increase in faculty members in certain areas, the need for additional or renewed facilities, or upgrades in technology, but such efforts are dependent on funding. SCC also illustrates the relationship between infrastructure needs and issues of structure and governance. As the institution has expanded to multiple campuses, questions of how to array people to do their work and whom to charge with making what decision have become more complicated. The same is true of policies or processes, but aligning these with improvements in infrastructure, such as by enhancing the management information system at SCC, is more straightforward. Additionally, even the seemingly basic matter of communicating within an academic or administrative unit is complicated when it is spread across multiple physical settings.

SCC illustrates most clearly that the primary challenge related to infrastructure shortages is in maintaining a positive institutional culture. Especially over time, shortages in staffing, buildings, computing, and funds tend to discourage people—eventually even the most committed ones within an institution. Infrastructure issues suggest several questions—the answer to which is most likely "no." Can an institution, like SCC, that is ultimately concerned with providing access to postsecondary education within its surrounding community, serve its mission if it does not continue to expand as demand dictates, even if it does not have sufficient resources to do so? Can any organization continue to function with persistently inadequate staffing levels, or will it partially shut down as components of the organization-as-system become overwhelmed and fail? How much can restructuring really accomplish in a situation where the necessary resources are not present? In the absence of critical infrastructure needs, can more robust processes, coupled with information to enable better decision support and assessment, be sufficient in and of themselves to provide needed capacity within an organization? Does it make sense to construct buildings, even when resources are available, if there is not enough staff to populate them? In the end, increases in enrollment and programs, even in the hardest economic times, require investments in human, physical, technological, and financial assets if an institution is going to prosper—or even maintain its current position.

CHAPTER TEN

Culture

Invigorating Undergraduate Education at the
University of Georgia

The University of Georgia (UGA) is enrolling increasingly accomplished classes of undergraduate students each year, coming over the past decade to be ranked in the top twenty among public research universities. However, the intellectual culture at the institution, including as measured by the National Survey of Student Engagement (NSSE), has not kept pace with changes in the composition of its students. In recognition, the UGA provost formed a task force to explore how to invigorate undergraduate education at the institution. The recommendations of the task force illustrate that addressing such a broad challenge requires attention to each of the eight BOC elements, particularly culture.

In attempting to change its character toward becoming more intellectually rigorous in its academic programs, the university considered structural adjustments, as in reducing the number of required courses within majors; reshaped policies and processes, as in having more tenured or tenure-track faculty teaching undergraduate students; and invested in infrastructure, as in enhancing study-abroad offerings. Given the academic nature of the reforms, involving faculty in their governance role was essential. Advancing an initiative such as reinvigorating undergraduate education requires aligning these elements with the mission and aspirations of the institution, contributing to the organizational capacity required to realize its purposes.

Culture as an Element

Culture is the essential character of an institution embodied in its shared norms, values, and beliefs and the ways in which these are made tangible (Toma, Dubrow, and Hartley 2005; Martin 2002). It conveys identity, facilitates commitment, enhances stability, guides sensemaking, and defines authority (Kuh and Whitt 1988). Culture has both substance and form, although its substance is less apparent, residing in what is explicitly understood or even implicitly held by those within a community. It assumes its form in the symbols, language, narratives, and practices that announce and reinforce meaning (Trice and Beyer 1993). These forms are the more observable actions—logos and colors, anecdotes and jokes, stories and myths, ceremonies and rituals—that affirm and communicate the character of a particular organization both to those within it and to outsiders (Toma, Dubrow, and Hartley 2005; Schein 1992). Nonetheless, without the substance of a distinctive set of norms, values, and beliefs behind them, such cultural forms mean little.

In both substance and form, culture is not static, but instead can either evolve or devolve, strengthening or weakening within an organization. As in the UGA case, leaders and senior managers commonly initiate efforts to change institutional culture. Hartley (2002a) suggests that attempting to manage institutional culture requires clarifying purposes. It also requires a recognition that culture, by definition, is so deeply ingrained within any organization that it is unlikely to transform overnight. Culture has been trumpeted as a panacea for a wide array of organizational needs and ills, but universities and colleges cannot simply impose a productive one (Toma, Dubrow, and Hartley 2005; Schein 1992). Sackmann (1997) argues that organizational culture is more pluralistic, diverse, paradoxical, and contradictory than is often thought; Harris and Ogbonna (2002) discuss unintended consequences associated with attempting to manage culture; Parker (2000) argues that culture cannot really be managed; and Ogbor (2001) describes corporate culture as corporate hegemony. Tierney (1988) suggests that culture is not an absolute, with people interpreting it in their own ways, as opposed to more functionalist conceptions in which shared understandings within an organization enable managers to predict and manipulate it. The opposites of consensus, consistency, and clarity may be just as likely to be present in an organization (Toma, Dubrow, and Hartley 2005).

Both Bergquist (1992) and Birnbaum (1988) pose typologies of dominant institutional cultures, with Bergquist categorizing institutions as either collegiate,
managerial, developmental, or negotiating, and Birnbaum describing them as collegial, bureaucratic, political, or anarchical. Both underscore that although one
culture may be dominant on a given campus, the other three will generally be
present to some degree. Collegial cultures feature lasting relationships and careful consensus within an organization-as-community. In a managerial culture, identity and meaning are derived from the structure of the organization, venerating
fiscal responsibility and effective supervision. Birnbaum frames this general type
as the bureaucratic institution, with legitimized authority and formal structure
as paramount values. Bergquist's developmental culture focuses on the personal
growth of its individual members, intending to address the shortcomings of the
collegiate culture. His negotiating culture is associated with how politics, through
negotiation and confrontation, determine the allocation of resources—and is a
reaction to a managerial culture. Birnbaum's political institution is similar, in
which the basis of institutional culture is shifting alliances founded on the competition for resources. He suggests that organized anarchy may be the model for
research universities, which have no single culture, with only the broadest values
being of real importance, such as the continued viability of the institution.

There are also subcultures within any institution, as with those associated
with faculty, administrators, and students. Faculty culture is influenced by the
various cultures associated with the overall society, professionals generally, the
academic profession, a particular discipline, a given institution, and a chosen inquiry paradigm (Toma 1997; Tierney and Rhoads 1993; Austin 1990; Clark 1987).
Across disciplinary domains—the humanities, the social sciences, the natural
sciences, and the professions—faculty members tend toward different personal
orientations and professional objectives, thus constituting various subcultures
(Gaff and Wilson 1971). Becher and Trowler (2001) draw the distinctions among
disciplines on two axes: applied versus pure and hard versus soft (see also Weidman, Twale, and Stein 2001; Biglan 1973). Applied disciplines focus on know-how
and the enhancement of professional practice, with engineers (hard) approaching their work more quantitatively and social work faculty (soft) concentrating on
qualitative distinctions (Stark, Lowther, and Haggerty 1987). Pure disciplines either are more cumulative and concerned with simplification and finding consensus, as in the sciences (hard), or are like the humanities in being reiterative and
concerned with complexity, rarely reaching agreement (soft). Administrators may
split into subcultures along similar orientations, such as academic affairs, student

Culture: A Perspective on the Research Literature

Greg Dubrow
University of California, Berkeley

Burton Clark was instrumental in introducing the idea of organizational culture into the study of higher education, using the concept to explain the nature of distinctive colleges (Clark 1970), as well as emphasize the importance of saga in the development of a cultural identity within an institution (Clark 1972). Clark defined the latter as a "collective understanding of unique accomplishment in a formally established group" (p. 500), arguing that sagas create the self-conception within a university or college that is so important in institutional governance. The mission and aspirations of an institution are central to understanding its culture, but so is the influence of history, such as with the sagas associated with the principles and influence of founders or early leaders (Kuh, Schuh, and Whitt 1991; Clark 1972). Tierney (1988) emphasized the relationship between organizational effectiveness and strong, congruent cultures. He suggested that writing on academic management be broadened from their focus on planning and marketing, identifying six areas as central to studying any university or college: environment, mission, socialization, information, strategy, and leadership.

Kuh and Whitt (1988), in another important early work, define the substance of institutional culture as the articulation of what constitutes acceptable behavior, the espoused and enacted ideals of an institution, and the tenets used to define roles and relationships. They describe institutional culture in higher education as "the collective, mutually supporting patterns of norms, values, practices, beliefs, and assumptions that guide the behavior of individuals and groups in an institution of higher education and provide a frame of reference within which to interpret the meaning of events and actions on and off campus" (pp. 12–13). According to Sackmann (1991), the substance of institutional culture is composed of common descriptions ("what exists"), common practices ("how things are done"), prescriptions for repair and improvement ("how things should be done"), and reasons and explanations given for an event ("why things are done the way they are"). Schein (1992) suggests that institutional culture consists of the attributes that come to be taken for granted by those within an organization, thus providing a shared framework for addressing all manner of problems of adaptation and integration.

These norms, values, and beliefs require tangible forms to encourage organizational members to understand them, according to Trice and Beyer (1993), whether as (1) symbols (objects, settings, performers), (2) language (jargon, gestures, songs, humor, metaphors, proverbs), (3) narratives (stories, legends, sagas, myths), and (4) practices (rituals, taboos, rites, ceremonials). Schein (1992) portrays these forms as artifacts, which provide a lens to examine the espoused values and underlying assumptions of an organization. However conceptualized, these tangible forms transmit culture and thus meaning to individuals and groups. Hartley (2002a) writes about organizational change, a topic also explored by Kezar (2001) that links organizational culture and organizational change (Kezar and Eckel 2002). Finally, Toma, Dubrow, and Hartley (2005) update Kuh and Whitt (1988), with the specific aim of linking culture with its uses for institutions, particularly in generating the institutional identification and brand equity that are important in resource acquisition (Dubrow 2003; Toma 2003; Hartley 2002a).

affairs, business services, institutional advancement, and so forth. They may also divide themselves based on hierarchy, with executives, managers, and support staff having different outlooks. Finally, matters such as valuing autonomy and creativity over material rewards also tend to define faculty culture, with acculturation as graduate students and participation in shared governance as important characteristics (Ruscio 1987; Blau 1973; Gaff and Wilson 1971).

Student culture, like that of faculty and administrators, is marked by commonalities as well as distinctive subcultures, while also contributing to the broader institutional culture. Astin (1993) identifies seven types of students (scholars, social activists, artists, hedonists, leaders, status strivers, and the uncommitted); Clark and Trow (1966) describe four student subcultures (collegiate, vocational, academic, and nonconformist), based on patterns of shared beliefs developed by predisposition and in-group socialization; and Horowitz's (1987) historical approach identifies three groups (the college man, the outsider, and the rebel). Students enroll at a university or college for a multitude of reasons, whether in pursuing knowledge for its own sake, obtaining credentials for later work, engaging in a pleasing social environment, or otherwise (Spitzberg and Thorndike 1992). Student culture is both a reflection and a subset of youth culture, particularly as students step in and stop out of college and take longer to finish their baccalaureate degrees (Hummon 1994; Moffatt 1989).

The University of Georgia and Invigorating
Undergraduate Education

As the first state-chartered university in the United States, established in 1785 and designated as a land-grant institution in 1862, the University of Georgia has been governed since 1931 by the University System of Georgia, which now oversees 35 public four- and two-year institutions in the state. The main campus is in Athens, a town of 100,000 located 60 miles northeast of Atlanta. Among public research universities nationally, UGA ranks in the top 20, assuming that position during the 1990s as Georgia became the ninth-most-populous U.S. state and Atlanta one of the ten largest metropolitan areas in the country.

The HOPE scholarship program, covering tuition and fees for those graduating from Georgia high schools with a B or better grade point average for as long as they maintain that standing in college, has also contributed to UGA's increased national prominence. HOPE enables the university to compete favorably for the best students from a large state, with all but a few in-state freshmen entering UGA on the scholarship. UGA admits about one-half of its applicants, with about one-half of those admitted enrolling. The average SAT score for about 5000 entering freshmen approached 1250 in 2006, an increase from 1190 a decade earlier. Students not admitted to UGA in 2006 had an average SAT score of 1136, which was roughly the average for students admitted to the university in 1990. The average SAT score for the roughly 2500 students in the honors program was approximately 1440.

UGA enrolls approximately 34,000 students, 90 percent of whom attend full time, including about 24,500 undergraduates, 7000 graduate students, 1500 professional students, and a small number at a few satellite campuses. For the 2006 academic year, 85 percent of new freshmen attended Georgia high schools, 58 percent of UGA undergraduates were women, 17 percent represented minority groups, and 6 percent came from over 130 countries abroad. The retention rate for new freshman going into their sophomore year in 2006 was 92 percent, and the graduate rate after six years was around 80 percent. The cost of attending UGA is low, over $1000 below the median at flagship institutions within the 16 Southern Regional Education Board (SREB) states. In 2006, undergraduate tuition and fees were about $5000 for in-state students and $18,000 for out-of-state students.

The university has a budget of $1.3 billion, about $400 million of which comes in an annual appropriation from the state of Georgia, with HOPE worth another $100 million annually. It has 16 colleges and schools, including new schools of public health and ecology, and offers baccalaureate degrees in 140 fields. About one-quarter of UGA students participate in study-abroad programs, including at university facilities in England, Italy, and Costa Rica. The Georgia Bulldogs compete in the Southeastern Conference in 21 varsity sports, several of which attract national attention.

UGA students reported satisfied with their overall experience, rating it as "highly favorable" on the 2003 NSSE survey in numbers significantly greater than those at institutions identified as being similar in nature.[1] However, UGA undergraduates, again relative to students at peer institutions, were not being adequately challenged in their courses and characterized their efforts as simply "memorizing facts, ideas, or methods so you can repeat them pretty much in the same form." Furthermore, the survey found UGA students study less than students at comparable institutions, averaging 12 to 13 hour per week, while the standard articulated by faculty is 30-45 hours weekly. The NSSE results also indicated that Georgia students write less than those elsewhere (and significantly less when considering the writing of lengthy papers), with fewer seniors enrolling in a capstone course.

With these results in mind, Provost Arnett Mace convened a task force in fall 2004 to evaluate undergraduate education at Georgia and offer recommendations for improving it. He named Del Dunn, the vice president for instruction and a longtime member of the faculty, and Jere Morehead, the vice-provost for academic affairs and former director of the honors program, as cochairs, appointing 24 additional task force members from across the university. The task force began its work by reading and discussing various reports, such as the *Greater Expectations* report by the American Association of College and Universities (2002), and documents related to general education from UGA and its peer institutions. The task force then conducted interviews and focus groups with and solicited e-mailed comments from various faculty, administrators, and students, as well as involving relevant experts.

In its September 2005 report, the task force identified globalization, community, diversity, and information as societal trends requiring students to complete a new set of deeper, as opposed to broader, general education courses. The task force highlighted the need for students to understand research and the construction of knowledge; know history and government, as well as literature and the fine arts; appreciate diversity, including through foreign language study and experiences abroad; and reason quantitatively and express themselves effectively in speech and in writing. The task force made several specific proposals to be considered by various faculty governance committees. In addition to improving general education, the recommendations addressed the overall learning environment at UGA, as with changes in faculty rewards and teaching approaches. The recommendations, grounded in purposes and focused, ultimately, on culture, required the UGA community to consider accompanying changes across the BOC elements, with structure, governance, policies, processes, information, and infrastructure each addressed.

NSSE prompted action at UGA in somewhat the same way that external accountability efforts can. There are challenges associated with trying to even measure something as inherently qualitative as intellectual engagement, but this has hardly prevented states and accreditors from attempting to have institutions do so. States, fundamentally, expect their public universities and colleges to balance access, affordability, and accountability (Altbach 2005). They are interested in matters such as transfers from two-year to four-year institutions and links between higher and secondary education; public-sector tuition prices; workforce preparation, as in improving teacher education, and other aspects of local economic development; and retention and graduation, especially for underrepresented groups (Toma 2007; Altbach, Berdahl, and Gumport, 2005; University of Texas 2005; Enders 2004; Coulter 2003; Heller 2002; Zumeta 2001). Influenced by financial pressures, states are also increasingly sympathetic to private-sector management ideas, as with experimenting with initiatives such as connecting funding with performance (McLendon, Hearn, and Deaton 2006; Gayle, Tewarie, and White 2003; Heller 2002).

In such an environment, institutions no longer expect that states will provide funds with no strings attached (McGuinness 2005). The real issue is not if there is accountability, but whether it will be limited to proper topics measured in proper ways (McGuinness 2005; Pusser 2003). Even though demands have not proven to be particularly onerous, institutions still must increasingly justify their impact to more skeptical publics (Schmidtlein and Berdahl 2005; Dill 2003). Zusman (2005) contends that institutional autonomy has remained largely intact:

> Most policy makers' demands for evidence of student learning, increased faculty workload, and institutional performance on state-determined criteria have left much discretion to institutions to determine appropriate responses, though sometimes after extensive negotiations or discussions. Moreover, higher education institutions, especially universities with strong alumni support, alternative

revenue sources, and complex, loosely coupled structures, have considerable ability to adopt strategies to help retain institutional autonomy. (p. 145)

Perhaps of greater importance to selective universities and colleges is the pressure associated with their standing relative to peer and aspirational institutions. At UGA, lagging against similar institutions on the voluntary NSSE may provide a more powerful impetus to improving undergraduate education than any state mandate or influence related to accreditation. (Improving NSSE results is also a preemptive strike against state accountability demands, of course.) Strengthening the intellectual culture at UGA thus was not only consistent with its academic values, but also associated with maintaining its competitive advantage.

Purposes and Culture at the University of Georgia

The mission of UGA, similar to that of other U.S. flagship state universities, is reflected in its motto: "to teach, to serve, and to inquire into the nature of things." UGA has statewide commitments as the land-grant institution in Georgia, particularly through its public service and outreach unit. UGA is the most comprehensive and diversified institution in the state, providing instruction and degree programs in the humanities, social sciences, basic sciences, and fine arts (but not medicine or engineering, apart from areas connected with agriculture). It joins the Medical College of Georgia, the Georgia Institute of Technology (Georgia Tech), and Georgia State University as the primary site for graduate and professional education in the University System of Georgia. UGA balances serving the needs of the state, as with educating its most accomplished students, while being recognized both nationally and internationally for its research.

Upon arriving in Athens a decade ago from the presidency at Centre College in Kentucky, UGA President Michael F. Adams framed aspirations for the institution as the people of Georgia deserving the same world-class flagship university as those in states like Michigan, Virginia, North Carolina, and Texas. At worst, UGA endeavors to maintain its ranking among public research universities, particularly as measured by *U.S. News and World Report*, and is interested, as is common across institutions, in continuing to advance. UGA developed as a leading research university much later than other leading public institutions, beginning in the 1960s and 1970s. During the decade between 1986 and 1996, under President Charles B. Knapp, the university shed many of its characteristics as a Southern football school, with faculty credentials improving and better students enrolling, particularly with the advent of HOPE scholarships in the 1990s. Relative to its peers, UGA lags somewhat in sponsored research, suffering from the lack of programs in medicine and engineering, and is far less impressive in endowment and annual fund raising than the leading public institutions Adams featured.

UGA has moved ahead in its aspirations, as measured in the rankings, primarily through enrolling the more accomplished undergraduate students that comprise its entering classes. The NSSE data confirmed a general recognition on campus that UGA students are improving, while the curriculum being offered to them has stagnated. The university has not developed an intellectual culture among its undergraduates to match the caliber of the students now attending the institution. There is too much "party school" and "jock school" remaining at UGA—as validated regularly in rankings by *Playboy* and the *Princeton Review*. About one-quarter of UGA undergraduates are members of fraternities and sororities; Athens has a robust bar and music scene; and a large proportion of UGA undergraduates live off campus. Football continues to attract intense interest on campus, as it does among alumni and others across the state.

These aspects of the UGA culture are appealing to many prospective and current undergraduate students, offering a strategic advantage in recruitment. Yet academic values also matter to the university. Rising in the *U.S. News and World Report* rankings is an empty accomplishment without this being accompanied by a robust intellectual life on campus. Only the most socially inclined students fail realize that four years at UGA is an incomplete experience if they fail to invest in academic pursuits. The task force report stated the challenge in developing intellectual culture clearly:

> While individual faculty members strive to make each class intellectually challenging, a culture of low expectations has been allowed to take root in the University. In order to counter this development, students must be challenged to devote more time to their academic responsibilities, and faculty must be encouraged and rewarded for offering rigorous courses. Faculty and administrators should consistently insist on rigor, and students should demand it in all their courses.

Will UGA faculty, administrators, and students commit to enlivening undergraduate education and building intellectual culture at the institution—and what will doing so entail? Attention to purposes and culture, as well as aligning the other six BOC elements offers a point of departure.

Connecting with the Other Elements

Developing a new set of general education courses toward invigorating undergraduate education at UGA involved questions of *structure*. The task force appreciated that as the general education curriculum constituted one-half of the 120 credit hours needed to earn a degree in most programs, adding further requirements was unworkable. It recommended instead that departments consider whether they could reduce requirements for majors, taking advantage, as possible, of increasing flexibility in accreditation requirements. It also proposed using upper-division courses, when appropriate, for general education, encouraging a reduction in the number of survey courses. Another set of structural propositions, focused on adding depth and rigor to the general education curriculum, was to designate more courses as being writing intensive. The task force further suggested specific additions to the structure of general education at UGA: adding a requirement in moral reasoning and ethical behavior, having students complete two courses with a significant quantitative component, and increasing requirements in basic science.

An additional structural recommendation was to restructure orientation to include a more substantial academic component, introducing incoming students more completely to expectations within an intellectual community. Recognizing that students too frequently left Athens for long weekends, the task force also encouraged departments to schedule more classes meeting on Fridays, and recommended that the university hold more activities and events during the weekends, expand the operating hours of libraries and the campus fitness center, and discourage parents from sending freshmen to Athens with cars.

The task force recognized the *governance* issue of University System of Georgia (USG) requirements possibly frustrating the implementation of some of the structural and other changes proposed for UGA. The provost assured the university community that he would seek "special dispensation," as needed, from various USG policies, with UGA contending that it required local control on certain matters particular to its broader mission and scope than other USG institutions. Having various faculty committees act upon the many task force recommendations is another illustration of appropriately allocating decision making within the institution by group and level.

Changes in *policies* also advanced the goal of invigorating undergraduate education and strengthening intellectual culture at the university. One proposal was to encourage departments, perhaps through incentives, to have more tenured and tenure-track faculty teach courses taken by undergraduate students in their first and second years. Doing so would reverse a trend in the credit hours taught by faculty in non-tenure-significant appointments, which had increased from 33 percent in 2002 to 40 percent in 2004. Another change involved creating incentives through how the university calculates teaching loads, toward offering more one- and two-credit seminars by senior faculty. The task force also proposed recognizing and rewarding high-quality undergraduate teaching in the faculty review system, as well as initiating sabbaticals for tenured faculty members.

Another recommended change in policies intended to enhance intellectual culture involved considering whether advanced placement credit at UGA should be more difficult to earn, using it to assign students to particular levels of courses as opposed to allowing it to replace college-level courses. A related suggestion was to increase the requirements for admission to UGA from two to three high school courses in the same foreign language. The task force additionally proposed that all students should complete a capstone course in their major, which would incorporate a research project, with students graduating with honors required to take more than one such course. Another suggested change was to implement a plus-minus grading system to allow for greater differentiation in academic performance and thus strengthen the rigor of undergraduate courses. In a move to diminish alcohol use, the task force raised the possibility of a parental notification policy connected with students committing two or more alcohol-related offenses. The task force also suggested policies to reward students who participated in cultural events and engaged in leadership activities.

The task force understood that the *process* of reforming the general education curriculum needed to reside in the faculty governance system; it could not simply be imposed through the provost. It recommended that the university curriculum committee implement procedures for the periodic review of courses used to meet general education requirements, ensuring that they are satisfying stated learning goals for general education. The task force also proposed reviewing policies and processes at various student organizations, including fraternities and sororities, to ensure that they would not conflict with the intellectual climate of the university. Sorority rush, for instance, occurs around the first day of classes each fall, providing a significant distraction for those participating in it. Another recommended procedural change was to reduce the allotted time period for dropping and adding courses, attempting to address the problem of students doing so late in the semester, as well as to combat grade inflation.

Using NSSE data and other assessment tools to identify problems and measure outcomes related to the learning environment at UGA illustrates the need for *information* in the strategic management of universities and colleges. The task force encouraged the specification and assessment of learning outcomes associated with general education at the department level, as well as in individual courses. Doing so would better enable drawing on data in making decisions and setting policies. The task force additionally proposed an online course evaluation system with a uniform set of questions for all undergraduate courses that would include an item about student perceptions of the academic rigor of each course. A related set of changes involved enhancing the peer assessment of teaching, midterm evaluations by students, and the development of teaching portfolios.

There were also *infrastructure* investments that the task force proposed toward improving intellectual culture among undergraduates. The task force recommended enhancing staffing within the various units on campus focused on acquainting students with information resources, as with those responsible for developing study skills, the libraries, information technology services, and instructional support. It also advocated enlarging the mission of the Center for Teaching and Learning to refine the abilities of those who teach at the university. The task force proposed directing more resources toward hiring additional faculty, in order to decrease class sizes and student-faculty ratios, and suggested recruiting alumni experts as adjunct faculty and drawing on emeritus and emerita faculty to further increase capacity in teaching. It additionally recommended expanding academic advising into the residence halls, and proposed beginning an Office of Service Learning.

UGA also made investments in physical and technological infrastructure, most prominently with the opening in 2003 of the Student Learning Center, a 200,000-square-foot facility housing classrooms, study rooms, and an electronic library. The task force suggested that UGA expand its international educational opportunities, continuing its infrastructure investments in its facilities in England, Italy, and Costa Rica. When constructing or renovating buildings, the task force called for including instructional technology. UGA also began requiring first-year students to live on campus, making a commitment to increasing on-campus housing opportunities.

➤CULTURE AND ALIGNING THE OTHER ELEMENTS: A CHECKLIST
In undertaking an initiative such as invigorating undergraduate education, as at UGA, those leading and managing institutions might consider the following:

☐   What is the institution attempting to achieve relative to undergraduate education? UGA found that the established intellectual culture at the university was insufficient for the more accomplished undergraduate students it was enrolling. In not sufficiently challenging these students, the university was both not entirely fulfilling its instructional mission, as well as failing to align practices with progress related to its national standing. When institutions begin to realize their aspirations toward becoming more prestigious, their culture must evolve. One example is when a comprehensive university seeks to enhance research, thus requiring a different type of work from its faculty.

☐   How important is culture in realizing institutional purposes? The UGA community had a clear sense of the culture it intended to build, making structural and operational changes toward realizing it. Without such certainty, reforms in areas such as policies and infrastructure can lack needed focus. As universities and colleges change in composition, as with enrolling more accomplished students, institutional culture must evolve accordingly.

☐   Are there structural means to improve culture? In attempting to enhance the undergraduate intellectual culture, UGA could make some relatively straightforward structural adjustments, such as changing when it offered courses. At a smaller institution seeking to assume more of the characteristics of a liberal arts college, restructuring academic divisions, with the intent of decentralizing them, might be merited. Even though restructuring can be disruptive, it is still likely to be achieved more readily than changing institutional culture.

☐   Does how the institution makes decisions contribute positively to institutional culture? Improving the intellectual culture associated with undergraduate education at UGA required investments by the faculty. It was thus essential to have the task force include faculty members and have faculty governance be central to approving and implementing its recommendations. Culture can rarely be imposed from above, but leaders and senior mangers can send practical and symbolic signals toward guiding change.

☐   Can policies and processes contribute to enriching undergraduate culture? Similar to restructuring, relatively straightforward changes in certain rules and in the approaches to implementing them can support change efforts, but these alone are insufficient.

☐ What about obtaining data for decision support and communicating it in an effective manner? The task force at UGA identified assessing outcomes, initially through the NSSE survey, as being important in understanding what needed to be done, what has been done, and what remains to do to strengthen undergraduate education.

☐ Are the people, facilities, technology, and finances in place to support the desired culture? UGA had to ask whether there were infrastructure investments required in matters such as faculty teaching loads, student advising, and teaching facilities—and whether there were sufficient resources available to address areas in need of enhancement. Concentrating on infrastructure alone is unlikely to build the culture an institution intends to develop, but not doing so often presents a formidable barrier.

Applying the Framework

In considering an initiative such as enhancing the intellectual culture among undergraduates at a research university, leaders and senior mangers can begin with who needs to be responsible for managing the project and monitoring its progress. UGA assigned the project to a task force, cochaired by the vice-provost and the vice president for instruction, that involved a representative group of faculty. Without the latter, the effort would have lacked the necessary credibility, and having the faculty governance process consider implementing the recommendations of the task force provided the same type of legitimacy. However, a strictly faculty-directed approach may have been less disciplined than required. Naming two senior academic administrators with university-wide portfolios to cochair the effort minimized the risk—and, as importantly, any reasonable perception—of parochialism. For instance, had there been a dean involved in coordinating this initiative, the process might have been seen by some as slanted toward a given school or college. In framing the final report of the task force, the cochairs were also well positioned to remind the group of political and financial realities within the institution, balancing academic sensibilities and administrative concerns.

Given their positions, the cochairs also had a clear sense of the institutional ambitions that the initiative was intended to advance. Matters involving the curriculum, especially at a research university, absolutely require the participation the faculty. Yet there is also a strategic aspect to curricular reform—a need to connect it not only with mission, but also aspirations. Faculty members typically have an acute understanding of the former. Spending the initial portion of the project exploring trends and issues in higher education caused the entire committee, including the faculty, to be more attuned to the ambitions of the university, as well as to the constraints under which it operates. It also put the work of the task force into the national perspective that UGA regularly operates within in its research and its student recruitment. The dichotomy here is that while there is a need for reality, there is also a particular benefit in expansive thinking. Therefore, in preparing to do its work, it was important for the task force to both explore realities and recall ideals. For example, curricular reform at a research university needs to connect faculty rewards with research productivity. It also must acknowledge that reputational rankings measure inputs (SAT scores), but not necessarily outputs (effective learning). Nonetheless, academic values also matter, and faculty members, as on the task force, are adept at emphasizing these.

Having a group that already had a sense of the purposes and culture of the university—and of research universities generally—was also essential. Even though these elements would emerge more strongly as the task force became immersed in its work, its members were clear from the outset about what the university was and where it was headed. They thus had the foundation required to delve into more complicated matters. For instance, task force members recognized the challenges associated with the party school aspects of UGA's culture, but they also knew what positive features of the university's campus life they wanted to preserve. Furthermore, from their own training, especially in graduate school, they had a sense of the ideals of academe and how these could be more completely realized at UGA. In short, the task force members had enough depth to appreciate the possibilities for reform at UGA and to gauge where their recommendations could be realized. They knew to whom they would need to sell their recommendations, both on the faculty and in the administration. The cochairs also understood the politics of a public research university, including the necessity of keeping relevant external constituents informed, even on a matter as seemingly insular as curriculum reform.

The membership of the task force was sufficiently representative to have a clear understanding of the elements in strategic management that were related to the initiative and how they potentially aligned. Both the faculty and the administrators involved demonstrated an appreciation of shared governance, which was essential, given the nature and complexity of the issues before them. The faculty appreciated the purposes and culture at UGA, but they also regularly worked with the policies and processes that the task force examined, so they realized both their importance and the need for them to be in sync in the context of the overall initiative. Serving on the front lines of instruction at the university, faculty are also aware of infrastructure needs, just as senior administrators tend to understand the costs associated with the people, facilities, and technology involved in instruction. Those with administrative portfolios are also likely to have developed a particular appreciation of information. For instance, the vice president for instruction at UGA oversees crunching numbers in allocating faculty and classrooms within the confines of the instructional budget of the university. Data also informed the deliberations and eventual recommendations of the task force, making their report more authoritative. Finally, spending so much time collecting information, as through interviews and focus groups, enabled those on the task force to identify gaps in their understanding about what was needed to support the initiative. For instance, some members might not have seen processes as being all that relevant to intellectual culture, but they may have changed their minds when hearing from students frustrated by shortcomings here.

The task force structure additionally imposed a sense of urgency on the project, allotting a set amount of time for it. A standing committee, perhaps within faculty governance, could have considered these issues, but it probably would also have had other concerns before it at the time. A subcommittee might have been too small to be seen as representative of the university as a whole. In approaching its assignment, a task force resembles a sprint, having a focused set of responsibilities to be completed within a relatively short time frame. When the intended result is a credible set of recommendations related to a discrete and pressing issue, a task force may represent a useful approach.

A task force may also be more likely to focus on implementation, emphasizing practicality in its recommendations. For example, UGA had several smaller colleges and schools, including some newer ones. Even if restructuring academic units seemed to be a sensible option, the task force was aware that combining academic units was a nonstarter, given that there was a strategic aspect to organizing prominent programs such as ecology or public administration into their own schools. Finally, a task force may more easily build in a back end to its work, not only identifying problems in a systematic manner, but also pursuing the implementation of solutions in the same way. Doing so addresses the question of what is needed to measure progress and, ultimately, the impact associated with an initiative. One indicator is whether the recommendations of the task force are implemented. A less tangible one, with a longer time horizon, is whether the institution's intellectual culture, as possible to measure, has improved.

The primary challenge with most task forces is not associated with their work, but instead resides in those with power and influence who need to act upon their recommendations. At UGA, the shared governance process addressed the task force's recommendations, implementing most of them. The outcome offers a reminder that governance, even within the "organized anarchy" of a research university, can often work well. Such results are not a given, however. It is fair to ask whether faculty governance at a typical research university is robust enough to really make a difference in the intellectual climate of an institution.

Faculty committees, especially when working with the relevant administrators, can readily develop policies and processes that address concerns and align with the overall efforts of the university. Harmonizing ideals and infrastructure may prove to be more difficult. The UGA task force knew that certain improvements would benefit the institution's intellectual culture—as with having more tenured faculty teach undergraduate courses—but they also knew that the university operated under severe financial constraints in this area. They were positioned to understand that funding for matters such as instructional technology, or even new facilities, was often more readily available than additional support for standing faculty lines. As in clarifying purposes, certain aspects of building organizational capacity through strengthening culture do not necessary require significant additional resources, as in improving structure, governance, policies, and processes to better align with mission and aspirations. Developing the data support network and, especially, the infrastructure required to support an invigorated culture can be expensive, however, requiring creativity among leaders and senior managers to ensure that deficiencies in these elements do not doom a complex initiative such as building undergraduate education at UGA.

Conclusion

Organizational capacity is the administrative foundation essential for establishing and sustaining the initiatives—and ultimately the transformation—embodied in an institution's vision. The case studies of various initiatives at different types of institutions illustrate an approach to strategic management intended to build such capacity. Strategic management requires leaders and senior managers both to identify a set of elements—eight in the BOC framework—and to ensure that they align.

Identifying and Aligning Elements

Each chapter identifies an element and suggests how it relates to others in the context of a given situation and initiative that is both generic and reflective of broader trends in American higher education.

Building capacity within an institution begins with identifying its *purposes*—its mission and aspirations. The College of New Jersey knew what it had become and where it was headed in launching the Academic Transformation initiative to make its curriculum more consistent with that of a selective liberal arts college.

Table 2   Identifying elements

Element	Basic Concept	Case Study	Basic Question
Purposes	Mission, aspirations	The College of New Jersey	Why are we here and where are we headed?
Structure	Configuration	Virginia Tech	How should we be configured to do our work?
Governance	Decisions	Valley City State University	Who should make what decisions?
Policies	Rules	LaGrange College	What rules should we proceed under?
Processes	Means	Paul D. Camp Community College	How do we get things done?
Information	Data, communication	University of Redlands	What do we need to inform our decision making?
Infrastructure	Capital	Seminole Community College	What are our human, physical, technological, and financial assets?
Culture	Character	University of Georgia	What is our essential character?

LaGrange College sought to enhance faculty scholarship and integrate student research into the curriculum, increasing its selectivity and prestige as a liberal arts college. The University of Redlands attempted to do the same in developing its mechanisms for decision support related to tuition discounting. Each institution also articulated a set of values that became embedded within it, employing both practical and symbolic means to do so. Paul D. Camp Community College similarly recognized that improving student retention was essential for expanding access. Invigorating undergraduate education to challenge more accomplished students was also deeply connected to the purposes of the University of Georgia in fulfilling its teaching mission. Seminole Community College hoped to maintain quality—another essential institutional purpose across higher education—even with static resources. The Math Emporium at Virginia Polytechnic Institute and State University was a similar attempt to expand both services and quality while using fewer resources to advance the ideals and ambitions of the institution. Finally, the implementation of an enterprise resource planning system at Valley City State University focused on the same ends relative to an administrative function.

Structure is how an institution is organized. Like all of the BOC elements, it must align with purposes as well as with the other six elements. La Grange and TCNJ restructured their institutions toward more of a liberal arts model, reducing the number of schools or departments. SCC, meanwhile, sought to remain "one college" through such devices as having single academic departments function across each of its several campuses. Structural considerations in improving student retention at PDCCC concentrated on such issues as whether to situate student advising with faculty members or professional advisors. VCSU implemented its management information system through a structure that did not include its faculty, knowing that they would be uninterested in a project that did not directly involve them, and that administrative personnel could manage it successfully without them. Redlands similarly assigned what it came to see as the administrative function of tuition discounting to a working group of administrators, with appropriate input from those responsible for academic affairs. Virginia Tech recognized the decentralized nature of a research university and the centrality of individual academic departments in developing and delivering curriculum, such as the mathematics department's role in structuring the Math Emporium. Similarly, UGA acknowledged the division of labor that puts setting curriculum policy primarily with the faculty, thus directing most of the recommendations of its university-wide Task Force on Undergraduate Education there.

Governance determines who makes what decisions within an organization and must align with purposes, structure, and the other elements. Given the nature of the ConnectND project and how the state structured it, VCSU approached decision making among the administrators involved in the initiative in an orderly, businesslike manner. Redlands did the same in delegating decisions related to tuition-discounting policy to its working group. LaGrange sought to do the opposite, flattening decision making to encourage the faculty governance that had not traditionally been robust at that institution, but that is associated with prestigious liberal arts colleges. The same was true at TCNJ, as it evolved from being a comprehensive institution to a selective liberal arts college. Virginia Tech knew that before moving forward with the Math Emporium, it needed support from relevant units, not only those with interested faculty members, but also the administrative offices connected with such an initiative. UGA did the same, locating decision making associated with enriching the intellectual climate of the institution within the faculty governance process. SCC recognized the governance difficulties, when staffing is thin, with lower-level personnel making increasingly complicated decisions out of necessity. At PDCCC, the primary governance question was whether to have someone directly responsible for retention issues.

Policies are rules under which an organization chooses to operate, and *processes* are how it accomplishes these, involving both formal and informal means. SCC formulated its one-college approach and drew on the capabilities associated with its new PeopleSoft management information system to establish processes that better enabled it to apply various rules it established toward maintaining consistency across its campuses. In much the same manner, Redlands established a set of broad principles for tuition discounting and implemented them through a five-stage annual process involving its working group. TCNJ required a new set of policies to align with its revised curriculum and instituted several accompanying processes related to budgeting and assessment. LaGrange similarly needed new tenure rules and faculty evaluation processes to incorporate its heightened expectations related to research and scholarship. PDCCC also looked at faculty-rewards policies and student-services processes in considering how to improve retention. UGA was interested in instituting various policies to enhance intellectual life, including having more tenured and tenure-track faculty teaching undergraduate courses, and implementing various processes to effect them. The Math Emporium sought to keep internal rules to a minimum and had to navigate university processes at Virginia Tech that were sometimes incompatible with it as a relatively freestanding unit. With ConnectND, VCSU needed to initiate certain policies and processes to be consistent with those in use statewide.

Information informs decision making and includes both generating and communicating data. The exchange of information through informal means filled gaps in the formal implementation plan for ConnectND at VCSU, especially in relation to training needs. At LaGrange, the president used the full sweep of practical and symbolic means at his disposal to communicate not only his vision for the college, but also the norms consistent with it that those at the institution would need to internalize for the college to advance. UGA had a related set of challenges in advancing a culture of intellectual rigor at the university. At PDCCC and SCC, poor data, a common problem across institutions, made needed assessment more difficult. Also, having a large part-time faculty was sometimes a barrier to effective communication at both institutions. Virginia Tech had the challenge of demonstrating how the Math Emporium contributed to efficiency and quality, while Redlands sought precision in the use of data to support decisions that would maximize "bang for the buck" in tuition discounting. Both UGA and TCNJ sought to improve assessment in connection with their curricular reform initiatives.

Infrastructure encompasses the human, physical, technological, and financial assets of an organization. Once again, it must align with purposes and the other BOC elements. TCNJ made a sustained investment in each infrastructure area over the past two decades, particularly in aligning its personnel and buildings with the evolved purposes of the institution. LaGrange needed to do what TCNJ had done, adding the kinds of faculty members and the facilities, such as a new library, to accommodate the teacher-scholar approach it was introducing. At SCC and PDCCC, shortages in staff (but not necessarily in facilities at SCC) were a particular challenge that threatened other elements, such as culture. Redlands used a consultant in providing specialized expertise in its tuition-discounting initiative. Virginia Tech took advantage of existing infrastructure— the physical space available to house the Math Emporium—and UGA made infrastructure investments toward its aspirations, as with enhancing its study-abroad programs.

Culture is the essential character of an institution. In leading the ConnectND effort across North Dakota, VCSU took advantage of the can-do administrative culture at the institution, as well as its comfort in being an early adopter of technology. PDCCC and SCC also saw their positive (but stretched) institutional cultures as an advantage in tackling the challenges before them. Virginia Tech similarly drew on the technologically savvy nature of its campus, as well as its entrepreneurial character, in launching the Math Emporium. At LaGrange, the faculty needed to internalize the culture of a selective liberal arts college, something that was further along at TCNJ, but still remained an issue in areas such as faculty governance. Redlands and UGA, respectively, developed a working group and a task force that acted in ways consistent with the cultures of their campuses. In each case, culture needed to operate in concert with the other elements in order to build the organizational capacity to support the initiative at issue, thus advancing the mission and aspirations of the institution.

Identifying the eight BOC elements is the initial task before leaders and senior managers in employing strategic management to build organizational capacity, but aligning them is its essence. The checklists at the end of each case study chapter summarize possibilities for doing both, reminding us that strategic management is best portrayed as a web consisting of connections between and among elements. Strategic management is thus at least as much an art as a science. It is a straightforward framework that enables those leading and managing universities and colleges to diagnose problems. Solving them requires aligning the various aspects of an organization with its countless moving parts.

Implementing Strategic Management

In applying strategic management in the context of a specific initiative at their given institution, leaders and senior managers might consider eight questions toward identifying and aligning the BOC elements.

1. *Given the nature and scope of the initiative, who needs to be responsible for managing it, including monitoring progress?* In several of the cases, the president of the institution led the initiative. At a small institution, such as LaGrange, the president's involvement was crucial, particularly given the significant cultural changes taking place across the college as it reframed its purposes toward a teacher-scholar model. An institution's president is best positioned to make the symbolic gestures and exercise the practical means that are significant in clarifying purposes and reshaping culture. At LaGrange, lowering faculty teaching load and identifying the library as a fund-raising priority were important symbols in aiding understanding about what it means to assume the characteristics of an elite liberal arts college. These efforts also had the practical impact of contributing to establishing the foundation for becoming a more selective institution. At TCNJ, its president led the college's curricular reform, which accorded with both its institution-wide impact and its connection, as at LaGrange, with advancing purposes and aligning the culture of the college with these. Also, TCNJ's provost, as the inside leader at the institution, was essential in orchestrating changes across various academic and most administrative functions. At VCSU and SCC, the president was again the best person to be involved, because the initiatives at these two institutions essentially concerned external affairs, whether interactions within the state higher educational system or negotiations for resources at the state capitol. Such issues are less likely to directly involve faculty members in their formal governance role. Finally, at small institutions, the president may become involved in any larger-scale project almost by default, as with the retention initiative at PDCCC or ConnectND at VCSU.

At larger institutions, even in more complex initiatives such as enhancing intellectual culture at UGA or developing instructional infrastructure at Virginia Tech, presidents are less likely to assume direct responsibilities, limiting their involvement to approving the initial idea and receiving updates on its progress. Had these two initiatives branched into external affairs, the respective presidents probably would have directed them or been more significantly involved. At Virginia Tech, the executive vice president and the deans of the relevant colleges, knowing that they had the support of the president, were best able to lead the project, working directly with the mathematics faculty. The administrators negotiated the funding for the Math Emporium and the faculty developed the its academic program. Once the project was established, the mathematics faculty could run it, with the senior administrators moving on to the next initiative. At UGA, developing a task force cochaired by two senior administrators and involving a representative group of faculty members allowed the effort to be focused, even with the complexity of the issues involved, while maintaining the faculty involvement and insight that is essential in any academic reform effort. Finally, assigning a set of technical decisions related to tuition discounting to a working group including relevant administrative units across Redlands situated the annual effort to maximize benefits such as efficiency and impact. As at VCSU, the Redlands effort did not need to involve the faculty, given the fundamentally administrative nature of tuition discounting.

2. *Do those managing the project have a clear sense of the mission and the aspirations that the initiative is intended to advance?* There are benefits to managing projects as locally as possible. At LaGrange, only the president could lead the initiative, setting its tone, as it was intrinsically connected with his vision for the institution. Moreover, changing the nature of faculty work, and thus institutional culture, is a significant and potentially controversial undertaking. Because TCNJ was further along in both areas, the provost could assume a more central role, especially given the academic nature of the reform. In addition, any case for garnering institutional resources, as from the state at SCC, is essentially an exercise in articulating purposes, with no one able do this as credibly as the president. The enterprise resource planning system installation at VCSU was not so closely connected with the institution's vision that its president had to take part in it, but this project was associated with enhancing the profile of the institution within the state system, so her participation made sense. At PDCCC, the president probably needed to be involved. Although people within the institution understood PDCCC's mission, it was difficult for any one of them, even at a small-town community college, to view the institution as a whole—and the retention problem was institution-wide in its scope.

At Redlands, the president and faculty did not need participate directly, instead receiving reports, as the working group was assigned a technical task—running the numbers to maximize the impact of tuition-discounting decisions—and was sufficiently representative and experienced to understand the university's mission and aspirations. The working group might have operated strictly as a technical exercise, but its efforts were more credible and persuasive when it was able to frame its decisions in terms of institutional purposes. The purposes and culture that allowed the creation of the Math Emporium were so embedded within Virginia Tech that the executive vice president, academic deans, and mathematics faculty were able to lead the project, speaking the same language (perhaps with different dialects) in doing so. The administrators, especially, understood its multiple facets: how the project, in stretching instructional resources, contributed to realizing the teaching mission at the institution through more efficient means; how the institution's ambitions depended on shifting instructional work away from core faculty; and how the culture at Virginia Tech was such that it could tolerate a decentralized approach. The mathematics faculty knew how to operate such a facility with academic integrity.

3. *Does the person or team managing the project have a clear understanding, relative to the initiative, of each element and how they align?* Having an associate provost and a vice-provost serve as cochairs ensured that UGA's task force would advance the university's aspirations, but faculty involvement guaranteed that its recommendations would also reflect the values embedded in its instructional mission. The cochairs, given their broad responsibilities, were also likely to appreciate how the other elements related to the initiative and how they aligned. Strategic management can be a challenge for those without responsibilities that require understanding the entire institution. Faculty members, like less-experienced administrators, often require guidance in discerning the elements and understanding how they interrelate, especially those more operational in nature. Business officers readily comprehend elements related to operations—policies, processes, information, and infrastructure—but sometimes overlook matters such as culture, an area where faculty members tend to have more facility.

Like the cochairs at UGA, the presidents who led various initiatives, because of their positions, were likely to appreciate the elements and their alignments—and be able to assist others in doing so. Individuals or groups with more local responsibilities can nevertheless organize their thinking by employing a strategic-management framework, but it may take them longer to grasp the concept and its components. For instance, had the PDCCC president decided to appoint a task force (or even a working group, as at Redlands) to address the retention problem, he might have overcome the more limited view its faculty had of the institution by offering some training in strategic management. Doing so would have provided such a task force with a framework to organize their deliberations and encouraged them to view the problem in its entirety. Finally, various vice presidents at SCC understood the logic, especially when working with teams, of employing strategic management and systems thinking in directing some of the initiatives, such as developing technological infrastructure or constructing facilities.

4. *Both among those responsible for a project, as well as across an institution, what kinds of efforts tend to further understanding about the elements and how they relate to one another?* Understanding what an institution is (mission) and where it is headed (aspirations) is the necessary first step in the application of any strategic management framework. Doing so usually occurs over time, with symbolic acts and practical means providing illustrations of purposes. Both TCNJ and LaGrange sought to associate themselves more completely with the most selective liberal arts colleges. The two colleges embedded curricular initiatives within a more collegial approach to governance and the accompanying institutional culture. The colleges also used infrastructure improvements, especially facilities, to emphasize their ambitions, such as TCNJ assuming more of the look and feel of a traditional liberal arts college and LaGrange planning a new library building. They also tended to signal their ambitions with their faculty hires, opting for those more likely to embrace the teacher-scholar ethos. TCNJ and LaGrange similarly restructured policies and processes, as in faculty evaluation, to better align with the selective liberal arts model, delivering another set of messages related to purposes in so doing.

Similarly, in directing the recommendations of its Task Force on Undergraduate Education to the faculty senate, UGA emphasized the importance of faculty in developing a rich intellectual life at the university. The policies and processes that UGA developed in response to the task force report signaled that the university was serious about change. SCC could readily connect support for additional faculty infrastructure to the realization of its access mission, as well as to resource needs threatening both institutional culture and more tangible functions, such as processes related to student services. The Math Emporium at Virginia Tech quite clearly served the mission and advanced the aspirations of the institution, fit neatly into its entrepreneurial and technologically-savvy culture, aligned with its decentralized structure and diffuse approach to governance, and addressed its infrastructure needs. The way in which VCSU framed and approached the implementation of ConnectND was similar, except that it was more systematic in structure and governance associated with the initiative. The tuition-discounting process at Redlands works because it so intentionally and obviously aligns with purposes and culture at the institution and is supported by the other elements, such as policies and processes. The same is true of the retention challenge at PDCCC. The prospects of addressing it successfully are increased when those across the institution come to understand it as a systemic issue, one involving not only every unit on campus, but also each of the BOC elements.

5. *How might such an understanding of the elements and their alignment differ in various parts of the university—and what are the possibilities for the elements, especially purposes and culture, to connect to the institution?* Individuals across units are likely to view a given initiative differently, just as they might have varying perceptions about the idea of strategic management and its possibilities in building organizational capacity. Purposes and culture have the potential to connect the multiple facets of even the most loosely coupled institution. The initiatives at UGA and Virginia Tech clearly served the aspirations of these universities, contributing to advancing their institutional stature, but they also supported deeply embedded academic values. They worked only because they were seen as improving undergraduate education and thus resonated across the institution, particularly with the faculty. The efforts also functioned in a manner consistent with the culture broadly associated with research universities, as well as that of the particular institutions involved. In addition, they required people across different orientations and with various responsibilities to work together—faculty, academic administrators, and administrators in other areas. The mathematics faculty at Virginia Tech could not simply consider values, but also had to emphasize operational matters, such as policies and processes, with those under the executive vice president being in the opposite situation. Having a shared sense of why the institution existed, where it was headed, and what its essential character was tended to bridge differences. At TCNJ and LaGrange, there was the same need to address any administrative-academic divide that existed, with purposes and culture contributing to doing so. (It may also be that because of the smaller size and more collegial nature of these latter two institutions, those involved in administrative work have more connections with academic efforts—and perhaps vice versa.)

At SCC, the challenge was not necessarily in having those with different functional responsibilities work in concert, but instead in needing purposes and culture to connect different campuses within a single institution. Common policies and processes, as well as governance and information spanning the campuses, were also of assistance in doing so. Purposes and culture similarly contributed to bringing together a cross-functional group of administrators at Redlands, ensuring they had a clear sense of the reason for their work and how the institution expected them to contextualize it. UGA had the same advantages with its task force. So did PDCCC, where those with either administrative or academic responsibilities tended to embrace retention as mission-specific. At VCSU, having an institutional culture inclined to welcome innovations in technology helped with the implementation of ConnectND, but the institution also kept the project narrow, involving only those in administrative roles.

6. *Apart from those leading the project, who else needs to be involved in it, including external constituents, so that each of the elements is addressed and aligned with the others?* The scope of the institutional change at LaGrange was so significant that the entire campus needed to be engaged, including alumni and friends. Even though the initiative focused on enhancing faculty scholarship and student research, it also involved remaking certain administrative functions to support these ends—and required significant fund raising. The same situation existed at TCNJ, but curricular reform there was more a matter of informing external constituents, rather than a need to involve them more directly. VCSU implemented ConnectND without involving faculty or students—or external constituents, other than those across state government who were expressly interested in the project.

At Virginia Tech, those launching the Math Emporium informed relevant people across campus, but the decentralized nature of the institution was such that few individuals needed to be directly involved. The same was true of many administrative personnel at UGA or faculty members at Redlands. They may have had a passing interest in the work of the task force or the working group, but their recommendations were only remotely connected with their work. In both situations it was actually useful to keep the projects bounded, with only relevant people involved. The opposite was true at PDCCC, as its retention problem cut across the institution, and the small size of the college made it best to keep everyone informed. SCC needed to focus externally in securing resources at the state level, helping those in Tallahassee understand that shortages in needed infrastructure had a negative influence on the overall functioning of the college and its ability to serve its mission. The college also sought to maintain the cohesion of its several campuses, which required investments by those across it, especially in the midst of tight resources.

7. *Given the initiative and the type of institution involved, where are breakdowns likely to occur, which connections between and among elements are the strongest, and which ones present the greatest challenges?* Strategic management not only identifies elements and encourages their alignment, but also suggests where there are

omissions and disconnects. At UGA, had the recommendations of the task force been perceived as administrative impositions rather than as the product of faculty governance, the project may have failed. Also, supporting infrastructure, policies, and processes were all needed to buttress the proposed reforms. Academic Transformation at TCNJ required similar accompanying means, as well as the same clarity in mission and aspirations and a culture that supported institutional purposes. The culture at LaGrange was still evolving, so breakdowns in governance were possible as faculty were still learning what it means to operate in a collegial environment. Developing policies and constructing facilities to support the ambitions of the college were likely to prove more straightforward (assuming the financing was in place for the latter). At PDCCC, the difficulty was in connecting the other elements with infrastructure, as even a perfectly developed plan is likely to fail without the staffing needed to realize it. There was a similar risk with ConnectND at VCSU, but those involved stretched, as needed, to complete the project, the difference being that implementing a management information system is more bounded and probably more readily accomplished than tackling a retention issue.

The challenge at Virginia Tech was that an infrastructure investment like the Math Emporium can be forgotten within a decentralized university, especially without policies and processes to connect the unit with the institution. SCC offers another decentralization challenge, with consistency within the various elements more difficult to achieve across multiple campuses. For instance, policies and processes may be similar on paper, but they could be implemented differently across campuses. Shortages in faculty and administrators can also cause an infrastructure breakdown, even when mission and aspirations are well understood and the institution has developed a productive culture. Finally, information is the crucial element at Redlands. The legitimacy of the tuition-discounting working group depended on producing the data needed for decision support, as well as on communicating the impact of its efforts.

8. *What is the time frame for planning and developing the initiative, what are the major steps along the way, and what is needed to measure progress and, ultimately, impact?* At Redlands, the tuition-discounting process was annual and the results could be measured with some precision, including through the various admissions numbers associated with each entering class. Measuring impact at VCSU was also fairly straightforward—was the new system up and running? The initiatives at VCSU, UGA, and Virginia Tech each had a relatively short timeline, with the faculty governance process eventually taking over at UGA and the Math Emporium reverting to the mathematics faculty. One measure of the success of the

UGA task force could be the number of its recommendations that were eventually implemented. However, a more meaningful assessment is also more nebulous—determining if the intellectual culture for undergraduates actually improved. The same is true at Virginia Tech. Measuring efficiency—the relative cost of serving a certain number of students—is simple enough, but assessing whether learning improved is considerably less tangible.

LaGrange's initiative was just beginning, so laying the proper foundation and early (and relatively easy) victories are the appropriate measures of its initial success, although the ultimate determination will only occur after several years. One measure will be how the college improves in regional and national rankings, but there is always the less certain question of whether the faculty scholarship and student research initiatives, as well as those projects related to them, actually enhance the student experience. At PDCCC, its retention initiative needs to be ongoing to some extent, perhaps following a flurry of initial activity to fix the more apparent problems, but determining its success is more concrete—are fewer students departing? The effort at SCC is similarly continuous. Institutions must constantly fight for resources, but eventually financial situations stabilize—and SCC can review increases in its staffing and enrollment in the context of fulfilling its mission. Finally, curricular reform at TCNJ occurred within a set period, but it was the product of the college evolving in purposes and culture over several years. Such a project, like that of the UGA task force, needs to maintain its momentum, so imposing deadlines can be useful. Rankings, once again, are one measure of the impact of the TCNJ initiative—and student satisfaction may be another. However, a more qualitative sense of whether the curriculum better fits what TCNJ has become—and where it wants to go—may prove more meaningful.

The questions raised by, and the realities associated with, implementation offer a reminder of the challenges that accompany leading or managing an organization as complex as a university or college. Institutional leaders articulate worthy missions and impressive ambitions, but they commonly direct less attention to developing the organizational capacity needed to support the initiatives intended to realize these purposes. Strategic management can help impose order and identify gaps in building an appropriate administrative foundation. Drawing on frameworks specific to corporations, nonprofits, and government is instructive, but Building Organizational Capacity grounds strategic management within the particular culture associated with universities and colleges, as well as placing it in the context of the trends and issues that are shaping strategies and tactics within them.

Higher education is increasingly operating within a neoliberal frame that emphasizes individual gain and return on investment and minimizes traditional arguments associated with universities and colleges serving the public good. Although competition between and among institutions had never been so intense, values continue to matter in higher education. As the case studies and responses to the implementation questions suggest, building capacity through strategic management does not inevitably lead to more managed institutions and diminished faculty influence, and to a de-emphasis of other traditional values such as access. In fact, leaders and senior managers can best employ strategic management in protecting these values, aligning the elements of an institution in ways that enable it to realize not only its aspirations, but also its long-standing ideals.

Appendix

Master Interview Protocol

How are you involved in [the initiative being studied]?

How does [the initiative being studied] connect with the mission of the institution (its fundamental purpose) as well as its vision and goals (its significant aspirations)?

How does the structure of the university—how it is configured to do its work—both generally and in terms of [the initiative being studied], further its fundamental purposes and significant aspirations?

How does governance—how the organization makes decisions—enable effective implementation of [the initiative being studied]?

Does how your institution is structured and governed tend to cause people to view the parts of the institution and decision making within them as connected with one another across the university?

How important is it to think in terms of systems as a way of establishing [the initiative being studied]?

How are policies—the rules that articulate how an institution will proceed—connected with processes, which are how the institution gets things done?

How does the university, and how do the various academic and administrative units within it, ensure that needed information is generated, disseminated, and assimilated to inform and support the policy setting and the decision making that advance the mission, vision, and goals (purposes) of the institution?

How does the university consider infrastructure—broadly defined as its human, physical, technological, and financial assets—in [the initiative being studied]?

How does the culture of the institution shape decisions related to [the initiative being studied]?

Looking at the Building Organizational Capacity framework, does it make sense to you? Do the elements seem to integrate into an effective whole? How important is it to have elements such as these integrate?

Might a framework like Building Organizational Capacity help you particularly, and your institution more generally, in advancing [the initiative being studied]?

Are you confident that improvements made over the past several years will be sustainable over time? Are they likely to continue with the next administration, and with succeeding administrations? Should they continue? Is what has been accomplished sufficiently adaptable? Will this really become the new business as usual at your institution?

Interview List

The College of New Jersey

33 interviews

> **R. Barbara Gitenstein, President***
> **Stephen Briggs, Provost and Vice President for Academic Affairs**
> Susan Albertine, Dean, Culture and Society
> Robert Anderson, Director, General Education
> Susan Bakewell-Sachs, Dean, Nursing
> Raymond Barclay, Director, Institutional Research
> Annelise Catanzaro, Alternate Student Trustee
> Walter Chambers, Immediate Past Chair, Board of Trustees
> Patrice Coleman-Boatwright, Director, College and Community Relations
> Dan Crofts, Professor and Chair, History, and President, Faculty Senate
> Laura DeLucia, Student Government Association (SGA) Vice President
> Ralph Edelbach, Professor, Technological Studies
> George Facas, Dean, Engineering
> Vivian Fernandez, Assistant Vice President, Human Resources
> Thomas Hagedorn, Professor, Mathematics and Statistics, and Vice-Chair, Middle States Self-Study Committee
> Lauren Lebano, SGA Vice President for Academic Affairs
> James Lentini, Dean, Art, Media, and Music
> Monique Manfra, Student Trustee
> Kevin McHugh, Director of Athletics
> Marcia O'Connell, Professor and Chair, Biology, and Vice President, Faculty Senate
> Terry O'Connor, Dean, Education
> Emmanuel Osagie, Vice-Provost, Academic Grants and Sponsored Research

*Boldface type indicates the key informant at each site—the person who arranged the visit.

Susanne Pasch, Vice-Provost, Academic Programs and Initiatives
Barbara Pelson, Trustee
Mary-Elaine Perry, Vice President for Student Life
David Prensky, Dean, Business
Christina Puglia, SGA President
Harry Reichard, Trustee
Gail Simmons, Dean, Science
Nadine Stern, Chief Information Officer
David Tiffany, Vice President, Development and Alumni Affairs
David Venturo, Professor, English, and Chair, Middle States Self-Study
    Committee
Barbara Wineberg, Treasurer

LaGrange College

13 interviews
Stuart Gulley, President
Phyllis Whitney, Executive Vice President
Jay Simmons, Vice President for Academic Affairs
David Ahern, Chair, Humanities
Kim Barber, Chair, Fine Arts
Linda Buchanan, Vice President and Dean, Student Life and Retention
Sandie Johnson, Director, Core Program
Chuck Kraemer, Director, Undergraduate Research
Greg McClanahan, Chair, Science and Mathematics
Bill McCoy, Chair, Biology and Chemistry
Kim Myrick, Vice President, Enrollment Management
Marty Pirrman, Comptroller
Maranah Sauter, Chair, Professional Programs

Paul D. Camp Community College

18 interviews
Douglas W. Boyce, President
Jean Britt, Secretary, Academic Division
Barbara Butler, Assistant, Enrollment Services
Carolyn Crowder, Director, Workforce Development
Joe Edenfield, Campus Dean, Franklin
Renee Felts, Assistant Professor, Information Systems Technology
Susan Francis, Data Specialist, Advancement Office (formerly with Student
    Support Services and Financial Aid)
Glenn Gabbard, Consultant (University of Massachusetts Boston)
Alan Harris, Counselor, Suffolk
Nita Holt, Coordinator, Recruitment and Financial Aid
Patsy Joyner, Vice President, Institutional Advancement

Martha Kello, Associate Professor, Reading and Early Childhood Education
Teresa King Harrison, Assistant, Financial Aid
John Patterson, Assistant Professor, Biology
Safianu Rabiu, Associate Professor, Biology
Bessie Smith, Associate Professor, Administrative Support Technology
Jerry Standahl, Director, Assessment and Institutional Research
Monette Williams, Coordinator, Student Support Services

Seminole Community College

29 interviews
E. Ann McGee, President
Carol Hawkins, Vice President, Institutional Effectiveness, Planning, and Information Services
Laura Aromando, Cochair, Nursing
Beverly Bailey, Faculty, English, and Coordinator, Honors Program
Bobbie Bell, Chair, Humanities, and Faculty, Theater and Speech
Ruth Corey, Cochair, Nursing
Susan Dooley, Chair, Health Information Systems, and Faculty Senate Officer
Patry English, Director, Counseling and Educational Planning
Barbara Entwistle, Faculty Senate President and Chair, Information Systems, Business, and Legal Studies
Michael Garlich, Director, Community Relations and Marketing
Elnora Gilchrist, Dean, Adult Education
Dan Gilmartin, Faculty, History
Dick Grant, Faculty, Computer Science
Dick Hamann, Associate Vice President, Technology Services
Jim Henningsen, Vice President, Student Success Services
Angela Kersenbrock, Dean, Career Programs
Bob Lynn, Director, Financial Aid
Nelda Malm, Faculty, Nutrition
Randy Pawlowski, Director, Student Life
Pamela Pelaez, Director of Admissions
Annye Refoe, Dean, Arts and Sciences
Christine Robinson, Dean, Business and Information Technology
Lynn Rudd, Coordinator, Hunt Club Campus
Joe Sarnovsky, Vice President, Administration and Business Services
Dede Schaffner, Board of Trustees
Bill Schmidt, Chair, English
Travis Spaulding, Director, Enrollment Services and Registrar
James Turner, Chair, Biology
Lane Vosbury, Chair, Mathematics

The University of Georgia

6 interviews

Jere Morehead, Vice President, Instruction
Del Dunn, former Vice President, Instruction
Josef Broder, Associate Dean and University Professor, Agriculture and
  Environmental Sciences
Michelle Cook, Associate Dean, Students, Franklin College of Arts and
  Sciences
Joe Crim, Associate Vice President, Instruction
Jan Hathcote, Associate Dean and Associate Professor, Family and Consumer
  Sciences

13 additional interviews primarily related to institutional ambitions at UGA*

Tom Landrum, Senior Vice President, External Affairs
Meg Amstutz, Chief of Staff to the President
Linda Bachman, Assistant Dean, External Affairs, Franklin College of Arts
  and Sciences
Paul Cassilly, Director, Design and Construction
Melinda DeMaria, Associate Director, Admissions
Kathleen DeMarrais, Associate Dean, Education
Bonnie Joerschke, Director, Student Financial Aid
Gerry Kowalski, Executive Director, University Housing
Eric Orbach, Executive Director, UGA Real Estate Foundation
Sean Rogers, Director, Capital Budgets
Hugh Ruppersburg, Senior Associate Dean, Franklin College of Arts and
  Sciences
Danny Sniff, Associate Vice President, Facilities Planning
Karen Watkins, Associate Dean, Education

The University of Redlands

15 interviews

Phillip L. Doolittle, Senior Vice President, Finance and Administration
James R. Appleton, President
Alisha Archibald, Associate Director, Financial Aid
Mark Bottoroff, Associate Dean, Admissions, Arts and Sciences
Nancy Carrick, Vice President, Academic Affairs

---

*Several UGA graduate students, working in teams, conducted these interviews. I extend my
thanks to David Dial, Erinn Floyd, Jennifer McGinnis, and Mary Michael Pontzer for interviewing the
architects; Alexander Cuenca, Wesley Fugate, Beth-Anne Leech, Pat Nodine, Yarbrah Peeples, and
Scott Rizzo for the other institutional ambition interviews; and Ann Duffy, Jennifer Leahy, Oksana
Parylo, and Laurel Richmond for the interview related to the task force. I collected addition information through conversations with people from across the university.

Bethann Corey, Director, Financial Aid (Working Group Coordinator)
Paul Driscoll, Dean, Admissions, Arts and Sciences
Kevin Dyerly, Assistant Dean, Admissions, Arts and Sciences
Hamid Etesamnia, Executive Director and Chief Information Officer,
    Integrated Technology
Wendy McEwen, Analyst, Institutional Research
Junelyn Peeples, Analyst, Senior Institutional Research
Betty Porter, Manager, Administrative Systems Technology
Craig Slaughter, Associate Director, Financial Aid (Kenyon College),
    Incoming Director, Financial Aid (University of Redlands)
Susan Traverso, Dean, Arts and Sciences
Kathy Wetherell, Associate Vice President, Finance and Administration

Valley City State University

21 interviews
Ellen Earle Chaffee, President
William Ament, Comptroller, Business Office
Skye Braun, Student
Margaret Dahlberg, Associate Professor, Communication Arts Faculty
Irene Groth, Division Assistant, Education and Psychology
Don Hoff, Assistant Professor, Science Faculty
Monte Johnson, Director, Office of the Registrar
LaDonna Kiser, Division Assistant, Business and Information Technology
Dan Klein, Director, Enrollment Services
Jody Klier, Assistant Registrar, Office of the Registrar
Joan Noeske, Payroll Specialist, Business Office
Connie Pedersen, Assistant Registrar, Office of the Registrar
Erika Peterson, Student
Marcia Pritchert, Assistant Director, Financial Aid
Glen Schmalz, Vice President, Student Affairs
Betty Schumacher, Director, Financial Aid
Charlene Stenson, Admission Counselor, Enrollment Services
Ann Thoreson, Accountant, Business Office
Joe Tykwinski, Chief Information Officer
Stacy Wendel, Admission Counselor, Enrollment Services
James Wigtil, Vice President, Academic Affairs

Virginia Polytechnic Institute and State University

21 interviews
**Minnis E. Ridenour, Executive Vice President and Chief Operating
    Officer**
**Michael Williams, Associate Professor, Mathematics, and Director, The
    Math Emporium**

Robert C. Bates, Provost and Academic Vice President, Washington State University (former Dean, Arts and Sciences, Virginia Tech)

Christopher A. Beattie, Professor, Mathematics

Monte B. Boisen, Professor and Chair, Mathematics, University of Idaho (former Professor, Mathematics, Virginia Tech)

Christi Boone, Coordinator, Academic Affairs, Engineering

Terri A. Bourdon, Instructor, Mathematics

Ralph M. Byers, Director, Government Relations

Lay Nam Chang, Dean, Science

Kenneth B. Hannsgen, Professor Emeritus, Mathematics

Charles Hodges, Instructor, Mathematics

Mark G. McNamee, University Provost and Vice President for Academic Affairs

Peggy S. Meszaros, Professor, Human Development, and Director, Center for Information Technology Impacts on Children, Youth, and Families (former University Provost and Senior Vice President)

Anne H. Moore, Associate Vice President, Learning Technology

Robert F. Olin, Dean, Arts and Sciences, University of Alabama (former Professor and Head, Mathematics, Virginia Tech)

Elizabeth Reed, Director, Real Estate Management

John F. Rossi, Professor and Head, Mathematics

M. Dwight Shelton, Jr., Vice President, Budget and Financial Management

Raymond D. Smoot, Jr., Chief Operating Officer, Virginia Tech Foundation, and University Treasurer

Bevlee Watford, Associate Dean, Academic Affairs, Engineering

Diane L. Zahm, President, Faculty Senate

Notes

Introduction

1. Among other foundational works on management, Balderston (1995) published the first edition of *Managing Today's University* in 1974, the same year that Cohen and March wrote *Leadership and Ambiguity* about the presidency of universities and colleges. In *How Colleges Work*, Birnbaum (1988) considers management, including applying systems thinking, within four archetypical institutions. More recently, he examines management fads (2001). Leslie and Fretwell (1996) write even more directly about the management of universities and colleges, and Tierney (1999) concludes that management challenges require structural reform. In writing that are more specific to strategy, Keller (1983) popularized strategic planning in higher education in *Academic Strategy* (and closed his career with a 2004 case study of strategy at a liberal arts college). In a series of articles in the mid-1980s, Chaffee (1984a, 1984b, 1985) looks at strategy. Clark's (1983b) writing on organizational issues has also been influential. Winston (1993) considers economic issues across his work on higher education; McPherson and Schapiro (1998) explore tuition pricing strategies in *The Student Aid Game*; and Ehrenberg (2002) examines the impact of such strategies on institutions. More recently, Slaughter and Leslie (1997) and Slaughter and Rhoades (2004) address institutional strategy in the context of the increasingly entrepreneurial university; Kirp (2003) focuses on marketing the university; Bok (2002) examines commercialism; and Geiger (2004), Newman, Couturier, and Scurry (2004), and Zemsky, Wegner, and Massy (2005) all explore the influence of markets on strategy.

2. Here I draw on the work of my colleague Karen Miller, who synthesized the literature on capacity building. For further insight on defining capacity building, please see Connolly 2006; Doherty and Mayer 2003; Sobeck and Agius 2003; Backer 2001; DeVita, Fleming, and Trombly 2001; and Letts, Ryan, and Grossman 1999.

3. There are other frameworks for building capacity within nonprofits, several of which I reference in chapter 1, most prominently the capacity assessment grid developed by McKinsey and Company (2001) and Robert Kaplan and David Norton's *The Balanced Scorecard* (1996), as adapted to nonprofits.

CHAPTER 1: Strategic Management and Systems Thinking

1. For another typology, Martinet (1996) divides strategy into four traditions: teleologic, sociologic, ideologic, and ecologic. Lauriol (1996) maps Mintzberg's ten schools onto Martinet's four. Also, Mintzberg and Lampel (1999) and Mintzberg, Lampel, Quinn, and Ghoshal (2003) challenge approaches to planning and management that they view as deterministically analytical, linear, and sequential. Chaffee (1984a, 1984b) divides strategic management into linear, adaptive, and interpretive strategies.

2. The McKinsey framework builds on its 7S model from the 1970s and 1980s, which included seven elements: (1) shared values, (2) structure, (3) systems (processes and operations), (4) style (the symbolic behavior of managers), (5) staff development, (6) skills (what an organization does well), and (7) strategy (actions aimed at gaining competitive advantage) (Peters and Waterman 1982; Waterman 1982). The seven-sided web diagram portraying BOC is similar to the one Waterman, Peters, and Phillips (1980) present in illustrating the 7S approach. Bigler (2004) updated the framework into a 10S model, also for use in the corporate world, and included the following: (1) strategy; (2) speed; (3) synchronization (with consumer needs); (4) simplicity (of solutions and responses); (5) savings (through efficiency and cost reduction); (6) success (demonstrating results to ensure shareholder confidence); (7) standards (baselines for measurement); (8) stratified similarity (in approaches across organizations); (9) shock effects (an early warning about changes in one area that will ripple across the system); and (10) self-confidence, self-esteem, and self-identity.

3. Other significant approaches include Aaker (1998), Alex Miller and Gregory Dess (1996), and Hammer and Champy (1993). In considering marketing, Aaker focuses on the strategic analysis of external environments, suggesting six elements for any strategy: (1) a definition of markets in which, and products with which, to compete; (2) the level of investment required; (3) the functional areas that a strategy requires, such as finance, marketing, e-commerce, and the like; (4) strategic assets or skills that provide sustainable competitive advantages; (5) the allocation of resources across units; and (6) the development of synergies across units. Miller and Dess contend that once an organization has determined its purposes through both internal and external analyses, implementation of a strategy depends upon three levers: context (structure, communication networks, culture), system (processes, including information, reporting, and control), and action (leadership). Hammer and Champy's reengineering approach focuses on complete processes within an organization, going from raw materials to distribution, and requires a reevaluation of assumptions and beliefs about processes, systems, structure, people, culture, practices, and technologies. Calori (1998) cautions that strategic-management models have biases toward binary logic and against considering emotions and morals.

4. The same concept would work in higher education, provided that a surrogate measure for stock performance could be developed to empirically demonstrate the

move from good to great relative to a twin organization. In addition, great organizations tend to have great early histories, which is certainly common across higher education, as well—something akin to the "first mover" advantage in the industry. But it is possible to adjust the Collins approach so as not to disadvantage newer corporations by analyzing firms that were once average and then, beginning at a certain point, improved.

5. Collins also focuses on managers and leaders. Great organizations first decide on "who," then on "what," as Collins argues that the best hedge against unpredictability is not strategy, but finding the right people to formulate the strategy—getting the right people on the bus, the wrong people off, and the right people into the right seats. In this regard, higher education is more constrained than corporations, especially given tenure and the generally lower turnover in faculty and administrators at universities and colleges. But meaningful change, particularly at the unit level, is possible through focused and disciplined hiring. Furthermore, the great firms, including each of those Collins studied, have "level-five" leadership. Leadership is not binary—having good leadership or lacking it—but, instead, is dependent on level of skill. All CEOs are capable, contribute to a team, can manage, and are effective leaders, Collins suggests. However, level-five leaders are distinct, because they are humble and have ambition not for themselves but for the firm, its work, and its cause—and they have the will to make a chosen strategy happen. Again, many university and college presidents are more constrained than CEOs, as the position of the former is often more legislative than executive, especially at the least bureaucratic institutions. Unlike higher education institutions, which almost always hire presidents from the outside, great companies typically have homegrown leaders who are more likely to be loyal to the firm than focused on their own ambitions. If nothing else, insider CEOs have an easier time sorting through who to have on the bus and where to place them, since they have worked with these people and come to know their capabilities.

6. Keller concentrates on the strategic uses of planning in higher education, arguing that planning must be (1) active, not passive; (2) look outward; (3) focus on markets and competition; (4) concentrate on decisions, not goals; (5) blend the rational, the political, and the psychological; and (6) ultimately focus on the fate of the institution. His model has three internal elements of analysis: (1) traditions, values, and aspirations; (2) academic and financial strengths and weaknesses; and (3) leadership. It also has three external ones: (1) environmental trends, (2) market preferences, and (3) the competitive situation. Like BOC, Keller emphasizes the complex interplay of elements and eschews a rational-linear model.

7. Keller (1983) continues to be relevant, though less for his approach to planning than for being outward looking, encouraging higher education to recognize external competition. He also recognizes the importance of considering the influence of politics and culture on what appears to be a rational process. Keller's argument supports several aspects of BOC, including an emphasis on the importance of information, personnel, and quality that extends beyond the planning process itself.

8. Sophisticated treatments of management in higher education are generally severely limited. One useful source is Shattock (2003), who writes from the United Kingdom.

9. I use *systems approaches* and *systems thinking* interchangeably, avoiding the terms *systems theory* and *systems dynamics*. Systems theory is more appropriate to the biological and physical sciences. Forrester (1994b) draws reasonable distinctions between his systems-dynamics approach to exploring organizations and management and what he characterizes as systems thinking. He suggests that systems thinking lacks the analytical rigor that he champions in systems dynamics, but it is useful both in serving as a general introduction (geared to popular audiences) to the existence and importance of systems, and in playing a constructive role as a door-opener to system dynamics. He cautions that systems thinking can lead to unquestioning and superficial enthusiasm.

10. For those in the sciences (and in philosophy), the concept of systems is more of a worldview, so there is suspicion about extending such a scientific notion involving biological and physical systems toward applied ends within social systems (Jackson 2003).

11. Systems thinking also can address the criticism that strategic-management theories are too aligned with economic theory and thus not sufficiently attentive to behavioral theory and approaches (Kelly and Booth 2004).

12. Systems thinking has influenced health management and medical treatment, which have moved toward a "whole person" approach. Researchers have explored various issues in the health sciences through systems thinking, including the treatment of childhood and adolescent obesity (Pronk and Boucher 1999); family therapy for adults with learning disabilities (Fidell 2000); residential child care (Gibson, Leonard, and Wilson 2004); and neonatal quality standards (Horbar, Plsek, and Leahy 2003). The *American Journal of Public Health* devoted its March 2006 edition to the application of systems thinking in public health (see Leischow and Milstein 2006). Recent applications in other fields include wildlife management (S. Riley et al. 2003), safety (Pierce 2002), and land reclamation (Haigh 2002).

13. Other contemporary general scholarly treatments of systems approaches include Richmond (2001), Goodman et al. (1997), and O'Connor (1997).

14. Haines, Aller-Stead, and McKinlay (2005) and Haines (2000a, 2000b, 1999) are guides to systems thinking for practitioners, not focusing on situating the approach more broadly, as does Jackson. They instead offer a solid basic review of key concepts and tools for use in the application of systems thinking. Sherwood (2002) provides another practical handbook on the basics of systems thinking and constructing causal loop diagrams. Gharajedaghi (1999) addresses practical questions in systems thinking, also offering a theoretical basis and proposing an approach he terms "iterative design."

15. For each approach in his typology, Jackson (1) offers a description, including its historical development, its philosophy and theory, its methodology, its methods, and its recent development; (2) explores the approach "in action"; (3) includes a critique; and (4) suggests its value to managers.

16. Stampen and Hansen (1999) provide an example of quantitative modeling using systems theory for a problem in higher education. Gilmore and Lozier (1987) focus on systems theory in planning and decision support in education. Walter Davis and Timothy Chandler (1998) look at Boyer's *Scholarship Reconsidered* (1990) in the context of a systems-based model for change.

17. In *The Fifth Discipline Fieldbook*, Senge et al. (1994) concentrate on the application of Senge's (1990) learning organization.

18. Galbraith (2001) offers an archetype drawn from education (introducing technology throughout a school curriculum) and focuses on systems thinking at universities, using funding as an illustration.

19. Petrides (2002) offers an interesting take on organizational learning and redesigning processes related to the flow of information throughout higher educational organizations, providing a framework for the integration of institutional research within the larger context of "the learning organization." Freed and Klugman (1996) study ten higher educational institutions to determine whether they have become "learning organizations." Brown (1997) provides a brief, accessible review of Senge's work and offers recommendations for its implementation in higher education; Brancato (2003) applies Senge's work to faculty development at universities and colleges; Cotter (1999) and Houston and Rees (1999) both apply systems thinking to the curriculum, the latter to analyze quality; and Cain (1999) considers community colleges in the context of systems thinking.

20. Cutright (1999) offers an intriguing discussion of strategic planning in higher education, applying chaos theory and drawing on metaphors.

21. Vanderstraeten (2000) has an interesting take on paradigm change in systems theory, focusing on socialization and education.

22. For those interested in directly applying a systems approach, perhaps Jackson has the right idea in encouraging leaders and managers to combine approaches, treating them like food in a cafeteria line.

CHAPTER 2: Managing Increasingly Complex Institutions

1. In addition to the standard works on the neoliberal university (Zemsky, Wegner, and Massy 2005; Geiger 2004; Newman, Couturier, and Scurry 2004; Slaughter and Rhoades 2004; Kirp 2003; Ehrenberg 2002; and McPherson and Schapiro 1998), there is a robust literature critical of contemporary higher education. In just the past few years, Lewis (2006) writes of the lack of coherence in the curriculum, the disconnectedness of faculty from students, and the coddled and infantilized students at Harvard; Bok (2007) and Kronman (2007) discuss what students are not learning (including, the latter argues, the meaning of life); Giroux (2007) and Newfield (2008) focus on the influence of conservatives in, respectively, chilling critical thought and suppressing democratizing impulses in higher education; Golden (2007) and Schmidt (2007) consider the advantages affluent applicants have in admissions to elite institutions; Rhode (2006) addresses the negative impact the pursuit of status has on the

pursuit of knowledge, as do, more generally, Hersh and Merrow (2006); Washburn (2006) discusses negative corporate influences; and Bousquet (2008) explores the concept of faculty as disposable workers within the low-wage sphere of the service economy.

2. LaGrange, Virginia Tech, and UGA all have examples of such programs, although the respective cases in this book do not focus upon these.

3. The Virginia Tech case in chapter 4 illustrates generating efficiencies through the establishment of the Math Emporium, which certainly uses personnel other than regular faculty, but which still has a significant degree of regular-faculty involvement and influence.

4. Trustees and statewide coordinating boards operate, by definition, not at the level of management, but instead by setting policy (and strategy, to some extent)—again, dealing with what, not how (McGuinness 2005).

5. Works by Clark (1970), Chaffee (1984a, 1984b), Birnbaum (1988), and Chaffee and Tierney (1988) initiated research on leadership in higher education.

6. One could also employ an inductive approach to develop a strategic-management framework, including by formulating a set of case studies that themselves suggest elements and their connections with one another.

7. We also conducted minicases at two other institutions (University of California, Davis and Arizona State Downtown), in the latter working with Mernoy Harrison, the vice president and provost. The appendix contains a list of those interviewed at the eight primary case study institutions, including their titles.

8. We triangulated our data collection through an extensive review of relevant documents from each site. We essentially asked the same set of questions at each institution, focusing on identifying the elements within that institution (viewed as a complex system) and testing and refining our emergent set of eight elements. The master interview protocol is in the appendix. In analyzing the collected data, I applied the standards associated with rigorous qualitative research (Toma 2005). I wrote each case study and circulated them to our host on each campus, to the other researchers, and to our project advisors as a form of member checking. I also synthesized the published research that Mike Massey and Theresa Wright, graduate assistants at the Institute of Higher Education, helped to gather during their appointments as graduate fellows, the product of which appears in chapters 1 and 2 and at the beginnings of chapters 3 through 10. The project team focused on the conceptual development of the project at several meetings—as during gatherings of the research team in Kansas City in November 2004, Atlanta in January 2005, and Athens, Georgia, in June 2005—as well as at meetings of NACUBO constituents in Chicago in October 2004 and in Baltimore in February 2005 that essentially served as focus groups. Jay and I also presented our emerging findings and conclusions in a variety of settings, including at the NACUBO annual meetings in Milwaukee in July 2004 and Baltimore in July 2005, encouraging reactions from those in attendance. Throughout the conceptual development of the project, as well as in the data collection and data analysis processes, the project team pushed and pulled at the Building

Organizational Capacity framework, suggesting ways for it to evolve in whole or in part.

9. I wrote the initial case studies using various styles, including building the narrative around quotations from individuals and around the biography of a significant individual in the initiative. I also structured the cases in different ways before settling on the more descriptive approach I ultimately used in the later one, reworking the earlier cases accordingly. Inserting "voice" into the narratives seemed forced—doing it just for the sake of doing it. Had the case studies been about institutions actually applying the BOC framework, as opposed to providing a generic situation to enable speculation about how the approach might apply and thus illustrating the possibilities for strategic management and systems thinking in higher education, I may have chosen to highlight individual voices more. Also, there is an efficiency that comes with a descriptive approach, as opposed to a more ethnographic one, that I found compelling, again given that the purpose of the cases is to illustrate the framework as opposed to critiquing the institutions, initiatives, or individuals featured. Within the case studies, I limited the discussion to two or three paragraphs per element, knowing that the elements would be mentioned again in each of the other seven cases.

10. The initiatives we explored were generally not particularly controversial, and where they were, I discuss this in the relevant chapter. Also, I arranged the interview schedule prior to our arrival on each campus, through a contact at that institution, requesting that we meet with those with relevant perspectives and knowledge related to the initiative we considered. Such an approach tends to produce interviews featuring supporters. As a research team, while we were on each campus, we relied on our own skepticism and experience, both as faculty members ourselves and as experienced qualitative researchers, to challenge assertions and seek out alternative perspectives when merited. Given the basically innocuous nature of the initiatives we explored, we rarely found the need to seek out perspectives beyond those in the scheduled interviews.

11. In addition, the systems element in the 7S approach (formal policies and processes, such as budgeting, performance measures, or information systems) cuts across policies, processes, and information, with skills (the distinctive competencies needed in management practices) incorporating both processes and information. Infrastructure in the 7S approach is both staffing (to find and develop the right people) and skills (the distinctive competencies needed by people and in technology), and culture is both style (the right leadership operating styles to shape norms) and shared values.

12. Perhaps there is merit in considering hierarchical or linear aspects within a strategic-management approach such as BOC, including whether it makes sense in applying the framework to examine some elements before looking at others.

CHAPTER 3: Purposes

1. Five members of the project team visited TCNJ in May 2004: Jay Morley, Doug Toma, Christopher Morphew, Matthew Hartley, and Greg Dubrow. We wish to thank

R. Barbara "Bobby" Gitenstein and Stephen Briggs for hosting us. Bobby also presented the case study, along with Jay and Doug, at the American Council on Education meeting in October 2004.

2. The College of William and Mary, a comprehensive institution with elite students and professional programs (including a law school), would not term itself a public liberal arts college, either.

3. As I discuss in chapter 2, through becoming more like universities and colleges at "the next level," as Americans commonly express the notion, educational institutions gain the legitimacy and autonomy that comes with greater prestige (DiMaggio and Powell 1983). They also attempt to minimize the influence of the external entities on which they rely for support by increasing their prestige, thus enhancing their independent resource base (Pfeffer 1982; Pfeffer and Salanick 1978).

4. Between 1999 and 2007, undergraduate enrollments at TCNJ increased slightly, from 5930 to 6205, with the proportion of white and African American students remaining nearly constant (at around 4500 for the former and 375 for the latter). The number of Hispanic students grew to 521 in 2007, a figure that was around 350 as late as 2003, and the students categorized as Asian increased from 278 to 469. Enrollments in the various schools have been generally steady, with a slight increase in the engineering and nursing schools (rising from 153 to 560 students between 1999 and 2007).

5. Here, there is an interesting connection with external governance. Given public policy in New Jersey, TCNJ has been able to underwrite an aggressive building program through a combination of fees and bonds, thus creating the physical infrastructure to support its goals.

CHAPTER 4: Structure

1. Five members of the project team visited Virginia Tech in June 2004: Jay Morley, Anthony Knerr, Doug Toma, Kelly Ward, and Kevin Kinser. We wish to thank Minnis Ridenour for hosting us, and Michael Williams for spending a morning discussing the Math Emporium and its development.

2. Other institutions, including the University of Alabama and the University of Idaho, have developed programs modeled on the Math Emporium.

CHAPTER 5: Governance

1. Three members of the project team visited VCSU in May 2005: Jay Morley, Doug Toma, and Lisa Wolf-Wendel. We wish to thank Ellen Chaffee for hosting us and Karen Paulson of the National Center for Higher Education Management Systems (NCHEMS) for suggesting Valley City State University as a possible case study.

2. There is a rich literature on state governance and higher education (McGuinness 2005; Hamilton 2004; Heller 2004; Lingenfelter 2004; MacTaggart 2004; McLendon 2003). The same is true of writing on trustees (Freedman 2004; Hermalin 2004; Chait, Holland, and Taylor 1996, 1991). Olivas (2004) offers an interesting perspec-

tive on the influence of various outside entities on higher education, including insurers, accreditors, consortia, and vendors.

3. Chait, Holland, and Taylor (1991) identify six areas in which effective boards of trustees—those with a constructive relationship with senior management—are particularly skillful: an understanding of context, an appreciation of educational values, interpersonal skills, analytical ability, political savvy, and strategic thinking. In their 1996 work, Chait, Holland, and Taylor examine the obstacles to effective board leadership across nonprofit organizations and discuss how their six earlier skill sets can be used for effective trusteeship, board development, board cohesion, trustee education, and the improvement of board processes.

CHAPTER 6: Policies

1. Four members of the project team visited LaGrange in September 2004: Jay Morley, Doug Toma, Lisa Wolf-Wendel, and Theresa Wright. We wish to thank Stuart Gulley, Jay Simmons, and Phyllis Whitney for hosting us.

CHAPTER 7: Processes

1. Three members of the project team visited PDCCC in March 2005: Jay Morley, Doug Toma, and Robert Rhea. We wish to thank Douglas Boyce and Peter Parker for hosting us.

CHAPTER 8: Information

1. Four members of the project team visited Redlands in May 2005: Doug Toma, Adrianna Kezar, Chris Morphew, and Jessica Shedd. We wish to thank Phillip Doolittle for hosting us.

CHAPTER 9: Infrastructure

1. Four members of the project team visited SCC in October 2004: Jay Morley, Doug Toma, Kate Shaw, and Theresa Wright. We wish to thank Ann McGee and Carol Hawkins for hosting us. Doug also visited Seminole during a campus-wide retreat in January 2005.

CHAPTER 10: Culture

1. These universities include Iowa State, Ohio State, Penn State, Illinois–Urbana-Champaign, Indiana–Bloomington, Iowa, Maryland–College Park, Michigan, Missouri–Columbia, Nebraska–Lincoln, North Carolina–Chapel Hill, Oklahoma, Texas–Austin, Virginia, Washington, and Wisconsin–Madison.

Bibliography

Aaker, D. A. (1998). *Strategic Market Management*, 5th ed. New York: John Wiley and Sons.

Albert, S., and D. A. Whetten (1985). Organizational identity. In L. L. Cummings and B. M. Staw (eds.), *Research in Organizational Behavior* (pp. 263–295). Greenwich, CT: JAI Press.

Alfred, R. L. (2006). *Managing the Big Picture in Colleges and Universities: From Tactics to Strategy*. Westport, CT: Greenwood.

Altbach, P. G. (2005). Patterns in higher education development. In P. G. Altbach, R. O. Berdahl, and P. J. Gumport (eds.), *American Higher Education in the Twenty-First Century: Social, Political, and Economic Challenges* (pp. 15–37). Baltimore: Johns Hopkins University Press.

Altbach, P. G., R. O. Berdahl, and P. J. Gumport (eds.) (2005). *American Higher Education in the Twenty-First Century: Social, Political, and Economic Challenges*. Baltimore: Johns Hopkins University Press.

American Association of College and Universities (2002). *Greater Expectations*. Washington, DC: American Association of College and Universities.

Argyris, C. (1990). *Overcoming Organizational Defenses: Facilitating Organizational Learning*. Needham, MA: Allyn and Bacon.

Argyris, C. (1993). *On Organizational Learning*. Cambridge, MA: Blackwell.

Argyris, C., and D. A. Schon (1978). *Organizational Learning: A Theory of Action Perspective*. Reading, MA: Addison-Wesley.

Aronson, D. (1998). *Overview of Systems Thinking*. www.thinking.net/Systems_Thinking/OverviewSTarticle.pdf.

Association of Governing Boards of Universities and Colleges (1996). *Renewing the Academic Presidency: Stronger Leadership for Tougher Times*. Washington, DC: Association of Governing Boards.

Astin, A. W. (1993). An empirical typology of college students. *Journal of College Student Development* 34(1): 36–46.

Austin, A. E. (1990). Faculty cultures, faculty values. In W. G. Tierney (ed.), *Assessing Academic Climates and Cultures* (pp. 61–74). San Francisco: Jossey-Bass.

Backer, T. E. (2005). Strengthening nonprofits: Foundation initiatives for nonprofit organizations. In C. J. DeVita and C. Fleming (eds.), *Building Capacity in Nonprofits* (pp. 31–83). Washington, DC: Urban Institute.

Baker, D. D., and J. B. Cullen (1993). Administrative reorganization and configurational context: The contingent effects of age, size, and change in size. *Academy of Management Journal* 36(6): 1251–1277.

Balderston, F. E. (1995). *Managing Today's University: Strategies for Viability, Change, and Excellence.* San Francisco: Jossey-Bass.

Baldridge, J. (1971). *Power and Conflict in the University.* New York: John Wiley and Sons.

——— (1982). Shared governance: A fable about the lost magic kingdom. *Academe* 68 (January–February): 12–15.

Bates, A. W. (2000). *Managing Technological Change: Strategies for College and University Leaders.* San Francisco: Jossey-Bass.

Baum, S., and L. Lapovsky (2006). *Tuition Discounting: Not Just a Private College Practice.* New York: College Board.

Becher, T., and P. R. Trowler (2001). *Academic Tribes and Territories: Intellectual Enquiry and the Culture of Disciplines,* 2nd ed. Buckingham, England: Open University Press and Society for Research into Higher Education.

Beer, S. (1966). *Decision and Control: The Meaning of Operational Research and Management Cybernetics.* London: John Wiley and Sons.

Bellinger, G. (2004). *Archetypes: Interaction Structures of the University.* www.systems -thinking.org/arch/arch.htm.

Benjamin, R., and S. Carroll (1998). The implications of the changed environment for governance in higher education. In W. G. Tierney (ed.), *The Responsive University* (pp. 92–119). Baltimore: Johns Hopkins University Press.

Bensimon, E. M., and A. Neumann (1993). *Redesigning Collegiate Leadership: Restructuring for High Performance.* Baltimore: Johns Hopkins University Press.

Bensimon, E. M., A. Neumann, and R. Birnbaum (1989). *Making Sense of Administrative Leadership: The "L" Word in Higher Education.* ASHE-ERIC Higher Education Report 1989, no. 1. San Francisco: Jossey-Bass.

Berdahl, R. O. (1991). Shared academic governance and external constraints. In M. W. Peterson, E. E. Chaffee, and T. H. White (eds.), *Organization and Academic Governance in Higher Education,* 4th ed. (pp. 167–179). Needham Heights, MA: Ginn Press.

Berdahl, R. O., P. G. Altbach, and P. J. Gumport (2005). The contexts of American higher education. In P. G. Altbach, R. O. Berdahl, and P. J. Gumport (eds.), *American Higher Education in the Twenty-First Century: Social, Political, and Economic Challenges* (pp. 1–11). Baltimore: Johns Hopkins University Press.

Bergan, M. (2004). Why governance? Why now? In W. G. Tierney (ed.), *Competing Conceptions of Academic Governance: Navigating the Perfect Storm* (pp. vii–xiv). Baltimore: Johns Hopkins University Press.

Berger, J. B. (2002). The influence of the organizational structures of colleges and universities on college student learning. *Peabody Journal of Education* 77(3): 40–59.

Bergquist, W. (1992). *The Four Cultures of the Academy: Insights and Strategies for Improving Leadership in Collegiate Organizations.* San Francisco: Jossey-Bass.

Bernhardt, V. L. (2005). Data tools for school improvement. *Educational Leadership* 62(5): 66–69.

Biglan, A. (1973). Characteristics of subject matter in different academic areas. *Journal of Applied Psychology* 57: 195–203.

Bigler, W. (2004). *The New Science of Strategy Execution: How Established Firms Become Fast, Sleek Wealth Creators.* Westport, CT: Praeger.

Birnbaum, R. (ed.) (1984). *Organization and Governance in Higher Education.* Lexington, MA: Ginn.

—— (1988). *How Colleges Work: The Cybernetics of Academic Organization and Leadership.* San Francisco: Jossey-Bass.

—— (1989). The cybernetic institution: Toward an integration of governance theories. *Higher Education* 18(2): 239–253.

—— (1992). *How Academic Leadership Works: Understanding Success and Failure in the College Presidency.* San Francisco: Jossey-Bass.

—— (2001). *Management Fads in Higher Education: Where They Come From, What They Do, Why They Fail.* San Francisco: Jossey-Bass.

—— (2004). The end of shared governance: Looking ahead or looking back. In W. G. Tierney and V. M. Lachuga (eds.), *Restructuring Shared Governance in Higher Education* (pp. 5–22). San Francisco: Jossey-Bass.

Blau, P. M. (1973). *The Organization of Academic Work.* New York: John Wiley and Sons.

Bok, D. C. (2002). *Universities in the Marketplace: The Commercialization of Higher Education.* Princeton, NJ: Princeton University Press.

—— (2007). *Our Underachieving Colleges: A Candid Look at How Much Students Learn and Why They Should Be Learning More.* Princeton, NJ: Princeton University Press.

Bolman, L., and T. Deal (2003). *Reframing Organizations: Artistry, Choice, and Leadership,* 3rd ed. San Francisco: Jossey-Bass.

Bousquet, M. (2008). *How the University Works: Higher Education and the Low-Wage Nation.* New York: New York University Press.

Boyer, E. L. (1987). *College: The Undergraduate Experience in America.* New York: Harper and Row.

—— (1990). *Scholarship Reconsidered: Priorities of the Professoriate.* Princeton, NJ: Carnegie Foundation for the Advancement of Teaching.

Brancato, V. C. (2003). Professional development in higher education. In K. P. King and P. A. Lawler (eds.), *New Perspectives on Designing and Implementing Professional Development for Teachers of Adults* (pp. 59–65). New Directions for Adult and Continuing Education no. 98. San Francisco: Jossey-Bass.

Brewer, D., S. M. Gates, and C. A. Goldman (2002). *In Pursuit of Prestige: Strategy and Competition in U.S. Higher Education.* New Brunswick, NJ: Transaction Press.

Brown, J. S. (1997). On becoming a learning organization. *About Campus* 1(6): 5–10.

Burgan, M. (2006). *What Ever Happened to the Faculty? Drift and Decision in Higher Education.* Baltimore: Johns Hopkins University Press.

Cain, M. S. (1999). *The Community College in the Twenty-First Century: A Systems Approach*. Lanham, MD: University Press of America.

Calori, R. (1998). Philosophizing on strategic management models. *Organizational Studies* 19(2): 281–305.

Cameron, K. S., and J. S. Smart (1998). Maintaining effectiveness amid downsizing and decline in institutions of higher education. *Research in Higher Education* 39(1): 65–86.

Chaffee, E. E. (1984a). Successful strategic management in small private colleges. *Journal of Higher Education* 55(2): 212–241.

—— (1984b). Three models of strategy. *Academy of Management Review* 10(1): 89–98.

—— (1985). The concept of strategy: From business to higher education. In J. C. Smart (ed.), *Higher Education: Handbook of Theory and Research*, vol. 1 (pp. 133–171). New York: Agathon Press.

Chaffee, E. E., and W. G. Tierney (1988). *Collegiate Culture and Leadership Strategies*. New York: Macmillan.

Chait, R. T., T. P. Holland, and B. E. Taylor (1991). *The Effective Board of Trustees*. Westport, CT: American Council on Education / Oryx Press.

—— (1996). *Improving the Performance of Governing Boards*. Washington, DC: American Council on Education / Oryx Press.

Checkland, P. (1999). *Systems Thinking, Systems Practice*. New York: John Wiley and Sons.

Clark, B. R. (1970). *The Distinctive College*. Chicago: Aldine.

—— (1972). The organizational saga in higher education. *Administrative Science Quarterly* 17 (June): 178–184.

—— (1983a). The contradictions of change in academic systems. *Higher Education* 12(1): 101–116.

—— (1983b). *The Higher Education System: Academic Organization in Cross-National Perspective*. Berkeley: University of California Press.

—— (ed.) (1984). Perspectives in higher education: Eight disciplinary and comparative views. Collection of papers presented at the University of California, Los Angeles.

—— (1987). *The Academic Life: Small Worlds, Different Worlds*. Princeton, NJ: Princeton University Press.

Clark, B. R., and M. Trow (1966). The organizational context. In T. M. Newcomb and E. K. Wilson (eds.), *College Peer Groups and Prospects for Research* (pp. 17–70). Chicago: Aldine.

Cohen, M. D., and J. G. March (1974). *Leadership and Ambiguity: The American College President*. New York: McGraw-Hill.

Cohen, M. D., J. G. March, and J. P. Olsen (1972). A garbage can model of organizational choice. *Administrative Science Quarterly* 17(1): 1–25.

Collins, J. C. (2001). *Good to Great: Why Some Companies Make the Leap . . . and Others Don't*. New York: HarperBusiness.

Collins, J. C., and J. I. Porras (1994). *Built to Last: Successful Habits of Visionary Companies.* New York: HarperCollins.

Collis, D. (2004). The paradox of scope: A challenge to the governance of higher education. In W. G. Tierney (ed.), *Competing Conceptions of Academic Governance: Navigating the Perfect Storm* (pp. 33–76). Baltimore: Johns Hopkins University Press.

Collis, D., and C. Montgomery (1997). *Corporate Strategy: A Resource-Based Approach.* New York: McGraw-Hill.

Connolly, P. M. (2006). *Navigating the Organizational Lifecycle: A Capacity-Building Guide for Nonprofit Leaders.* Washington, DC: BoardSource.

Connolly, P. M., and C. Lukas (2002). *Strengthening Nonprofit Performance: A Funder's Guide to Capacity Building.* St. Paul, MN: Amherst H. Wilder Foundation.

Cooper, B. (1995). Systems thinking: A requirement for all employees. Paper, Center for Collaborative Organizations, University of North Texas. Web link no longer available.

Cotter, M. (1998). Using systems thinking to improve education. *About Campus* 2(6): 9–14.

Coulter, T. (2003). *Issue Priorities and Trends in State Higher Education.* Denver: State Higher Education Executive Officers.

Crampton, F. E., and D. C. Thompson (eds.) (2003). *Saving America's School Infrastructure.* Greenwich, CT: Information Age Publishing.

Cutright, W. M. A. (1999). Chaos-Theory metaphor for strategic planning in higher education: An exploratory study. Ph.D. diss., University of Tennessee at Knoxville.

David, F. R. (1995). *Strategic Management,* 5th ed. Englewood Cliffs, NJ: Prentice Hall.

Davies, G. K. (1986). The importance of being general: Philosophy, politics, and institutional mission statements. In J. C. Smart (ed.), *Higher Education: Handbook of Theory and Research,* vol. 2 (pp. 85–101). New York: Agathon Press.

Davis, J. S. (2003). *Unintended Consequences of Tuition Discounting.* Indianapolis: Lumina Foundation.

Davis, W. E., and T. J. L. Chandler (1998). Beyond Boyer's *Scholarship Reconsidered. Journal of Higher Education* 69(1): 23–64.

Delucchi, M. (1997). "Liberal arts" colleges and the myth of uniqueness. *Journal of Higher Education* 68(4): 414–426.

DeVita, C. J., C. Fleming, and E. Trombly (2001). Building nonprofit capacity: A framework for addressing the problem. In C. J. DeVita and C. Fleming (eds.), *Building Capacity in Nonprofits* (pp. 5–32). Washington, DC: Urban Institute.

Dill, D. D. (2003). Allowing the market to rule: The case of the United States. *Higher Education Quarterly* 57(2): 136–157.

Dill, D. D., and K. P. Helm (1988). Faculty participation in policy making. In J. Smart (ed.), *Higher Education: Handbook of Theory and Research,* vol. 4 (pp. 319–355). New York: Agathon Press.

DiMaggio, P. J., and W. W. Powell (1983). Iron cage revisited: Institutional isomorphism and collective rationality in organizational fields. *American Sociological Review* 48: 147–160.

Doherty, S., and S. E. Mayer (2003). *Results of an Inquiry into Capacity Building Programs for Nonprofit Programs*. Minneapolis: Effective Communities Project. www .effectivecommunities.com/articles.html.

Dubrow, G. (2003). It's just the way things are done here: The role of institutional culture in the process of general education curriculum reform. Ph.D. diss., University of Pennsylvania.

Duderstadt, J. J. (2004). Governing the twenty-first century university: A view from the bridge. In W. G. Tierney (ed.), *Competing Conceptions of Academic Governance: Navigating the Perfect Storm* (pp. 137–157). Baltimore: Johns Hopkins University Press.

Duryea, E. D. (1973). Evolution of university organization. In J. A. Perkins (ed.), *The University as Organization* (pp. 15–37). Princeton, NJ: Carnegie Foundation for the Advancement of Teaching.

Eckel, P., M. Green, B. Hill, and W. Mallon (1999). *Taking Charge of Change: A Primer for Colleges and Universities*. Washington, DC: American Council on Education.

Education Commission of the States. (2002). *Data-Driven Decisionmaking*. No Child Left Behind Issue Brief. Denver: Education Commission of the States.

Ehrenberg, R. G. (2002). *Tuition Rising: Why College Costs So Much*. Cambridge, MA: Harvard University Press.

Enders, J. (2004). Higher education, internationalisation, and the nation-state: Recent developments and challenges to governance theory. *Higher Education* 47: 361–382.

Fidell, B. (2000). Exploring the use of family therapy with adults with a learning disability. *Journal of Family Therapy* 22(3): 308–323.

Fink, I. (2005). Offices on campus. *Facilities Manager* 21(2): 23–28, 32–36.

Forrester, J. W. (1991). Systems dynamics and the lessons of 35 years. Unpublished paper, Massachusetts Institute of Technology. http://sysdyn.clexchange.org/sdep/papers/D-4224-4.pdf.

——— (1994a). Learning through systems dynamics as preparation for the 21st century. Address at the Systems Thinking and Dynamic Modeling Conference for K–12 Education, Concord, Massachusetts.

——— (1994b). Systems dynamics, systems thinking, and soft OR. *Systems Dynamics Review* 10(2): 245–256.

——— (1998). Designing the future. Address at the Universidad de Sevilla, Spain.

Freed, J. E., and M. R. Klugman (1996). Higher education institutions as learning organizations: The quality principles and practices in higher education. Paper presented at the Association for the Study of Higher Education, Memphis, Tennessee.

Freedman, J. O. (2004). Presidents and trustees. In R. G. Ehrenberg (ed.), *Governing Academia* (pp. 9–27). Ithaca, NY: Cornell University Press.

Gaff, J. G., and R. C. Wilson (1971). Faculty cultures and interdisciplinary studies. *Journal of Higher Education* 42(3): 186–201.

Galbraith, P. L. (2001). Systems thinking: A lens and scalpel for organizational learning. Unpublished paper, No. ED453186, ERIC [Education Resources Information Center]. www.eric.ed.gov.

Gayle, D. J., B. Tewarie, and A. Q. White, Jr. (2003). *Governance in the Twenty-First Century University: Approaches to Effective Leadership and Strategic Management.* ASHE-ERIC Higher Education Report, vol. 30, no. 1. San Francisco: Jossey-Bass.

Geiger, R. (2004). *Knowledge and Money: Research Universities and the Paradox of the Marketplace.* Stanford, CA: Stanford University Press.

Gharajedaghi, J. (1999). *Systems Thinking: Managing Chaos and Complexity; A Platform for Designing Business Architecture.* Burlington, MA: Butterworth-Heinemann.

Gibson, J., M. Leonard, and M. Wilson (2004). Changing residential child care: A systems approach to consultation and development. *Child Care in Practice* 10(4): 345–357.

Gilmore, J. L., and G. G. Lozier (1987). Managing strategic planning: A systems theory approach. *Educational Planning* 6(1): 12–23.

Giroux, H. A. (2007). *The University in Chains: Confronting the Military-Industrial-Academic Complex.* Boulder, CO: Paradigm.

Gladieux, L. E., J. E. King, and M. E. Corrigan (2005). The federal government and higher education. In P. G. Altbach, R. O. Berdahl, and P. J. Gumport (eds.), *American Higher Education in the Twenty-First Century: Social, Political, and Economic Challenges* (pp. 163–197). Baltimore: Johns Hopkins University Press.

Golden, D. (2007). *The Price of Admission: How America's Ruling Class Buys Its Way into Elite Colleges—and Who Gets Left Outside the Gates.* New York: Three Rivers Press.

Goodman, M., R. Karash, C. Lannon, K. W. O'Reilly, and D. Seville (1997). *Designing a Systems Thinking Intervention.* Waltham, MA: Pegasus Communications.

Green, K. C. (1996). The coming ubiquity of information technology. *Change* 28(2): 24–29.

Gross, E., and P. V. Gramback (1968). *University Goals and Academic Power.* Washington, DC: American Council on Education.

Gumport, P. J. (1991). E pluribus unum? Academic structure, culture, and the case of feminist scholarship. *Review of Higher Education* 15(1): 9–29.

——— (2000). *Academic Governance: New Light on Old Issues.* AGB Occasional Paper 42. Washington, DC: Association of Governing Boards of Universities and Colleges.

Gumport, P. J., and B. Pusser (1999). University restructuring: The role of economic and political contexts. In J. Smart (ed.), *Higher Education: Handbook of Theory and Research,* vol. 14 (pp. 146–200). New York: Agathon Press.

Gumport, P. J., and B. Sporn (1999). Institutional adaptation: Demands for management reform and university administration. In J. Smart (ed.), *Higher Education: Handbook of Theory and Research,* vol. 14 (pp. 103–145). New York: Agathon Press.

Haigh, M. J. (2002). Land reclamation and deep ecology: In search of a more meaningful physical geography. *Area* 34(3): 242–252.

Haines, S. G. (1999). *The Manager's Pocket Guide to Systems Thinking and Learning.* Amherst, MA: HRD Press.

——— (2000a). *The Complete Guide to Systems Thinking and Learning.* Amherst, MA: HRD Press.

——— (2000b). *The Systems Thinking Approach to Strategic Planning and Management.* Boca Raton, FL: CRC Press.

Haines, S. G., G. Aller-Stead, and J. McKinlay (2005). *Enterprise-Wide Change: Superior Results through Systems Thinking.* San Francisco: Pfeiffer.

Hamilton, N. W. (2004). Faculty involvement in system-wide governance. In W. G. Tierney (ed.), *Competing Conceptions of Academic Governance: Negotiating the Perfect Storm* (pp. 77–103). Baltimore: Johns Hopkins University Press.

Hammer, M., and J. Champy (1993). *Reengineering the Corporation: A Manifesto for Business Revolution.* New York: HarperCollins.

Hardy, C. (1990). Putting power into university academic governance. In J. C. Smart (ed.), *Higher Education: Handbook of Theory and Research*, vol. 6 (pp. 393–426). New York: Agathon Press.

Harris, L. C., and E. Ogbonna (2002). The unintended consequences of culture interventions: A study of unexpected outcomes. *British Journal of Management* 13(1): 31–49.

Hartley, M. (2002a). *A Call to Purpose: Mission Centered Change at Three Liberal Arts Colleges.* New York: RoutledgeFalmer.

——— (2002b). Supplemental or shadow governance structures? The promise and peril of task forces during times of change. Paper presented at the Research Forum, Center for Higher Education Policy Analysis, University of Southern California, held in Santa Fe, New Mexico.

——— (2003). "There is no way without a because": Revitalization of purpose at three liberal arts colleges. *Review of Higher Education* 27(1): 75–102.

Harvard Business Review (2000). Perspectives from the Editors: Redraw the line between the board and the CEO. In W. J. Salmon et al. (eds.), *Harvard Business Review on Corporate Governance* (pp. 187–211). Boston: Harvard Business School Press.

Hasenfeld, Y. (2002). The making of the black box: An organizational perspective on implementing social policies. Paper presented at the Workshop on Organizations and Social Policy, Chicago, Illinois, June 2002.

Heller, D. E. (2002). State governance and higher education outcomes. Paper presented at the Cornell Higher Education Research Institute Conference, Ithaca, New York, June 2002.

——— (2004). State oversight of academe. In R. G. Ehrenberg (ed.), *Governing Academia* (pp. 49–70). Ithaca, NY: Cornell University Press.

Hermalin, B. E. (2004). Higher education boards of trustees. In R. G. Ehrenberg (ed.), *Governing Academia* (pp. 28–48). Ithaca, NY: Cornell University Press.

Hersh, R. H., and J. Merrow (2006). *Declining by Degrees: Higher Education at Risk.* New York: Palgrave Macmillan.

Horbar, J. D., P. E. Plsek, and K. Leahy (2003). NIC/Q 2000: Establishing habits for improvement in neonatal intensive care units. *Pediatrics* 111(4): e397–e410.

Horowitz, H. L. (1987). *Campus Life: Undergraduate Cultures from the End of the Eighteenth Century to the Present.* Chicago: University of Chicago Press.

Hossler, D., G. Kuh, and D. Olsen (2001). Finding (more) fruit on the vines: Using higher education research and institutional research to guide institutional policies and strategies (parts I and II). *Research in Higher Education* 42(2): 221–235.

House, R. J. (1998). Leadership. In C. L. Cooper and C. Argyris (eds.), *The Concise Blackwell Encyclopedia of Management* (pp. 355–358). Malden, MA: Blackwell.

Houston, D., and M. Rees (1999). Developing a quality management system for a postgraduate education programme: A case study. *Journal of Higher Education Policy and Management* 21(2): 227–238.

Hummon, D. M. (1994). College slang revisited: Language, culture, and undergraduate life. *Journal of Higher Education* 65(1): 75–98.

Jackson, M. C. (2003). *Systems Thinking: Creative Holism for Managers*. West Sussex, England: John Wiley and Sons.

Kaplan, G. E. (2004a). Do governance structures matter? In W. G. Tierney and V. M. Lachuga (eds.), *Restructuring Shared Governance in Higher Education* (pp. 23–34). San Francisco: Jossey-Bass.

——— (2004b). How academic ships actually navigate. In R. G. Ehrenberg (ed.), *Governing Academia* (pp. 165–208). Ithaca, NY: Cornell University Press.

Kaplan, R. S., and D. P. Norton (1996). *The Balanced Scorecard: Translating Strategy into Action*. Boston: Harvard Business School Press.

——— (2004). *Strategy Maps: Converting Intangible Assets into Tangible Outcomes*. Boston: Harvard Business School Press.

Keller, G. (1983). *Academic Strategy: The Management Revolution in American Higher Education*. Baltimore: Johns Hopkins University Press.

——— (2001). Governance: The remarkable ambiguity. In P. G. Altbach, P. J. Gumport, and D. B. Johnstone (eds.), *In Defense of American Higher Education* (pp. 304–322). Baltimore: Johns Hopkins University Press.

——— (2004a). A growing quaintness: Traditional governance in the markedly new realm of U.S. higher education. In W. G. Tierney (ed.), *Competing Conceptions of Academic Governance: Navigating the Perfect Storm* (pp. 158–176). Baltimore: Johns Hopkins University Press.

——— (2004b). *Transforming a College: The Story of a Little-Known College's Strategic Climb to National Distinction*. Baltimore: Johns Hopkins University Press.

Kelly, L., and C. Booth (2004). *Dictionary of Strategy: Strategic Management A–Z*. Thousand Oaks, CA: Sage Publications.

Keup, J. R., A. A. Walker, H. S. Astin, and J. A. Lindholm (2001). *Educational Digest on Institutional Transformation and Institutional Culture*. ERIC Digest ED464521. Washington, DC: ERIC Clearinghouse on Higher Education.

Kezar, A. J. (2001). *Understanding and Facilitating Change in Higher Education in the 21st Century*. San Francisco: Jossey-Bass.

——— (2004). What is more important to effective governance: relationships, trust, and leadership, or structures and formal processes? In W. G. Tierney and V. M. Lachuga (eds.), *Restructuring Shared Governance in Higher Education* (pp. 35–46). San Francisco: Jossey-Bass.

——— (2005). Consequences of radical change in governance: A grounded theory approach. *Journal of Higher Education* 76(6): 634–668.

Kezar, A. J., R. Carducci, and M. Contreras-McGavin (2006). *Rethinking the "L" Word in Higher Education: The Revolution in Research on Leadership.* ASHE Higher Education Report, vol. 31, no. 6. San Francisco: Jossey-Bass.

Kezar, A. J., and P. D. Eckel (2002). *Taking the Reins: Institutional Transformation in Higher Education.* Phoenix: American Council on Education / Oryx Press.

——— (2004). Meeting today's governance challenges: A synthesis of the literature and examination of a future agenda for scholarship. *Journal of Higher Education* 75(4): 371–399.

Kirp, D. (2003). *Shakespeare, Einstein, and the Bottom Line: The Marketing of Higher Education.* Cambridge, MA: Harvard University Press.

Kotter, J. P. (1990). What leaders really do. *Harvard Business Review* 68(3): 103–111.

——— (1995). Why transformation efforts fail. *Harvard Business Review* 73(2): 59–67.

——— (1999). *On What Leaders Really Do.* Boston: Harvard Business School Press.

Kronman, A. T. (2007). *Education's End: Why Our Colleges and Universities Have Given Up on the Meaning of Life.* New Haven, CT: Yale University Press.

Kuh, G. D., J. Schuh, and E. J. Whitt (1991). *Involving Colleges: Successful Approaches to Fostering Student Learning and Development Outside the Classroom.* San Francisco: Jossey-Bass.

Kuh, G. D., and E. J. Whitt (1988). *The Invisible Tapestry: Culture in American Colleges and Universities.* ASHE-ERIC Higher Education Report 1988, no. 1. Washington, DC: Association for the Study of Higher Education.

Lauriol, J. (1996). Cognition et organisation: Quelques repères pour un paradigme en émergence. *Revue Internationale de Systémique* 10(1-2): 9–38.

Lee, B. (1991). Campus leaders and campus senates. In R. Birnbaum (ed.), *Faculty in Governance: The Role of Senates and Joint Committees in Academic Decision-Making* (pp. 41–62). New Directions for Higher Education 75. San Francisco: Jossey-Bass.

Lee, J., and S. Clery (2004). Key trends in higher education. *American Academic* 1(1): 21–36.

Leischow, S. J., and B. Milstein (2006). Editorial: Systems thinking and modeling for public health practice. *American Journal of Public Health* 96(3): 403–405.

Leslie, D., and L. Fretwell (1996). *Wise Moves in Hard Times: Creating and Managing Resilient Colleges and Universities.* San Francisco: Jossey-Bass.

Letts, C. W., W. P. Ryan, and A. Grossman (1999). *High Performance Nonprofit Organizations: Managing Upstream for Greater Impact.* New York: John Wiley and Sons.

Levin, J. S. (ed.) (1998). *Organizational Change in the Community College: A Ripple or a Sea Change?* San Francisco: Jossey-Bass.

Lewis, H. R. (2006). *Excellence without a Soul: How a Great University Forgot Education.* New York: PublicAffairs.

Lingenfelter, P. E. (2004). The state and higher education: An essential partnership. In W. G. Tierney and V. M. Lachuga (eds.), *Restructuring Shared Governance in Higher Education* (pp. 47–60). San Francisco: Jossey-Bass.

Lohmann, S. (2004). Darwinian medicine for the university. In R. G. Ehrenberg (ed.), *Governing Academia* (pp. 71–90). Ithaca, NY: Cornell University Press.

Longanecker, D. A. (2004). *Exploring Trends in Higher Education*. Boulder, CO: Western Interstate Commission on Higher Education.

Lorenz, E. (1993). *The Essence of Chaos*. Seattle: University of Washington Press.

Lumina Foundation (2004). A shared commitment to increase opportunity: National initiative aims to enhance the success of community college students. Press release, Lumina Foundation for Education, Indianapolis, Indiana.

MacTaggart, T. J. (2004). The ambiguous future of public higher education systems. In W. G. Tierney (ed.), *Competing Conceptions of Academic Governance: Negotiating the Perfect Storm* (pp. 104–136). Baltimore: Johns Hopkins University Press.

Maltz, L., and P. B. DeBlois (2005). Top 10 issues. *Educause* 40(3): 14–29.

Manns, D., and R. Opp (2005). A fifty-state assessment of capital needs for public higher education: Policy objectives. *Facilities Manager* 17(4): 39–49.

March, J. G., and J. P. Olsen (1981). Organizational choice under ambiguity. In O. Grusky and G. A. Miller (eds.), *The Sociology of Organizations* (pp. 248–262). New York: Free Press.

Marginson, S. (2006). Enabling democratic education in the neoliberal age. *Educational Theory* 56(2): 205–219.

Markowitz, M. (2006). *State Trends and Issues in Higher Education: Accessing State Funds for Psychology*. Washington, DC: American Psychological Association.

Marshall, C. (ed.) (1997). *Feminist Critical Policy Analysis: A Perspective from Post-Secondary Education*, vol. 2. Washington, DC: Falmer Press.

Martin, J. (2002). *Organizational Culture: Mapping the Terrain*. Thousand Oaks, CA: Sage Publications.

Martin, J., M. S. Feldman, M. J. Hatch, and S. B. Sitkin (1983). The uniqueness paradox in organizational stories. *Administrative Science Quarterly* 28(3): 438–453.

Martinet, A. C. (1996). Pensée stratégique et rationalités, un examen épistémologique. Paper presented at the 6th Annual Conference of the Association Internationale de Management Stratégique (AIMS), Montreal, Quebec, Canada.

Mazzeo, C., S. Rab, and S. Eachus (2003). Work-first or work only: Welfare reform, state policy, and access to postsecondary education. *Annals of the American Academy of Political and Social Science* 586(1): 144–171.

McGee, R. (1971). *Academic Janus*. San Francisco: Jossey-Bass.

McGuinness, A. C. (2005). The states and higher education. In P. G. Altbach, R. O. Berdahl, and P. J. Gumport (eds.), *American Higher Education in the Twenty-First Century: Social, Political, and Economic Challenges* (pp. 198–225). Baltimore: Johns Hopkins University Press.

McKinsey and Company (2001). *McKinsey Capacity Assessment Grid*. http://vppartners.org/learning/reports/capacity/assessment.pdf.

McLendon, M. K. (2003). Setting the governmental agenda for state decentralization of higher education. *Journal of Higher Education* 74(5): 1–37.

McLendon, M. K., J. C. Hearn, and R. Deaton (2006). Called to account: Analyzing the origins and spread of state performance-accountability policies for higher education. *Education Evaluation and Policy Analysis* 28(1): 1–24.

McLendon, M. K., D. E. Heller, and S. Young (2005). State postsecondary education policy innovation: Politics, competition, and the interstate migration of policy ideas. *Journal of Higher Education* 76(4): 363–400.

McPherson, M. S., and M. O. Schapiro (1998). *The Student Aid Game: Meeting Need and Rewarding Talent*. Princeton, NJ: Princeton University Press.

——— (2002). Changing patterns of institutional aid: Impact on access and education policy. In D. E. Heller (ed.), *Condition of Access: Higher Education and Lower Income Students* (pp. 73–94). Westport, CT: Praeger.

Meyer, J. W., and B. Rowan (1985). Institutionalized organizations: Formal structure as myth and ceremony. *American Journal of Sociology* 83(2): 340–63.

Meyer, J. W., W. R. Scott, and T. E. Deal (1981). Institutional and technical sources of organizational structure: Explaining the structure of educational organizations. In H. D. Stein (ed.), *Organization and the Human Services* (pp. 151–178). Philadelphia: Temple University Press.

Middlehurst, R. (1993). *Leading Academics*. Buckingham, England: Society for Research into Higher Education and Open University Press.

Miller, A., and G. G. Dess (1996). *Strategic Management*, 2nd ed. New York: McGraw-Hill.

Miller, M. T. (2003). *Improving Faculty Governance: Cultivating Leadership and Collaboration in Decision Making*. Stillwater, OK: New Forums Press.

Mintrom, M. (1997). Policy entrepreneurs and the diffusion of innovation. *American Journal of Political Science* 41(3): 738–770.

Mintzberg, H. (1979). *The Structuring of Organizations: A Synthesis of Research*. Englewood Cliffs, NJ: Prentice Hall.

——— (1987a). The strategy concept I: Five Ps for strategy. *California Management Review* 30(1): 11–24.

——— (1987b). The strategy concept II: Another look at why organizations need strategies. *California Management Review* 30(1): 25–32.

Mintzberg, H., B. Ahlstrand, and J. Lampel (2005). *Strategy Safari: A Guided Tour through the Wilds of Strategic Management*. New York: Free Press.

Mintzberg, H., and J. Lampel (1999). Reflecting on the strategy process. *Sloan Management Review* 40(3): 21–30.

Mintzberg, H., J. Lampel, J. B. Quinn, and S. Ghoshal (2003). *The Strategy Process: Concepts, Contexts, Cases*, 4th ed. Upper Saddle River, NJ: Prentice Hall.

Moffatt, M. (1989). *Coming of Age in New Jersey: College and American Culture*. New Brunswick, NJ: Rutgers University Press.

Morecroft, J. D. W., and J. D. Sternman (1994). *Modeling for Learning Organizations*. Portland, OR: Productivity Press.

Morgan, G. (1997). *Images of Organizations*. Thousand Oaks, CA: Sage Publications.

Morphew, C. C. (2007). Fixed tuition pricing: A solution that may be worse than the problem. *Change* 39(1): 34–39.

Morphew, C. C., and B. J. Taylor (2009). College rankings and dueling mission statements. *Chronicle of Higher Education*, Aug. 19.

Morphew, C. C., and J. D. Toma (2004). Becoming name brand: Case studies of emerging U.S. public liberal arts colleges. Paper presented at the 2004 European Association for Institutional Research (EAIR) Annual Forum, Barcelona, Spain, September 2004.

Mortimer, K. P., and T. R. McConnell (1978). *Sharing Authority Effectively: Participation, Interaction, and Discretion.* San Francisco: Jossey-Bass.

Nanus, B. (1992). *Visionary Leadership: Creating a Compelling Sense of Direction for Your Organization.* San Francisco: Jossey-Bass.

National Center for Academic Transformation (2001). *Program in Course Redesign: Virginia Tech.* www.thencat.org/PCR/R1/VT/VT_Overview.htm.

Newfield, C. (2008). *Unmaking the Public University: The Forty-Year Assault on the Middle Class.* Cambridge, MA: Harvard University Press.

Newman, F., L. Couturier, and J. Scurry (2004). *The Future of Higher Education: Rhetoric, Reality, and the Risks of the Marketplace.* San Francisco: Jossey-Bass.

Newsom, W., and C. R. Hayes (1991). Are mission statements worthwhile? *Planning for Higher Education* 19(2): 28–30.

O'Connor, J. (1997). *The Art of Systems Thinking: Essential Skills for Creativity and Problem Solving.* London: Thorsons.

Ogbor, J. O. (2001). Critical theory and the hegemony of corporate culture. *Journal of Organizational Change Management* 14(6): 590–608.

Olivas, M. A. (1992). The political economy of immigration, intellectual property, and racial harassment: Case studies of the implementation of legal change on campus. *Journal of Higher Education* 63(5): 570–598.

—— (2004). The rise of nonlegal legal influence on higher education. In R. G. Ehrenberg (ed.), *Governing Academia* (pp. 258–275). Ithaca, NY: Cornell University Press.

—— (2005). Higher education as "place": Location, race, and college attendance policies. *Review of Higher Education* 28(2): 169–190.

Ouchi, W. G. (1980). Markets, bureaucracies, and clans. *Administrative Science Quarterly* 25(1): 129–141.

—— (1981). *Theory Z: How American Business Can Meet the Japanese Challenge.* Reading, MA: Addison-Wesley.

Pappas Consulting Group (2007). *Proposing a Blueprint for Higher Education in Florida: Outlining the Way to a Long-Term Master Plan for Higher Education in Florida.* Report to the Florida Board of Governors.

Parker, M. (2000). *Organizational Culture and Identity: Unity and Division at Work.* Thousand Oaks, CA: Sage Publications.

Perna, L. W., P. Steele, S. Woda, and T. Hibbert (2005). State public policies and the racial/ethnic stratification of college access and choice in the state of Maryland. *Review of Higher Education* 28(2): 245–272.

Peters, T., and R. Waterman (1982). *In Search of Excellence.* New York: Harper and Row.

Peterson, M. W. (1985). Emerging developments in postsecondary organization theory and research: Fragmentation or integration. *Educational Researcher* 14(3): 71–82.

—— (2001). Change and transformation in higher education: An annotated bibliography. Ann Arbor: Center for the Study of Higher and Postsecondary Education, University of Michigan.

Peterson, M. W., and L. A. Mets (eds.) (1987). *Key Resources on Higher Education Governance, Management, and Leadership: A Guide to the Literature.* San Francisco: Jossey-Bass.

Peterson, M. W., and M. G. Spencer (1990). Understanding academic culture and climate. In W. G. Tierney (ed.), *Assessing Academic Climates and Cultures* (pp. 3–18). San Francisco: Jossey-Bass.

Petrides, L. A. (2002). Organizational learning and the case for knowledge-based systems. In A. M. Serban and J. Luan (eds.), *Knowledge Management: Building a Competitive Advantage in Higher Education* (pp. 69–84). New Directions for Institutional Research 113. San Francisco: Jossey-Bass.

—— (2004). *The Democratization of Data in Higher Education: A Case Study of the Challenges That Institutions Face As They Seek to Improve Student Success.* www.iskme.org.

Petrides, L. A., L. Nguyen, and E. Doty (2005). *A Tale of Two Colleges.* www.iskme.org.

Petrides, L. A., and T. R. Nodine. (2003). *Knowledge Management in Education: Defining the Landscape.* www.iskme.org.

Pettigrew, A. M. (1979). On studying organizational cultures. *Administrative Science Quarterly* 24: 570–581.

Pfeffer, J. (1982). *Organizations and Organization Theory.* Marshfield, MA: Pitman.

Pfeffer, J., and G. R. Salanick (1978). *The External Control of Organizations: A Resource Dependence Perspective.* New York: Harper and Row.

Pierce, F. D. (2002). Applying systems thinking to safety. *Professional Safety* 47(6): 49–52.

Pope, M. L. (2004). A conceptual framework of faculty trust and participation in governance. In W. G. Tierney and V. M. Lachuga (eds.), *Restructuring Shared Governance in Higher Education* (pp. 75–84). San Francisco: Jossey-Bass.

Porter, M. E. (1979). How competitive forces shape strategy. *Harvard Business Review* 57(2): 137–145.

—— (1987). From competitive advantage to corporate strategy. *Harvard Business Review* 65(3): 43–59.

—— (1996). What is strategy? *Harvard Business Review* 74(6): 61–78.

Pound, J. (2000). The promise of the governed corporation. In W. J. Salmon et al. (eds.), *Harvard Business Review on Corporate Governance* (pp. 79–104). Boston: Harvard Business School Press.

Powell, W. W., and P. J. DiMaggio (eds.) (1991). *The New Institutionalism in Organizational Analysis.* Chicago: University of Chicago Press.

Presley, J. B., and D. Leslie (1998). Understanding strategy: An assessment of theory and practice. In J. Smart (ed.), *Higher Education: Handbook of Theory and Research,* vol. 14 (pp. 201–239). New York: Agathon Press, 1999.

Pronk, N. P., and J. Boucher (1999). Systems approach to childhood and adolescent obesity prevention and treatment in a managed care organization. *International Journal of Obesity* 23(2): S38–S42.

Pusser, B. (2003). Beyond Baldridge: Extending the political model of higher education organization and governance. *Higher Education Policy* 17(1): 121–140.

Redd, K. E. (2000). Discounting toward disaster: Tuition discounting, college finances, and enrollment of low-income undergraduates. Indianapolis: USA Group Foundation.

Rendon, L. I., V. Novack, and D. Dowell (2005). Testing race-neutral admissions models: Lessons from California State University–Long Beach. *Review of Higher Education* 28(2): 221–244.

Rhoades, G. (1995). Rethinking and restructuring universities. *Journal of Higher Education Management* 10(2): 17–23.

——— (2005). Capitalism, academic style, and shared governance. *Academe* 91(3): 38–42.

Rhoads, R. A., V. Saenz, and R. Carducci (2005). Higher education reform as a social movement: The case of affirmative action. *Review of Higher Education* 28(2): 191–220.

Rhode, D. (2006). *In Pursuit of Knowledge: Scholars, Status, and Academic Culture.* Stanford, CA: Stanford Law and Politics.

Rice, R. E., and A. E. Austin (1988). High faculty morale: What exemplary colleges do right. *Change* 20(2): 51–58.

Richardson, G. P. (1991). *Feedback Thought in Social Science and Systems Theory.* Philadelphia: University of Pennsylvania Press.

Richmond, B. (2001). *An Introduction to Systems Thinking.* Hanover, NH: High Performance Systems.

Riley, G., and J. V. Baldridge (eds.) (1977). *Governing Academic Organizations: New Problems and Perspectives.* New York: McCutchan.

Riley, S. J., W. F. Siemer, D. J. Decker, L. H. Carpenter, J. F. Organ, and L. T. Berchielli (2003). Adaptive impact management: An integrative approach to wildlife management. *Human Dimensions of Wildlife* 8: 81–95.

Rosovsky, H. (1991). *The University: An Owner's Manual.* New York: W. W. Norton.

Ruscio, K. (1987). Many sectors, many professions. In B. Clark (ed.), *The Academic Profession: National, Disciplinary, and Institutional Settings* (pp. 331–368). Berkeley: University of California Press.

Rush, S., and S. Johnson (1989). The decaying American campus: A ticking time bomb. Alexandria, VA: Association of Higher Education Facilities Officers and National Association of College and University Business Officers.

Sackmann, S. A. (1991). *Cultural Knowledge in Organizations: Exploring the Collective Mind.* Newbury Park, CA: Sage Publications.

——— (ed.) (1997). *Cultural complexity in organizations: Inherent contrasts and contradictions.* Thousand Oaks, CA: Sage Publications.

Sample, S. B. (2003). *The Contrarian's Guide to Leadership.* San Francisco: Jossey-Bass.

Schein, E. H. (1992). *Organizational Culture and Leadership*, 2nd ed. San Francisco: Jossey-Bass.

Schmidt, P. (2007). *Color and Money: How Rich White Kids Are Winning the War over College Affirmative Action*. New York: Palgrave Macmillan.

Schmidtlein, F. A., and R. O. Berdahl (2005). Autonomy and accountability: Who controls academe? In P. G. Altbach, R. O. Berdahl, and P. J. Gumport (eds.), *American Higher Education in the Twenty-First Century: Social, Political, and Economic Challenges* (pp. 71–90). Baltimore: Johns Hopkins University Press.

Schuster, J., D. Smith, K. Corak, and M. Yamada (1994). *Strategic Academic Governance: How to Make Big Decisions Better*. Phoenix: Oryx Press.

Scott, W. R. (1970). *Social Processes and Social Structures: An Introduction to Sociology*. New York: Holt, Rinehart, and Winston.

——— (1998). *Organizations: Rational, Natural, and Open Systems*, 4th ed. Englewood Cliffs, NJ: Prentice Hall.

Selznick, P. (1957). *Leadership in Administration*. New York: Harper and Row.

Senge, P. M. (1990). *The Fifth Discipline: The Art and Practice of the Learning Organization*. New York: Doubleday.

Senge, P. M., A. Kleiner, C. Roberts, R. Ross, and B. Smith (1994). *The Fifth Discipline Fieldbook*. New York: Doubleday.

Shattock, M. (2003). *Managing Successful Universities*. Berkshire, England: Society for Research into Higher Education and Open University Press.

Shaw, K. M., and S. Rab (2003). Market rhetoric versus reality in policy and practice: The Workforce Investment Act and access to community college education and training. *Annals of the American Academy of Political and Social Science* 586(1): 172–193.

Sherwood, D. (2002). *Seeing the Forest for the Trees: A Manager's Guide to Applying Systems Thinking*. London: Nicholas Brealey.

Simpson, W. B. (1991). *Cost Containment for Higher Education: Strategies for Public Policy and Institutional Administration*. New York: Praeger.

Slaughter, S., and L. L. Leslie (1997). *Academic Capitalism: Power, Politics, and the Entrepreneurial University*. Baltimore: Johns Hopkins University Press.

Slaughter, S., and G. Rhoades (2004). *Academic Capitalism and the New Economy: Markets, State, and Higher Education*. Baltimore: Johns Hopkins University Press.

Smith, D. C., and C. H. Reynolds (1990). Institutional culture and ethics. In W. W. May (ed.), *Ethics and Higher Education* (pp. 21–31). New York: American Council on Education / Macmillan.

Sobeck, J., and E. Agius (2003). Organizational capacity building: Addressing a research and practice gap. *Evaluation and Program Planning* 30(3): 237–246.

Society for College and University Planning (2005). *Trends in Higher Education*. Ann Arbor, MI: Society for College and University Planning.

Spitzberg, I. J., and V. V. Thorndike (1992). *Creating Community on College Campuses*. Albany: State University of New York Press.

Stampen, J. O., and L. W. Hansen (1999). Improving higher education access and persistence: New directions from a systems perspective. *Educational Evaluation and Policy Analysis* 21(4): 417–426.

Stark, J. S., M. A. Lowther, and B. M. K. Haggerty (1987). Faculty perceptions of professional preparation environments. *Journal of Higher Education* 58(5): 530–561.

Sternman, J. D. (2000). *Business Dynamics: Systems Thinking and Modeling for a Complex World.* Boston: Irwin/McGraw-Hill.

Stroup, H. (1966). *Bureaucracy in Higher Education.* New York: Free Press.

Sweezy v. New Hampshire, 354 U.S. 234 (1957).

Tierney, W. G. (1988). Organizational culture in higher education: Defining the essentials. *Journal of Higher Education* 59(1): 2–21.

——— (1992). Cultural leadership and the search for community. *Liberal Education* 78 (5): 16–21.

——— (1999). *Building the Responsive Campus: Creating High Performance Colleges and Universities.* Thousand Oaks, CA: Sage Publications.

——— (2004). Improving academic governance: Utilizing a cultural framework to improve organizational performance. In W. G. Tierney (ed.), *Competing Conceptions of Academic Governance: Negotiating the Perfect Storm* (pp. 202–216). Baltimore: Johns Hopkins University Press.

Tierney, W. G., and G. C. Hentschke (2007). *Same Players, Different Game: Understanding the Rise of For-Profit Colleges and Universities.* Baltimore: Johns Hopkins University Press.

Tierney, W. G., and J. T. Minor (2004). A cultural perspective on communication and governance. In W. G. Tierney and V. M. Lachuga (eds.), *Restructuring Shared Governance in Higher Education* (pp. 85–94). San Francisco: Jossey-Bass.

Tierney, W. G., and R. A. Rhoads (1993). *Enhancing Promotion, Tenure, and Beyond: Faculty Socialization as a Cultural Process.* ASHE-ERIC Higher Education Report 1993, no 6. Washington, DC: Association for the Study of Higher Education.

Tolbert, P. S. (1985). Institutional environments and resource dependence: Sources of administrative structure in institutions of higher education. *Administrative Science Quarterly* 30(1): 1–13.

Toma, J. D. (1997). Alternative inquiry paradigms, faculty cultures, and the definition of academic lives. *Journal of Higher Education* 68(6): 679–705.

——— (2003). *Football U.: Spectator Sports in the Life of the American University.* Ann Arbor: University of Michigan Press.

——— (2006). Necessary infrastructure—or mission inflation? *Chronicle of Higher Education,* Jan. 27, B10.

——— (2007). Expanding peripheral activities, increasing accountability demands, and reconsidering governance in U.S. higher education. *Higher Education Research and Development* 26(1): 57–72.

——— (2008). Aspirational U.: Positioning for prestige in American higher education. Paper presented at the Association for the Study of Higher Education (ASHE) Annual Meeting, Jacksonville, Florida, November 2008.

Toma, J. D., G. Dubrow, and M. Hartley (2005). *The Uses of Institutional Culture: Strengthening Identification and Building Brand Equity in Higher Education.* ASHE Higher Education Report, vol. 31, no. 3. San Francisco: Jossey-Bass.

Toma, J. D., and C. C. Morphew (2001). The public liberal arts college: Case studies of institutions that have bucked the trend . . . and what it says about mission and market for all institutions. Paper presented at the Association for the Study of Higher Education (ASHE) Annual Conference, Richmond, Virginia, November 2001.

Townsend, B. K., L. J. Newell, and M. D. Wiese (1992). *Creating Distinctiveness: Lessons from Uncommon Colleges and Universities.* ASHE-ERIC Higher Education Report, vol. 21, no. 6. San Francisco: Jossey-Bass.

Trice, H. M., and J. Beyer (1993). *The Cultures of Work Organizations.* Englewood Cliffs, NJ: Prentice Hall.

Trow, M. A. (1989). American higher education: Past, present, and future. *Studies in Higher Education* 14(1): 5–22.

Twale, D. J., and B. M. DeLuca (2007). *Faculty Incivility: The Rise of the Academic Bully Culture and What to Do About It.* San Francisco: Jossey-Bass.

Underwood, J. C., and J. O. Hammons (1999). Past, present, and future variations in community college organizational structure. *Community College Review* 26(4): 39–60.

University of Texas System (2005). *Trends Affecting Higher Education.* www.utsystem .edu/OSM/planning.htm.

Vanderstraeten, R. (2000). Luhmann on socialization and education. *Educational Theory* 50(1): 1–23.

Washburn, J. (2006). *University, Inc.: The Corporate Corruption of American Higher Education.* New York: Basic Books.

Waterman, R. H. (1982). The seven elements of strategic fit. *Journal of Business Strategy* 2(3): 69–73.

Waterman, R. H., T. Peters, and J. Phillips (1980). Structure is not organization. *McKinsey Quarterly* (Summer): 2–20.

Weick, K. E. (1976). Education organizations as loosely coupled systems. *Administrative Science Quarterly* 21(1): 1–19.

——— (1979). *The Social Psychology of Organizing.* Reading, MA: Addison-Wesley.

——— (1993). The collapse of sensemaking in organizations: The Mann Gulch disaster. *Administrative Science Quarterly* 38: 628–652.

——— (1995). *Sensemaking in Organizations.* Thousand Oaks, CA: Sage Publications.

Weidman, J. C., D. J. Twale, and E. L. Stein (2001). *Socialization of Graduate and Professional Students in Higher Education: A Perilous Passage?* ASHE-ERIC Higher Education Report, vol. 28, no. 3. San Francisco; Jossey-Bass.

Williams, D., W. Gore, C. Broches, and C. Lostski (1987). One faculty's perception of its academic governance role. *Journal of Higher Education* (58)6: 629–657.

Wilson, J. D. (2004). Tiebout competition versus political competition on a university campus. In R. G. Ehrenberg (ed.), *Governing Academia* (pp. 139–164). Ithaca, NY: Cornell University Press.

Winston, G. C. (1993). The capital costs conundrum: Why are capital costs ignored by colleges and universities and what are the prospects for change? *Business Officer* 26(12): 22–27.

Zemsky, R., G. R. Wegner, and W. F. Massy (2005). *Remaking the American University: Market-Smart and Mission-Centered.* New Brunswick, NJ: Rutgers University Press.

Zumeta, W. (2001). Public policy and accountability in higher education: Lessons from the past for the new millennium. In D. E. Heller (ed.), *The States and Public Higher Education Policy: Affordability, Access, and Accountability* (pp. 155–197). Baltimore: Johns Hopkins University Press.

Zusman, A. (2005). Challenges facing higher education in the twenty-first century. In P. G. Altbach, R. O. Berdahl, and P. J. Gumport (eds.), *American Higher Education in the Twenty-First Century: Social, Political, and Economic Challenges* (pp. 115–160). Baltimore: Johns Hopkins University Press.

Index

alignment, BOC elements, 2–4, 6–8, 10–12, 207–12, 213–17, 220; and culture as an element, 201–3, 205–6; and governance as an element 109, 114–16; and information as an element, 166–69; and infrastructure as an element, 185–89; and policies as an element, 120, 126–32; and processes as an element, 135–36, 141, 147–49; and purposes as an element, 55, 57, 60, 62, 64, 65–67, 69–72, 74; and strategic management theory, 15, 19, 25; and structure as an element, 76–77, 85, 91–93, 95–96; and systems thinking, 41–42, 44, 51, 53

application, BOC framework, x, 2–3, 9–14, 212–20, 234nn2–3, 235n10; and culture as an element, 203; and developing the BOC approach, 49–51, 53; and governance as an element, 115–16; and information as an element, 168; and infrastructure as an element, 187; and leading organizational change, 44–49; and policies as an element, 132; and processes as an element, 148; and purposes as an element, 55, 72; and strategic management theory, 15, 20, 24–25; and structure as an element, 76, 81, 93, 95; and systems thinking, 28, 30, 32, 34; and trends and issues in higher education, 35, 42–44

Building Organizational Capacity (BOC), vii–x, 1–4, 6–14, 207, 209, 211–12, 216, 231nn5–6, 235nn9–10; and culture as an element, 198, 205; developing the approach, 49–53; and information as an element, 154, 169; and infrastructure as an element, 189; and leading organizational change, 44, 45; and policies as an element, 122; and

purposes as an element, 55–57, 65–66, 72; and strategic management, 15–25; and structure as an element, 76–77, 85, 93; and systems thinking, 25–28, 31–32, 34; and trends and issues in higher education, 35

College of New Jersey, The (TCNJ), 12–13, 37, 39, 42–43, 50, 54–74, 207–13, 215–19, 235–36nn1–5; applying the framework, 72–74; checklist, purposes and aligning the elements, 70–71; and culture as an element, 69–70; and governance as an element, 66; and information as an element, 68–69; and infrastructure as an element, 69; introduction as an element, 54–55; overview of Academic Transformation, 54, 55, 60–63; and policies as an element, 66–67; and processes as an element, 67–68; and purposes as an element, 54–55, 63–65; and structure as an element, 65–66

culture, as BOC element, ix–xi, 1, 5–6, 8–9, 11–14, 208, 210, 211–19, 221, 231n7, 235n1 (chap. 10); as an element (research literature), 190–91, 193; applying the framework, 203–6; checklist, culture and aligning the elements, 201–3; and developing the BOC approach, 49, 52; Dubrow note, 192–93; and governance as an element, 98–101, 105, 107, 111, 113, 115–16, 199–200; illustrated as an element, 189–93, 196–206; and information as an element, 152, 163, 165–66, 168–69, 171, 201; and infrastructure as an element, 182–84, 186–88, 201; introduction to featured chapter, 189–90; and leading organizational change, 45; and policies as an element, 119–20, 122, 126–34,